POETRY WITH A
PURPOSE

Indiana Studies in Biblical Literature

Herbert Marks and Robert Polzin,
general editors

POETRY WITH A PURPOSE

Biblical Poetics and Interpretation

HAROLD FISCH

INDIANA UNIVERSITY PRESS
BLOOMINGTON & INDIANAPOLIS

First Midland Book edition 1990

Copyright © 1988 by Harold Fisch
All rights reserved

Manufactured in the United States of America

Library of Congress Cataloging-in-Publication Data

Fisch, Harold.
Poetry with a purpose.

(Indiana studies in biblical literature)
Includes indexes.
1. Hebrew poetry, Biblical—Themes, motives.
I. Title. II. Series.
BS1405.2.F57 1988   809′.93522 87-45338
ISBN 0-253-34557-X
ISBN 0-253-20564-6 (pbk)

2 3 4 5 6   94 93 92 91 90

In memory of
Solomon Fisch, scholar and man of God
(1889–1985)
אָבִי אָבִי רֶכֶב יִשְׂרָאֵל וּפָרָשָׁיו
2 Kings 2:12

CONTENTS

ACKNOWLEDGMENTS

Many friends and colleagues have given me the benefit of their comments on this or that portion of this book. I am particularly indebted to Marcel L. Mendelson and Richard E. Sherwin for their helpful criticism. Except where otherwise indicated, biblical quotations are drawn (with occasional adaptation) from *The Holy Scriptures,* the English text revised and edited by Harold Fisch, © copyright by Koren Publishers Jerusalem Ltd., Jerusalem, 1969, with the kind permission of the publisher. Chapter and verse divisions, however, are as in the standard English versions. I must here record my gratitude to the Oxford Centre for Postgraduate Hebrew Studies and to its president, Dr. David Patterson, for an opportunity to spend the spring months of 1984 as a Visiting Scholar at Yarnton Manor while writing the Job chapter. Thanks are due to Shirley Shaiak, who carefully typed out the manuscript, guiding it (and me) through the mysterious world of Bar-Ilan University's computer. Finally, I would like to express my special thanks to the staff of the Indiana University Press. We have been discussing this book for some years and they have borne with me patiently as it went through its many stages of preparation. It is finally here and the reader must judge the result.

POETRY WITH A
PURPOSE

INTRODUCTION

Writers and critics over the centuries have perceived in the Hebrew scriptures a model of literary excellence. Longinus in his day found there the highest reach of the sublime; for Petrarch, David was the supreme poet; Auerbach found in its narratives an ultimate standard of realism. Critics in our own day do not speak much of sublimity or even of realism but they have found other literary qualities to praise. J. P. Fokkelman in his unsurpassed micro-exegesis of selected biblical pericopes has shown how the verbal symmetries, especially those organized according to the pattern of the chiasmus, descend to the most minute particulars of the text.[1] At the other end of the spectrum, Northrop Frye in his macro-criticism has demonstrated the literary power of the Bible in the larger visionary sweep of its unifying images or myths. "The city, the garden, and the sheepfold are the organizing metaphors of the Bible," he declares.[2] Balancing the apocalyptic or paradisal imagery of the Bible there is, he says, a vast system of demonic imagery: against the Garden of Eden, we have the vision of the wasteland; instead of the rivers of paradise, the burning fires of Sheol.[3] Such critics are not mistaken. The Bible does have such literary power and even without the critics we would know this from reading the many poets and novelists whose lips have been touched with its burning coals. Indeed Mr. Frye came to emphasize the mythopoeic power of the biblical narratives and prophecies through observing that power at work in the writings of Milton and Blake and many others.

And yet those writers who have had difficulty in accommodating the Bible to any normal aesthetic have also not been mistaken. They include the Augustine of the *Confessions,* and they include Dr. Johnson, who taught that "the intercourse between God and the human soul cannot be poetical." And nearer our own time, C. S. Lewis finds the Bible "so remorselessly and continuously sacred that it does not invite, it excludes or repels, the merely aesthetic approach."[4] On the Jewish side, the medieval philosopher Yehuda Halevi points out in his *Kuzari* that the Bible removes itself from the normal sphere of poetry by placing the category

1

of significance above that of harmony and beauty.[5] How, it may be asked, can both groups be right? It is the argument of this book that they are. Because if the Bible is literature, even supreme literature, it is also anti-literature. And this is not because it is rough or uncouth, as Augustine thought in the early days after his conversion, but because its authors, capable of all the richness of the epic, all the sophistication of the romance and the lyric as they were known in their time, were also conscious of being involved in an enterprise that called into question, banished, and condemned all merely "literary" effects.

Northrop Frye's archetypal criticism has been mentioned. That has been seen as a basis for viewing the Bible as an integral part of literature-in-general. Myth or archetype is the common ground, it is claimed, between the Bible and other forms of imaginative writing: "Since archetypes belong not only to the Bible but are the basic constituent elements of literature itself, the archetypes of biblical literature allow us to relate it to other literature. . . ."[6] But we can be misled by the fearful symmetry of the archetypal world as summoned up by the prophets and psalmists. The grand mythological vision is there, but it contains its own antithesis. We may take the example of the vision of Sheol in Isaiah 14. The prophet there utters his scorn of the King of Babylon, likening him to Helel, son of Shahar, the god of the dawn in Canaanite mythology, who is thrown down by Baal:

> How art thou fallen from heaven,
> O bright star, son of the morning!
> How art thou cut down to the ground,
> that didst rule over the nations!
>   (14:12)[7]

This not only echoes mythological sources; it also in its turn inspired Milton's myth-epic vision of the fallen Beelzebub addressed by Lucifer:

> If thou beest hee; But O how fall'n how chang'd
> From him, who in the happy Realms of Light
> Cloth'd with transcendent brightness didst outshine
> Myriads though bright.
>   (*Paradise Lost* I, 84–87)

Isaiah 14 in short is an example of literary osmosis, the free flow of mythological motifs to the Bible and, from the Bible, to other writings. But if we pay closer attention to this chapter, especially to the verses immediately preceding and following 14:12, we may suggest that the scorn is directed not only against the King of Babylon but actually against the mythological inflation of such kingship. We observe the pitiful remains of the kings of the east communing together in Sheol:

Thy pomp is brought down to Sheol,
the sound of thy harps;
maggots are spread under thee,
and worms cover thee.

(14:11)

The words seem to be directed against the "high" poetry of the Canaanite texts themselves—the more clearly so because of the actual reference to harp-songs. They urge a reassessment of myth in favor of something more (literally!) down-to-earth. The maggots eat the remains of the kings of the east; they also devour the remains of the poetic system in which their exploits had achieved a proper epic resonance. God will sweep Babylon with "the broom of destruction"; the homely metaphor drives home the mock-epic or anti-epic message.[8]

But Milton too seems to have understood the self-negating character of the mythological poetry of the Bible. In the first books of *Paradise Lost,* Lucifer and Beelzebub are accorded full epic honors, as in the passage quoted above. But in the ninth book of the epic, the art of eloquence is seen as belonging to the armory of Satan and later, in *Paradise Regained,* Book IV, the art of eloquence and the charm of poetry constitute the Devil's final temptation and one that Jesus, the epic hero of that poem, naturally rejects. Poetry and the distrust of poetry go together in Milton's work.

The paradox we are discussing is thus not confined to the Hebrew Bible. It communicates itself to those writings which have taken the deepest imprint from Hebrew psalm, prophecy, and narrative. In the same letter to the Corinthians in which he achieves his most poetic utterance ("Though I speak with the tongues of men and angels . . ."), the apostle Paul also explicitly renounces the use of "the excellency of speech" or "the enticing words of man's wisdom" (1 Cor. 2:1, 4, AV). Protestant writers of the seventeenth century were fond of quoting this chapter of the first Epistle to the Corinthians as well as the chapter in the second epistle that speaks of the apostle using "great plainness of speech and not as Moses, which put a vail over his face" (2 Cor. 3:12–13, AV).[9] The "vail of Moses"—the reference is to Exod. 34:33—stands for the "enticing" poetry of the Bible itself, especially that of the prophets, which might conceal from us the clear, unadorned ideal of discourse for which Paul is here arguing. But Paul cannot escape the enchantment of the "vail of Moses" and neither could his followers. They stressed the renunciation of course and were reluctant to acknowledge that poetry was a component of the spiritual life; nevertheless, when we examine their work, we see that they inherited the paradox. George Herbert in his two "Jordan" poems pronounces a farewell to the art of poetry, to "quaint words and trim invention," to "metaphors" that "deck the sense."

He concludes that all that matters is a "plain intention" and that "There is in love a sweetnesse readie penn'd: / Copie out onely that, and save expense." But the paradox is that these poems gain their power from the devices that they renounce. "Herbert cannot let go."[10] Similarly, John Bunyan writes an allegorical novel filled with colorful adventures drawn from the black-letter romances of an earlier day but denies in his prefatory verses that he is writing a mere "romance," a "novelty": "It seems a Novelty, and yet contains / Nothing but sound, and honest Gospel-strains."[11] Tolstoy offers us in the nineteenth century the crowning achievements of the novel genre, its maximum range of feeling, its maximum opulence of detail, and yet in his tract "What is Art?" written toward the end of his career, he dismisses as vanity all that is not spare and controlled and does so by an appeal to a biblical "sincerity" that shuns the merely aesthetic as false.

Can then anything intelligible be said about biblical poetics? Or are all such attempts doomed to be frustrated? Certainly, if we stick to "categories" and "genres," the conventions of classical and European literature, we are likely to find ourselves deceived. Christian humanism in its search for a harmonizing principle often falls into this trap. Jerome thought that the poetry of the Bible was written in regular hexameters like the Homeric epics, but Robert Lowth in the eighteenth century found no difficulty in demonstrating that the prosody of Isaiah was utterly different from that of the Greeks, and, in our own century, Erich Auerbach has discussed the Homeric epics and the Genesis narratives as diametrically opposed models of realism.[12] Milton in one of his more expansive humanistic moods proposed a whole list of equations: the book of Job, he said, was an example of the "brief epic"; the Song of Songs was a "divine pastoral drama" with two persons and a double chorus; and the Psalms accommodated themselves to the kinds of lyric poetry that we know.[13] These are large claims, but Milton's own practice as a poet of biblical inspiration shows how slippery and undependable they are, for it is the *tension* between the high Virgilian epic mode and the biblical mode of *unepic* domestic realism that we chiefly note in *Paradise Lost*.[14] Such tension may be a source of dramatic interest but it nevertheless tends to stultify all such equations as Milton himself proposed.

Nor do the literary forms of the ancient Middle East prove to be much more reliable from this point of view. Scholars of our century have sought (and found) in the Bible the outlines of enthronement rituals, laments, taunt-poems, wisdom literature, and the rest. As in Isaiah 14, ancient Canaanite mythologies and the literary patterns that go with them have come into view as aspects of the biblical text. But as we noted, these forms often have a traitor in the house. The reader is encouraged to see the hollowness of those same mythological patterns which the text so grandly exhibits. Imagination and the distrust of imagination go together.[15] Perhaps it is on this very tension itself that we should focus. Here, it may well be, is the specific determinant of biblical poetics. The text summons the reader to respond in an accustomed literary fashion to a familiar form but at the same instant undermines that response. The forms will be there but the text will encourage the reader to call them into question. This will explain something of the problematical nature of the attempt to read "the Bible as Literature" down the centuries and the varied, indeed contradictory, results this attempt has yielded.

By focusing on the tension, the dialectic of likeness and unlikeness that the Bible exhibits when set beside other literatures, we may succeed in saying something about the specific nature of biblical texts or rather about the nature of the contract that governs them. They tell us a gripping story of olden times, one that "holds children from play and old men from the chimney corner," but in the end what we thought of as a story turns out to be a warning. We can of course treat it if we wish as pure "story" and ignore the warning element, but then it will cease to be "Bible" and will have become something else. Likewise, the Bible gives us poems: if we are sensitive, we are "smit with the love of sacred song"— but the same song demands that we resist its enchantment. The last chapter of Ecclesiastes offers such a song. It summons up in verses of haunting beauty the pathos of our earthly existence; it speaks of approaching death but it does so by means of the images of life itself seen in a kind of golden sunset:

> and the almond tree blossoms,
> and the grasshopper drags itself along,
> and the caperberry fails;
> because the man goes to his eternal home,
> and the mourners go about the streets.
> Before the silver cord is loosed,
> and the golden bowl is shattered,
> or the pitcher is broken at the fountain,
> or the wheel is broken at the cistern. . . .
> (12:5–6)

But we are not allowed to remain with the charm, the sadness, the human grace and frailty of this great elegy. The poet, or whoever was responsible for the text as we have it, sums up and dismisses the Preacher's "pleasing words" (*dibrê hēpeṣ*). Fine as they are, they are not what we are ultimately to take to heart: "Of making many books there is no end; and much study is a weariness of the flesh. The end of the matter, when all is said and done: Fear God, and keep his commandments, for that is the whole of man"(12:12–13). In the end, it would seem that texts are sacred because they command and because we assent to their commands. That is what the author of Ecclesiastes is here evidently trying to say. The first eighteen chapters or so of Leviticus are not poetical; one wonders whether they can be classed as literature at all in the sense of *belles lettres,* but they do manifestly command. That is what makes them "Bible." This has disturbing implications for the whole enterprise of leveling the Bible with other kinds of literature.

Of course other kinds of literature can also hint at such purposes. Shakespeare points in that direction when in *Hamlet* he has his hero dismiss "all trivial fond records"—his juvenile love-poetry, for instance— and dedicate himself single-mindedly to his task:

> And thy commandment all alone shall live
> Within the book and volume of my brain,
> Unmixed with baser matter.

This is a great and moving sentence; it is also in a sense very biblical in its tone and setting.[16] But the point is that the ghost of Hamlet's father does not command even the most devout Shakespeareans among us. More than that, he does not even command Hamlet himself. He proves to be an ambiguous and misleading ghost and Hamlet ends by seeking his own wavering and uncertain path to the life of dialogue. He has no external guide. In this sense the play is not only about a man facing his task; it is about the limitations of secular art itself, about the purposes that it can conceive but that it is ultimately, of itself, unable to follow through.

One more word about the "vail of Moses." What seems to be involved in the phrase also is a contrast between the density, the opaqueness of the Hebrew Scriptures and what the author of Corinthians conceived as the clear unmediated light of the gospel. Pure presence, the transparency of vision, is here opposed to the mediation of language, the imperviousness of the verbal texture of the Old Testament. We do not meet Moses in the Old Testament; we meet the words of Moses, the interposed web of textuality. It is all that we have and it is all that is given us for interpretation. The Hebrew prophets and psalmists worked with words, fashioning them plastically to their needs, working with and sometimes against the grain of the language. As a result, meaning is often hidden in the play of words; close attention is needed to puns and ambiguities, to the seemingly endless inflections of the Hebrew three- and two-letter roots with their subtle variations of sound and sense. We can call this a species of metaphysical wit or we can call it a "demonstration of spirit and power"—as in the angry denunciation of the prophet Isaiah: "He looked for justice *(mišpāṭ),* and behold, a scab *(mišpāḥ)*! for righteousness *(ṣĕdāqâ)*, and behold, a scream *(ṣeʿāqâ)*!" (5:7). Words are often fragmented, blown apart as the prophet grimly pursues his purpose. We shall find this when we come to look at the intense play on the roots of the names Ephraim and Asshur by the prophet Hosea.[17] He uses language there as a weapon. This may not be poetic in the commonly understood senses of that word, but the language nevertheless draws attention to itself, weaves its web. And it is of course the Hebrew language.

In the following pages we shall try to do justice to the "significant and sinewy" quality of the Hebrew Bible[18]—a quality often lost in translation. In order to give the reader a sense of this we shall frequently transcribe the Hebrew verbal forms that lie behind the English text of the passages we shall be discussing. It is hoped that the thoughtful reader, even if he lacks all knowledge of Hebrew, will find this an aid rather than an obstacle to his understanding.

·1·

ESTHER: TWO TALES
OF ONE CITY

An example of a text that undermines its own structure and style is the book of Esther. We recall the definition of Hebrew realism offered by Erich Auerbach in his discussion of the Binding of Isaac (Genesis 22). In contrast with the manner of Homer in his epics, the aim of such narratives, he declares, "is not to bewitch the senses." All but the most essential details are left in darkness, all but the most essential words are left unsaid. The three days of the journey to Moriah pass in silence.[1] But Auerbach's categories manifestly do not apply to the narrative strategy and style of the opening chapter of Esther. If the three days of Abraham and Isaac's journey from Beer-Sheba are bare of all reference to things said or seen, the seven days of King Ahasuerus's great drinking festival are filled with the most elaborate detail—the kind of detail that *does*, in spite of Auerbach, bewitch the senses. There is a careful placing of the occasion, a careful inventory of the more notable items of the decor:

> And when these days were fulfilled, the king made a feast for all the people that were present in Shushan the capital, both for great and small, seven days, in the court of the garden of the king's palace: there were hangings of white, of fine cotton, and blue, fastened with cords of fine linen and purple on silver rings and pillars of marble: the divans were of gold and silver, upon a pavement of alabaster, marble, pearl and precious stone. And they gave them drink in vessels of gold, (the vessels being diverse from one another,) and royal wine in abundance, according to the king's bounty. And the drinking was according to the law; none did compel: for so the king had appointed to all the officers of his house, that they should do according to every man's pleasure. Also Vashti the queen made a feast for the women in the royal house which belonged to King Ahasuerus. (Esther 1:5–9)

Homer could not have been more lavish in his account of a feast. S. D. Goitein pointed out some years ago how similar the book of Esther is in this respect to the work of the great tenth-century Persian poet Firdausi, especially in his epic *Shah-Nama,* reflecting no doubt much earlier poetic traditions going back possibly even to the period of Ahasuerus (Xerxes) himself.² Firdausi's epic is marked by opulent descriptions of week-long drinking festivals during which the nobles and the king are entertained by the minstrel who regales them with festive tales and songs. There is a mirror effect here as the details of the narration are reflected by the action of the poem itself, its indolent, ritualistic movement. The following passage is typical; in it we have an account of the harem as seen by a visitor, the prince Siyavosh:

> The harem occupants all approached in a body, gaily arrayed, the house from end to end being covered with musk and gold coins and filled with saffron. Silver coins were poured in his path and mingled together with rubies and emeralds. Chinese brocade covered the floor and the surface of the ground was strewn with pearls of purest lustre. Everywhere to be found were wine, music and minstrels' songs, and each lady of the harem wore a diadem on her head. The whole apartment was a paradise richly dight, with lovely women and precious objects in abundance.
>
> As Siyavosh entered, he beheld a throne of shining gold inlaid with emeralds, over it being laid a cover of brocade.³

The first chapter of Esther not only evokes a similar world of lavish, sensual delights but employs the same descriptive luxuriance to match that world. Moreover, the narrative hinges on some of the same central symbols and features. Goitein notes that the focus on King, Wine, and Women in the book of Esther corresponds exactly to the major concerns of the Persian epic as we know it.

The same thematic pattern is found in another text, viz., the apocryphal book of Esdras where three young men at a great feast in the court of Darius engage in a competition "to name the thing which he judges the strongest." (1 Esd. 3:5). The first declares that "Wine is the strongest"; the second declares, "the strongest of men is the King." The third, Zerubabel, who proves to be the wisest and whom the king rewards accordingly, chooses women: "Sirs, it is true the King is great, men are many, and Wine is strong, but who rules over them? Who is the sovereign power? Women, surely!" (1 Esd. 4:13–14, NEB). In keeping with these priorities, the first chapter of Esther, after the description of the seven-day drinking bout, describes how "on the seventh day, when the heart of the king was merry with wine," he commands his chamberlains to bring the queen to his presence that he might display her beauty (according to the rabbis, her naked beauty)⁴ before the assembled notables. Vashti refuses to come, thus defying the king's command! The king determines to replace Vashti in order to show an example of how husbands should rule their wives throughout all the provinces of the Persian empire (1:22). But the reader is made to feel—much in the spirit of

Zerubabel's contention—that the king is due to be disappointed. In spite of the royal firman, wives are destined to rule over their husbands just as Zerubabel had noted in the book of Esdras.

But when in the sequel Esther becomes queen in place of Vashti, we have something more than a demonstration of female power. Ironically, Esther, whom the king prefers to Vashti, proves to be, in spite of her meekness and undemanding simplicity, more skillful in manipulating his authority; she uses her position in the palace to pursue the interests of her people, making the king look even more foolish in the process than he had looked when Vashti had refused to obey his summons. But the irony is not only at the expense of the king. The world he represents and its system of values is made to look foolish. The whole fashion of Arabian nights' entertainment, so well caught in the opening chapter and elsewhere, is revealed as empty and alien.[5] I am arguing that the elaborate filling in of trivia, the festive style for a festive occasion, contains within itself its own antithesis. And it is Esther who, through her behavior and bearing, comes to signify this antithesis.

Esther, we recall, is conscripted under the order issued by the king to gather all the beautiful virgins of the kingdom to his harem (2:3–8). Their one night spent with the king was preceded by an elaborate ritual of anointing and beautifying with spices and ornaments (2:12). Moreover, the lady whose turn it was, "was given whatever she desired to take with her out of the house of the women into the king's house"—the intention being some extra jewel or special item of dress or other cosmetic adornment. Esther has been until now entirely passive (it is remarkable how much of this book is conducted in the passive voice, the Hebrew *nipʿal* or *puʿal*). She now makes her will known for the first time in three simple words—*loʾ biqĕšâ dābār,* "she asked for nothing"—nothing, that is, except what Hegai the eunuch indicated to be the regulation procedure (2:15). This too, is a kind of passivity, but one eloquent with resolution. Esther, who had submitted herself to the selection process and all it entailed, distances herself now from the pomp and ceremony of the court in those three words. Like Cordelia she demands nothing, bids for nothing. But King Ahasuerus, unlike Lear, is enchanted precisely by Esther's simplicity, which is in such striking contrast to the prevailing style of display around her. As the story proceeds, Esther is required (or rather chooses) to make even more startling deviations from established custom. Hearing from Mordecai the shocking news of the calamity about to befall her people, she decrees a three-day fast. In contrast to the great feasts and potations that mark the life of the court, she bids the Jews hold a fast "and neither eat nor drink for three days, night and day" (4:16). She and her maidens will do likewise. But the more daring break will come when she approaches the king without being summoned—a serious violation of law and custom, as we are twice told, and one whose penalty is death. Having greatly dared and nevertheless succeeded in this first step, she now decides that the way to compass her aims is to first adopt the style of the court. She will invite the king and Haman to a feast as elaborate as any to which the court is accustomed. She not only puts on a two-day banquet but uses the coquetry that she had earlier eschewed by coyly withholding her request to the king and reserving it for the second day of the feast (5:8). When that request is revealed, however, it is shown to be one that shatters the conviviality of the occasion. It is not a request for some royal favor or bounty of the kind that might suit the atmosphere of the banqueting hall. It is life she is begging—for herself and her people: "Let my life be given at my petition, and my people at my request" (7:3).

Attention should be given to the sudden change in style in the above half-verse. The master narrative, a novel of love and intrigue set in the fifth-century Persian court of Xerxes, is conducted in elaborate prose, labored, descriptive, and repetitive as in the first chapter of the book, but here in this short passage we have the more urgent poetic rhythm of the parallelism. We abandon here the brocaded language of the Persian "novel" for a simpler and sharper statement, an anti-novel whose essential terms are: "life," "people," "request." Poetry here proves to be simpler and sharper than the prose in which the main narrative is conducted. The poetic passages stand out in the stark simplicity of their language and the urgency of their rhythm. This parallelistic rhythm of urgency is picked up again in 8:6: "For how can I endure to see the evil that shall befall my people? Or how can I endure to see the destruction of my kindred?" Ahasuerus is uncharacteristically abrupt in his response. When hearing that Haman was the culprit (forgetting of course that he himself had given the order), he orders him to be hanged in two words— *tělûhû ʿālāyw*. I am arguing that Esther not only dares to undermine existing customs; her few initiatives in the book (there are only two or three of them altogether) become the focus of a kind and style of narration sharply at odds with the prevailing mode and style of the master narrative.

Mordecai is even more sharply at odds with this style than Esther. In the semiotic pattern of the book, he stands for the alien: he is the one man out. Sitting at the king's gate to see what will become of Esther, he neither bows nor prostrates himself to Haman as he passes. Later he will violate custom even more startlingly by rending his garments and stationing himself at the king's gate in sackcloth and ashes. We may say that here, in the "Hebrew" counterplot, we have—in contrast to the "Persian" narrative—the working out of Auerbach's categories of biblical simplicity. In the account of Mordecai's doings we note that economy of detail which Auerbach perceived as the mark of the akedah story. All we learn of Mordecai's behavior are three things, and, unlike the accumulated and superfluous details in the account of the feasting of the court, they are utterly necessary and utterly significant, since on them the movement of the counterplot hinges: they are his being at the king's gate—for that is where he overhears the conspiracy of Bigthan and Teresh; his refusal to bow to Haman—that is what provokes Haman to his plan of massacring the Jews; and his putting on of sackcloth and ashes—for that is what stirs the queen to action. It is like the fire, the knife, the wood, and the ram caught in the thicket in the akedah; they are the details on which the story hinges and this is why they are there. Not a word or detail is superfluous. Thus, in the book of Esther is imbedded a Hebrew type of narrative, marked by a realism in which nothing is on the surface, everything standing out against the darkness of its own background. Mordecai is the sign of this other narrative, Mordecai shrouded in darkness beyond the gate of the palace while the feasting goes on within, a feasting to which he is totally indifferent and from which he is totally cut off.

But there is one point in the book where Mordecai is astonishingly made to figure in a "Persian" display of royal ceremony. In the night between the two days of Esther's feast, the king, finding himself unable to sleep, calls for the chronicler to entertain him with some stories from the royal archives. It is a little like the function of the minstrel in the epic of Firdausi, though of course we do not have to do here with "mere" minstrelsy but with something more purposive. The item that stays in the king's mind is the discovery by Mordecai of the plot by Bigthan and Teresh to assassinate him. Esther had revealed this plot to the king in the name of Mordecai. As a consequence, Mordecai is lifted out of his obscurity (both senses of that word), arrayed in royal robes and a royal crown, and, riding on the royal charger, is escorted through the streets by Haman as "the man whom the king delights to honor." It is of course the turning point of the whole novel. But if the aspect of pomp and display here reaches a climax, in the festive parade of Mordecai and Haman through the streets with Mordecai dressed like the king himself, his own reaction or rather nonreaction marks this same episode as the climax of what may be termed the subtext or counterplot. Mordecai is here entirely passive, as wordless as Abraham and Isaac on the way to Moriah. It is what is done to him that is recorded. The passive voice (e.g., "thus shall it be done to the man . . .") is not merely a way of telling the story; it is the matter of the story itself. The reader is challenged to seek the agent concealed by these passive constructions, by these silences, by this obscurity. He is caught in the tension created by these two contrasting narratives, one of which undermines and questions the other.[6]

The phrase of maximum significance for this "other" narrative is achieved in 6:12. The procession over, the narrator states simply, "And Mordecai came back to the king's gate." Those words cry out for interpretation as peremptorily as does the phrase "the two of them went together" of the akedah narrative in Genesis 22. What are his thoughts as he returns to his post, resuming perhaps his sackcloth and ashes and crouching, as before, at the door of the palace? Is it expectation, or wonder, or puzzlement, or alarm? What—he may be asking himself— does this sudden elevation portend, this freakish change of circumstances, which, unlike that of Joseph when called likewise to the king's presence, is accompanied by no explanation and followed by no royal communication?[7] And why should his mortal enemy of all people have been chosen to escort him? Nothing of all this is actually expressed, but it is the silences of the story which now become eloquent. We are made aware that Mordecai cannot plan his further moves: he is, so to speak, being taken over. The *nip'al* or passive voice now comes into its own in a deeper sense than in the rest of the story. As Silas Marner says in George Eliot's novel, "There's dealings!"

It is in this context that we may consider the most eloquent silence in the whole book; it is of course the silence relating to God himself. He lurks behind the counterplot but nothing is said of him and his name is never mentioned. But his presence is hinted at by the silent waiting of Mordecai—the suspense that hangs in the air following that extraordinary ride through the streets. Only thus are we made aware of an agency concealed behind those passive constructions which govern the whole narrative. What is done to Esther and Mordecai and what is related to the king in the name of Mordecai are the result of a power at work in the story, a real King in contrast to the king of shreds and patches who presides over the overt narrative. In the covert narrative another kingship is at work, one about which nothing is said and yet which shows itself able to manage the entire business of the kingdom and steer it in a direction different from that which any of the actors could have anticipated.

The nearest we get to an allusion to the workings of providence is in Mordecai's warning to Esther in chapter 4: "Do not think in thy heart that thou shalt escape in the king's house any more than all the other Jews. For if thou dost at all remain silent at this time, then shall relief and deliverance arise to the Jews from another quarter [lit. 'from another place']" (4:14). And if Esther is being warned against succumbing to the luxury of the life of the court and thereby forgetting her "Jewish" responsibilities, the reader is likewise being warned against the same court-style and the arts of language that go with it. Providence works through a less ostentatious mode of narration, directs us to "another quarter."

There is also a more subtly revealing indication of the presence of a divine stage manager. The rabbis gloss 6:1, "On that night the king could not sleep," with the remark —"it was the King of the World whose sleep was disturbed."[8] This phrase "on that night the king could not sleep" marks in their view the coming together of the plot and counterplot, the latter being destined to overcome the former. Kingship is at the center of the Persian-style narrative, the ceremony and pomp of an earthly kingship. This is never totally displaced—even Mordecai at the end will become viceroy to the king. But the royal language is subtly undermined. A greater power than Ahasuerus can comprehend is at work disturbing his sleep because his own divine sleep is disturbed by what is done in Susa. There is need for only one tug of the string—a sleepless night for Ahasuerus, a record recited, a moment of honor for Mordecai, and the world is steered into a new direction. This is *Heilsgeschichte* as evidently as the story of Joseph and his brethren or of Ruth the Moabitess, but it is conducted by means of indirections. In the subtext, silence takes the place of noisy proclamations; the haste of the couriers mounted on their horses and posted on the king's service to the one hundred and twenty-seven provinces of the kingdom makes way for the unhurried action of a king who has no need of satraps or couriers to govern his kingdom and who will find other ways of compassing his aims if Mordecai and Esther will not see fit to help.

Above all, the undermining of the epic of the royal Persian court is achieved by the very devices that most characterize it—those of repetition and amplification. How many times are we told that the laws of the Medes and the Persians are unchanging, that the king's decree once issued can never be revoked! And yet as the formal phrases are again and again repeated they sound more and more hollowly in the reader's ears. We come to realize that the king takes no independent decisions and that those he does take are nearly all revoked one way or another. Instead of ruling, he is ruled by others—his chamberlains, Haman, Esther, Mordecai. In the end there is only one ruler whose commands, never officially promulgated, are unchanging and whose will prevails. He lurks behind the costly hangings of the court and whispers in the ear of Ahasuerus in the night. It is of him that the subtext speaks and whose deeds it records.

·2·

WHAT IS BEAUTIFUL?

Esther, we are told, is beautiful. It is that which gives her her chance—not so much to gain wealth and status as to help her people. But is Ruth beautiful? She is the heroine of an equally, if not more romantic story and yet the book of Ruth makes no reference to her physical charms. This is a little curious because the average reader has a clear impression that she is fair and graceful. Novelists too. Thus Eppie, the child heroine of George Eliot's *Silas Marner* who, in the manner of Ruth (and with deliberate echoing of the biblical text), turns her back on her natural family and determines to stay with her foster father, is, as everyone terms her, a pretty child—"a round fair thing with soft yellow rings all over its head." Ruth amid the alien corn also figures in the work of many visual artists and she is invariably beautiful. And yet nothing of this is said in the text. She is complimented on her loyalty, never on her appearance. The Shulammite of the Song of Solomon is, by contrast, praised repeatedly and abundantly for the perfection of her form and features—"Behold, you are beautiful, my love; behold, you are beautiful" (1:15). And yet it is difficult to recall many examples of artists who have been inspired to paint her.[1]

Beauty in the Bible is an elusive quality. It affirms itself even when not directly invoked. It is not true that the biblical writers show no interest in beauty in art and nature. They surely do. Esther's beauty is a key factor in her story. Bezalel the artist is given more titles of honor than are accorded to any hero, prophet, or king. God had "called him by name" and had "filled him with the Spirit of God, with ability and intelligence, with knowledge and all craftsmanship, to devise artistic designs . . ." (Exod. 31:2–3). All but one of the heroines of the patriarchal narratives in Genesis are singled out as beautiful and lovely: Leah, who isn't, suffers in consequence. But it can work the other way. When Rachel dies, her physical charm passes to Joseph: he too is beautiful and lovely—a tribute rarely paid to male characters in the Bible. Joseph pays for his good looks with much suffering. And yet looked at from the perspective to which the narrative ultimately directs us, his beauty represents the thread of grace out of which salvation history is woven. Had his brothers not been

15

aroused by it to jealousy and had his master's wife not desired him for it, Jacob and his sons would not have come down to Egypt thence to be so marvelously delivered. Joseph's beauty accompanies them, it would seem, in their ongoing history; it will not be forgotten.

The elusiveness of the beautiful is a matter of its direction. Ruth becomes beautiful through her posture, her movement, her direction. That sheds grace on her even without the notion of beauty being directly invoked. The Shulammite is more static; she and her lover seem to circle around a still center; their presence, visual, tangible, and also, olfactory—as well as their relationship to each other—is established by the repetition of set phrases and gestures. They seem to end where they begin. Perhaps that is why her beauty is less of a stimulus to the imagination of writers and painters. Direction and purpose are important. The tabernacle in the wilderness executed by Bezalel was, we are to believe, a marvelous artistic achievement. But unlike the Golden Calf (another artwork mentioned in close textual proximity to it), it is characterized by the feature of mobility. It moved with the people on their journeyings. The heavier objects, altars, table, and ark, had rings attached to them into which poles were fitted to facilitate their removal from place to place. Indeed, those fitted into the rings of the ark were never to be taken out (Exod. 25:15). Movement and the ever-present potentiality for movement, rather than fixity, are of the essence. Biblical beauty is not arrested in a still moment of aesthetic contemplation; it is caught, so to speak, in passage.

What therefore, is beautiful? We have the clearest of all definitions in Isa. 52:7:

> How beautiful upon the mountains
> are the feet of him that brings good tidings,
> that announces peace; that brings good tidings of good,
> that announces victory;
> that says to Zion, Thy God reigns!

This passage has been much praised as a high-water mark in the biblical perception of the beautiful. James Muilenburg finds it and the verses immediately following to be "the center and climax of the entire collection of poems" by this particular poet-prophet.[2] Another critic finds in the passage "a scene of breathtaking poetical beauty."[3] A third critic declares that there the prophet sees "the most beautiful sight in the world."[4] However, we should note the precise locus of this beauty: it is the *feet* of the herald which are said to be beautiful and that is because they run swiftly, bringing tidings of salvation. Of course, there is a scene and there is a figure; we glimpse the mountains around Jerusalem over which the fleet runner approaches to bring the message of victory. The watchman of the city spots the runner from his point of vantage (ibid., v. 8), much as the watchman sees the approaching runners in 2 Sam. 18:25–27. But it is not (in either case) the picture that arrests us by its grace and symmetry; what matters is the message that the herald is yet to deliver and which, in fact, he will deliver only when his feet have stopped running. In the meantime, that undelivered message sheds beauty on his moving feet—the beauty of an annunciation.

If we can think of this scene in Isa. 52:7 in terms of the art of painting, then the figure of the messenger will have to be striving for something outside the painting, some yet-to-be disclosed image of glad tidings. The nature of those tidings is intimated in the verse in the climactic movement of the words *šālôm, ṭôb, yěšûʿâ,* i.e., peace, good, and victory. But the ultimate term of the climax is in the final phrase—"that says to Zion, Thy God reigns." This is not merely beyond the frame of the picture; it seems to set aside all mere pictures. More than that, it transcends and, in a manner, abolishes the category of the beautiful. The expression *mah-nāʾwû* (how beautiful) used here of the feet of the herald and the same *nāʾwâ* used elsewhere of Jerusalem (Song of Sol. 6:4) or of the temple (Ps. 93:5) is an attribute of places and people, of things that touch the ground. But with the triumphant conclusion of the verse in the words "that says to Zion, Thy God reigns," the concept of *nāʾwâ* has been left behind. This is not because we are beyond visible beauty in some region of abstraction. Indeed, the affirmation of visibility remains. In the following verse we are told pointedly and startlingly that "They shall see eye to eye, / the Lord returning to Zion" (52:8)—but there is no hint of the aesthetic, of anything remotely suggestive of beauty in the blinding glare of that revelation. The eyeball to eyeball image in fact seems to interdict the beautiful; the eye is too close to the eye that it confronts to be aware of any shape or form, of anything beyond visibility itself. It is visibility, we may say, pared down to its essence, where all the shading, all the charm of a representable posture, have been banished. It is here at the limits of the seen that the epiphany will occur. It is a little like Job declaring that after his skin has been stripped from his body, in his flesh (or it may even be—for the prepositional *mem* is ambiguous—without his flesh) he will see God (Job 19:26). If that verse from Job gives us the lower limits of the seen, then Isa. 52:8 gives us its upper limits. Either way, there is no place for beauty, only the absoluteness of seeing itself.

Beauty, we have suggested, is the thread on which salvation is strung, but if we follow that thread it takes us away from the beautiful into some other region. The beauty of the temple leads us to holiness (Ps. 93:5). Through the beautiful sound of praise—the *nāʾwâ* of Ps. 147:1—we attain the knowledge of him to whom praise is due, and yet in that knowledge beauty is eclipsed. It is through the beautiful feet of the runner speeding to Jerusalem that we come to know the message of salvation, but the message, when it is delivered, will be that charm is deceitful and beauty vain.

We may set against the elusiveness of such contradictions a famous image of beauty from a text of a very different kind. Hamlet is speaking of his dead father:

> See what a grace was seated on this brow;
> Hyperion's curls, the front of Jove himself,
> An eye like Mars, to threaten and command,
> A station like the herald Mercury
> New-lighted on a heaven-kissing hill. . .
>
> (*Hamlet* III, iv)

As a matter of fact, Hamlet is not speaking of his father directly but of a picture of his father, perhaps one contained in the frame of a medallion. In this aesthetic space he sees comprised the beauty of the gods of the Greek and Roman pantheon. These gods do not elude the category of the beautiful by affirming some extra-aesthetic standard; quite the contrary, they situate themselves within the boundaries of that which can be rendered by a clear, visual symmetry. They are in fact more clearly outlined than the figure of Hamlet's father with whom they are being compared, and more beautiful. It might even be argued that the evocation here of the grace of the gods, the fair brow of Jupiter, the lovely hair of Hyperion, is a way of diverting attention from the far-from-beautiful characteristics of Hamlet senior. It is only through linking his memory imaginatively to the vision of the gods (elsewhere in the play, to Hercules) that Hamlet can think of his father as beautiful. Without that divine penumbra, we should see him merely as a "dead corse . . . making night hideous" or as a morally flawed monarch whose "foul crimes" must be "burnt and purged away"—phrases that suggest something far other than the beautiful.

In the quoted lines from Shakespeare's play, therefore, we have a dialectic, but one opposite to that which we found in Isa. 52:7–8. There, as we have said, the messenger's feet had pointed us—more correctly, speeded us—beyond the frame of the picture toward an epiphany where the category of *nā'wâ* no longer applied, toward an extra-aesthetic space. The *měbaśśēr* is exactly what that term implies—an announcer, an instrument for communicating tidings of salvation. That is why his feet are beautiful. But the seeing of God, the revelation itself that he announces, has nothing to do with beauty. By contrast, in the movement of Shakespeare's lines, the human agent has little grace or charm of his own: these are bestowed on him vicariously by bringing into the picture, indeed into the space of the medallion, the fair features of the gods who are the true source of beauty.

The parallel between the two passages we are discussing is made more pointed by the fact that both have to do with heralds and with the special beauty of the herald who brings his message of divine blessing to men. Shakespeare speaks of "the herald Mercury / New-lighted on a heaven-kissing hill. . . ." The descent of Hermes or Mercury is a central motif for all the epic writers from Homer to Milton,[5] just as the coming of the messenger of salvation is a central motif for the author of Isaiah 52, Nahum 1, and other great passages of biblical prophecy. The task of the herald in all these cases is to communicate the will of God and the coming of God. He is thus in a special sense a persona of the prophet: one critic has in fact suggested that the herald of Isaiah 52 is the prophet himself as he reflexively dramatizes his role in the history of salvation.[6] Mercury or Hermes has a similar metapoetic role for the poets of antiquity and the Renaissance. He comes to signalize the function of poetry. Beauty is for that reason properly associated with him—it is the beauty of the poet and of his poetry.

Surprisingly, in both the biblical and pagan sources our attention is fastened on the *feet* of the herald. In Virgil the description is already fairly stereotyped: "The god [Mercury] made ready to obey his mighty father's bidding, and first binds on his feet the golden shoes which carry him upborne on wings over seas or lands, swift as the gale. Then he takes his wand . . . on this relying, he drives the winds and skims the stormy clouds."[7] It will be seen that the winged feet and golden sandals of Mercury are a main feature in Virgil. The Hebrew poet as we have seen also draws our attention to the feet of the herald. The affinity is striking. Nevertheless the difference between the two *topoi*, however obvious, must be stated: it is that Mercury is a god, while the *měbaśśēr* of Isaiah 52 is all too obviously a human agent whose feet do not fly in the air on golden wings but touch the ground as do our own. And that, we may add, is why he is beautiful—he can be beautiful because he is not God! Mercury by contrast is beautiful because he *is* a god and as such can communicate something of the beauty of the gods to human affairs.

But there is another more important distinction between the biblical notion of the herald and the classical "descent of the god." The beauty of the herald Mercury in the very hellenically inspired passage from *Hamlet* that we have been considering is a beauty of *situation*. Of course, Mercury's task signifies movement; he is the god of travelers. But to discover his beauty we have to "freeze" him, to arrest his movement. In Shakespeare's words he is "new-lighted on a heaven-kissing hill." He is eternally held in that pose of consummate charm like the figures painted on Keats's Grecian Urn. Ultimately, we see that Mercury reveals the perfection of his form not by his swift flight but by his "station." That word in Shakespeare's line is extraordinarily powerful. He speaks of "a station like the herald Mercury." The image is one of stasis, of order; it suggests a moment never to be surpassed, we may even say—never to be attained. It is a beauty closed in upon itself, a kind of Platonic idea of the beautiful that we glimpse here in Hamlet's memory of his father, though—and here is the source of the wistful, elegiac tone of the passage—it has little relevance to the real figure of Hamlet's father in his habit as he lived.

We thus return to the question that we began with: what does the Bible see as beautiful? To answer negatively we may say that assuredly it is not a beauty of stasis. It is not the "station" of Isaiah's herald that charms us but, most emphatically, his movement, the promise implied by his purpose, a purpose not yet fulfilled as we glimpse him. It is a beauty not of being but of becoming, not of rest but of motion. It points us forward to what still has to be done in historical time.

II

This dynamic conception of a beauty that defies stasis may be applied to a much larger matter than we have so far considered, namely the biblical account of the world itself and its creation. The sun, the moon, and the stars are of course a standard of beauty in various passages of the Hebrew scriptures. The Shulammite is "fair as the moon, bright as the sun" (Song of Sol. 6:10). The first adjective here is *yāpâ*. Elsewhere, all that God has made, i.e., the world itself, is described as *yāpeh běʿittô* ("beautiful in its time," Eccles. 3:11). Often the adjective *ṭôb*, "good," is used as a synonym for *yāpeh*. This is clearly so in the combination *ṭôbat marʾeh*, "fair to look on" (Esther 1:11, 2:7; Gen. 24:16, etc.) and in such a phrase as *wěṭôbâ ʾănî běʿênāyw*, "if I have found favor in his sight" (Esther 8:5). When in Genesis 1, God sees that the world he is creating is "good," the repeated phrase *kî-ṭôb* surely has something of the same force. The world is fair, pleasing, or lovely; in the same way the mother of the infant Moses saw that the child she had brought into the world was "goodly" (*kî-ṭôb hûʾ*) in Exod. 2:2. He was fair to possess and to hold.

A case might thus be argued, on the basis of the six-times repeated phrase "and God saw that it was good" in Genesis 1, that the created world of the Hebrew Bible, like the *kosmos* of the Greeks, is supremely the seat of *to kalon*, i.e., the principle of beauty. Moreover, it would seem to be a rounded and perfected beauty. We remember that the account of creation in Genesis 1 rises upwards in an orderly process from the mineral to the vegetable world and thence to the world of animated creatures, to reach a climax with the production of Man himself. The final accolade is then given; it is not simply *kî-ṭôb* but *wĕhinnēh-ṭôb mĕʾōd* (Gen. 1:31), not *to kalon*, but *to kalliston*. We might suppose that here we have a whole that we can contemplate much in the manner of a work of art, having unity and perfection of form. That is in fact the way Cassuto understands the phrase:

> He perceived that not only were the details, taken separately, good, but that each one harmonized with the rest; hence the whole was not just *good*, but *very good*. An analogy might be found in an artist who, having completed his masterpiece, steps back a little and surveys his handiwork with delight, for both in detail and in its entirety it had emerged perfect from his hand.[8]

And yet there is surely something wrong with a scheme that makes the "very good" (*ṭôb mĕʾōd*) of Gen. 1:31 the moment of supreme aesthetic gratification that comes when a work of art has been completed. If the art-creation analogy of Cassuto is to hold, that moment of which he speaks should surely come not on the sixth day but on the seventh day! The moment when "the artist steps back a little and surveys his handiwork with delight" would more fittingly correspond with the contemplative posture of the day of rest, when indeed there is a *completion,* conveyed by the twice-repeated "were finished . . . God finished" (*wayĕkullû . . . wayĕkal*) of Gen. 2:1–2, as though to say that the work of creation had been well and truly completed. But the truth is that in 2:1–3 nothing is said of surveying the handiwork of the creation and nothing is said of the seventh day being *ṭôb* or *ṭôb mĕʾōd*. As in the example of the *mĕbaśśēr*, it seems that here we have gone beyond the beauty principle altogether. The accomplishments of the six days are beautiful and are defined as such, just as the feet of the herald are beautiful, but when those feet finally accomplish their purpose and his message is delivered, there is, as we saw, no further room for the beautiful. Likewise the "goodness" of the six days carries us to the supreme moment of completion of the seventh day. But when we get to that moment, we find not a moony space of aesthetic delight, not the category of *ṭôb* at all, but rather that of holiness (2:3). For God declares the seventh day not *yāpeh* or *ṭôb*, but *qādôš*. For six days the work had been beautiful; to the seventh day, when it arrives, he awards the title of holy.

This leads one to wonder whether the rounding off of the work of creation on the seventh day really carries with it the sense of closure that we would associate with a completed work of art. If completion is conveyed by the anaphoric *wayĕkullû . . . wayĕkal*, then something other than completion is conveyed by the verbs *bārāʾ . . . laʿăśôt* at the end of verse 3—literally "which God had created to make." Nahmanides in his comment on this verse suggested that the word *laʿăśôt* carried with it the notion that the world would go on being made throughout the six thousand years of its existence. The talmudic rabbis too had a sense of an open-ended act of creation that would be renewed daily,[9] and this is a thought that has occurred to more modern students of the Old Testament scripture.[10] If that is so, the thrust of the passage is one that denies closure. But the really critical term that points to continuing activity rather than a posture of aesthetic contemplation is the second verb of verse 3, namely *wayĕqaddēš*. We have suggested that it means, "he declared it holy," giving the root *qdš* an adjectival meaning corresponding with *ṭôb* in the six days of creation. The six days are "good," the seventh day is "holy." This, however, does not exhaust the meaning of the *piʿēl* form, *wayĕqaddēš*. God does not simply declare the seventh day holy; he actively hallows it, sets it apart, and marks it for ever as having a special character and function. The *piʿēl* form *qiddaš* has elsewhere the meaning of opening a campaign (Jer. 6:4; Joel 3:9) or mobilizing an army (Jer. 51:28). It powerfully conveys the sense of a beginning rather than an ending. In short we are speaking of a day invested with purposes still to be fulfilled.

Thus, far from completing the symmetry, the three verses that speak of the completion of the creation on the seventh day actually disturb the symmetry, introducing a note of urgency and purpose into what is otherwise an orderly and majestic narration. This urgency is conveyed also by the five verbs in the imperfect that follow one another in rapid order in vv. 1–3: *wayĕkullû . . . wayĕkal . . . wayišbōt . . . wayĕbārek . . . wayĕqaddēš*, "were finished . . . God finished . . . rested . . . blessed . . . sanctified." Paradoxically, the day of rest is announced by a group of signifiers that suggest ceaseless activity, a willed intention to shape a future.

The sense that we have to do here with a beginning rather than an ending, with openness rather than closure, becomes stronger if we set these verses against what follows in chapters 2 and 3. Ongoingness is immediately emphasized in Gen. 2:4. The narrator begins now to set forth the "generations" *(tôlĕdôt)* of heaven and earth as they were "in the process of creation" *(bĕhibbārĕʾām)*. That *bĕhibbārĕʾām*, with its *nipʿal* construction suggestive of continuing activity, will govern the whole subsequent history of struggle, of trial and error, of advances and reverses, light and darkness, in the chapters that follow. Ultimately, in spite of the moment of aesthetic gratification caught in the phrase "and God saw everything that he had made, and behold, it was very good," it is not closure but the inauguration of a historical program that we are dealing with here. And the creator God who sets this program in motion does not much resemble an artist who surveys his completed handiwork. If analogies from art are to be of any relevance, we would do better to think of a divine stage manager or dramatist who improvises as he goes along and never really discloses the completed pattern.

Of course, not to treat Gen. 1–2:3 alone but to relate that passage to what follows from 2:4 onwards, as we have just done, raises the whole question of the propriety of discussing the Bible (or even one single book of the Bible) as a single text. For if ever there is a break, it will be claimed, here it assuredly is in the transition from Gen. 2:3 to 2:4. Here indeed is the *locus classicus* for the whole documentary hypothesis regarding the composition of the Pentateuch.[11] Here is the seam between the P and J documents—the very *Urpunkt* of the kind of historical-philological scholarship that aims at exposing the different layers of text and their different origins and authorships. How then is one to justify the bringing together of verses that philologists tell us should be seen as distinct from one another? We may simply say here with Sir Philip Sidney that he who affirms nothing cannot be guilty of an untruth. We are saying nothing about the authorship or original dates of composition of the different verses and chapters. We are in this study affirming nothing about the archeology of the text or its later development, nor are we even trying to establish the boundaries of any particular poem or narrative with a view to defining its formal characteristics. All these are proper and legitimate concerns, but the enterprise on which we are embarked is simply that of trying to determine how the text, *as we find it delivered to us*, works and what it is trying to say.[12] On the other hand, we are not talking about an accidental concourse of atoms. The assumption is that whoever put the text together in the form in which we have it was trying to say something. Or rather, that is not only an assumption, it is more in the nature of a legitimate conclusion arising out of the discovery of analogies, echoes, and continuities binding texts and parts of texts to one another. We are talking about internal evidence to be sure, but then the philological-historical criticism done on the Bible is for the most part founded on internal evidence only. We may claim to be employing a similar mixture of pragmatism and intuition.

With that legitimating principle in mind, let us now take an even longer leap forward, from Genesis into Exodus. The dialectic of a completion that is not a completion emerges even more clearly from the analogy between Genesis 1–2 on the one hand and the story of the work of the tabernacle by the artist Bezalel on the other (Exodus 35–40), especially the account of the apparent completion of that work in Exod. 39:42–40:33. The analogy itself was discerned by the rabbis of the Talmud.[13] In modern times the link between creation and temple-building has been forcefully argued by Martin Buber,[14] by Umberto Cassuto[15] in his commentaries on Genesis and Exodus, and by others.[16] It is perhaps worth summarizing the salient features of the analogy. First, the key words of Gen. 1:31–2:3 seem to be present in the story of the completion of the tabernacle. The *work* (*mĕlā'kâ*, as in Gen. 2:2) is said to be *complete* (*wattēkel*, as in Gen. 2:1 and 2:2). Moses now performs the task that God had performed in the work of creation: he *sees all that has been done* and he *blesses* them (i.e., the workers) (39:43). And then, having performed the act of blessing *(wayĕbārek)*, he is bidden to *hallow* or *declare holy* (the same *piʿēl* form, *qaddēš*, as in Gen. 2:3) both Aaron the priest and the various completed articles of the sanctuary (Exod. 40:9, 10, 11, 13).

Here then is a work of man corresponding to the work of God in the days of creation. Moreover, we have before us, explicitly, an *artwork*. Bezalel the human artist is a craftsman who is filled with the "spirit of God" (Exod. 35:31), the same *rûaḥ ʾĕlōhîm* mentioned in Gen. 1:2 as moving over the waters of the primordial world of creation. What we have here is indeed more than a literary analogy. Jewish tradition deduces all the thirty-nine forms of work *(mĕlāʾkâ)* forbidden on the Sabbath from the various operations connected with the design and execution of the tabernacle, thus identifying the work from which God rested on the seventh day (and which we in consequence are bidden to desist from likewise) with that work which Bezalel, the master builder, performed in miniature in his creative role as builder of the tabernacle. Moses, who declares the work finished and blesses it, participates likewise in the work of God, especially God's hallowing of the seventh day. The hallowing of time is now paralleled by the hallowing of space as Moses utters the summarizing words of blessing over the completed sanctuary.

The manifest relation between the two accounts, that of world-creation and that of sanctuary-building, may also be regarded as a key to the system of metaphor in other parts of scripture, notably Psalms 24, 29, and 93. But it is worth pointing out a significant difference between the two accounts and one that lights up the subject on which we are here embarked, viz., the place of the category of the beautiful in the Bible. While the sanctuary in the wilderness is emphatically an artwork and Bezalel is emphatically the artist—more so than any other person named in the Bible—the key word *ṭôb* and its parallels, *yāpeh* and *nāʾweh*, are nevertheless missing from the account of his work! Exod. 39:43 actually cries out for the appropriate rounding off of the phrase that it echoes. In Gen. 1:31 it had been said, "And God saw everything that he had made, and behold, it was very good." Here in Exod. 39:43 we read, "And Moses saw all the work, and behold, they had done it; as the Lord had commanded, so had they done it. And Moses blessed them." The verse leaves us, as it were, hanging; it features a kind of anacoluthon. Instead of the ending that we expect, viz., *wĕhinnēh ṭôb-mĕʾōd*, "and behold it was very good," we have *wĕhinnēh ʿāśû ʾōtâ*, "and behold, they had done it. . . ." And then, as though to fill in the gap left by the missing words *ṭôb mĕʾōd*, we have the rather lame conclusion "as the Lord had commanded, so had they done it."

It is as though the summarizing phrase from Gen. 1:31, suggesting what Cassuto had referred to as the artist's delight in a perfectly executed design, were missing. We have spoken of the denial of the merely aesthetic in the verses that follow Gen. 1:31, of the ongoingness and the lack of closure in the work of creation, picked out especially by the verb *wayĕqaddēš* with its connotation of a program still to be implemented. This aspect, it now appears, is very much more to the fore in the matter of the tabernacle in the wilderness. The tabernacle is above all things a temporary structure, not a final resting place. While Moses may well bestow his blessing on the work of Bezalel, the artist, it is not a final blessing. No work of man, it seems, is final. There will be no room for purely aesthetic contemplation, for a perfected Sabbath of peace. The poles remain in place in the rings of the ark and the people remain in an ever-present state of watchfulness and readiness. There is no word of closure to round off the work of Bezalel, no *ṭôb mĕʾōd*. There will be advances and reverses in the ongoing history of the attempt to hallow the places of the earth, Jerusalem is indeed *kĕlîlat yōpî*, "the perfection of beauty" (Lam. 2:15), but the temple at Jerusalem will be built, destroyed, and built again—and that indeed is what the book of Lamentations records. The work remains incomplete. True, the cloud covers the tabernacle and the glory of the Lord fills it in the concluding verses of Exodus, but even they will be no permanent presence. They will move away from the tent from time to time, and when they do, the children of Israel will continue on their journey (Exod. 40:36, 37).

·3·

JOB: TRAGEDY IS NOT ENOUGH

No other question coming under the heading of "The Bible as Literature" has generated so much heat as the question of whether the book of
Job is or is not a tragedy. The question arises in all manner of discussions
of tragedy. Richard B. Sewall finds that "the book of Job has the basic
elements of the tragic form."[1] "Tragic vision," he declares, "is fulfilled in
tragic form."[2] Helen Gardner a little more cautiously argues that while it
is "not designed to please," Job's proximity to tragedy is such that "it is
not wholly improper to set it beside Greek Tragedy as a work of literary
art."[3] The view has ancient authority. Theodore of Mopsuestia in the
fourth century regarded Job as modeled on Greek drama and Theodore
Beza in the sixteenth century had similar notions.[4] But there have been
equally categorical objections. Robert Lowth, who certainly was centrally
involved in the whole enterprise of presenting the Hebrew Bible as a
document worthy of attention for the student of literature, went out of
his way to deny that Job had a formal resemblance to ancient tragedy.[5]
Karl Jaspers was emphatic that in the religion of the Christian, "the
darkness of terror is pierced by the radiance of blessedness and grace."[6]
This would evidently apply to Job as much as to the gospels. Tragedy is
thus inhibited. On the Jewish side, Baruch Kurzweil, following Franz
Rosenzweig, sees biblical man, and specifically Job, as the antithesis of
the tragic hero. Against the self-sufficiency (and ultimately, the silence)
of the tragic hero, we have the life of dialogue, the humble acceptance of
a divine absolute. To confuse the two is to engage in apologetics![7] True,
biblical norms penetrated Western literature from the Middle Ages on,
but the effect of this, as George Steiner has argued, has been the "death
of tragedy."[8] According to I. A. Richards, where there is a "compensating heaven" or even a valid program of salvation for man in society,
there can be no tragedy in the true sense.[9] For the tragic hero is doomed:
he is not marked for redemptive purposes. Classicists too will often deny
the likeness between Job and the tragic heroes of the ancient world, but
for other reasons. Gilbert Murray, for instance, declares that Job is made

of less heroic stuff than the Prometheus of Aeschylus, because unlike Prometheus, Job submits in dust and ashes.[10] Nietzsche would have agreed. Biblical man is puny and self-effacing; the Greek hero is strong and self-reliant. Murray Krieger gets past this by showing that the root of tragedy (whether in its Greek or non-Greek forms) is the hero's suffering and despair. It is not the hubris or pride of Oedipus that counts but the absoluteness of his misery.[11]

What emerges from all this is that there is no consensus. And that is the interesting thing. As many passionate (and I would add, convincing) voices have been raised on behalf of the one thesis as of the other. And what I would want to argue is that both sides are right. Just as the book of Esther is a novel and also a kind of anti-novel, so Job both is and is not a tragedy. It is that paradox itself that we need to consider.

Let us start with that most attractive and persuasive of the parallels that have been adduced in the long and continuing debate about Job as tragedy. I refer to the parallel with the *Prometheus Bound* of Aeschylus. The likeness both in outline and in detail is striking, so much so that more than one thoughtful student of the subject has been prompted to suggest that the author of Job may actually have known the work of the fifth-century tragedian and been influenced by it.[12] The Titan fettered to a rock in Scythia by the order of Zeus becomes for the literary tradition of the West an archetypal image of unmerited suffering precisely analogous to Job on his dunghill covered with sores and subjected to unbearable pain by the will of the high God. If the play of Aeschylus makes its point by a powerful visual image designed for the stage, then Job on his dunghill lamenting his fate is no less adaptable to dramatic presentation; and the agon conducted between Prometheus and his three main visitors is neither more nor less dramatic than the debate enacted between Job and his three friends. The dramatic climax of the two works is comparable. The play of Aeschylus closes with a thunderstorm in which Zeus makes known his will. In Job there is the stormwind in which, at the climax, God finally speaks. Job does not indeed vanish like Prometheus, but he submits himself to the wisdom of heaven. The essential situation with which the two "plays" begin and end, as well as the dramatic shape of the "plot," reveal a more than fanciful resemblance. To draw attention to these resemblances is not a matter of eccentricity or apologetics. They are there for all to see.

It is indeed tempting to suppose that the author of Job had seen (or read) *Prometheus Bound* or something very like it, just as the author of Isaiah 14 had surely read or heard a Canaanite poem about the fall of Helel from heaven. But what we noted there was not simply the likeness but the sharp swerve that the Hebrew author seems to take as he travels

along the same path as his predecessor. The same applies to Job and
Aeschylus. We may take a simple detail from both texts. Prometheus
wishes he could be with the dead and bemoans the ills and miseries that
have made him a laughingstock for his enemies:

> Oh, that he had hurled me below the earth, aye 'neath Hades, the
> entertainer of the dead, into impassable Tartarus, and had ruthlessly
> fastened me in fetters no hand can loose, that so no god nor other kind
> had now gloated over my agony! But as it is, a plaything of the winds,
> to my misery, I suffer ills whereat my foes exult. (Lines 152–59)[13]

Again and again Job likewise longs for death. "Oh, that I had perished,
and no eye had seen me" (10:18), he declares. He wishes that he were in
Sheol: "There the wicked cease from troubling; / and there the weary are
at rest" (3:17). He could lie down there with the stillborn as well as with
the kings and counselors of the earth. Job's misery (like that of Prometheus) is compounded by the thought that God has given him over into
the hands of the wicked, who can now heap their taunts and blows upon
him (16:10). It is as though the Hebrew poet were showing how his hero
could perform the same tragic gestures as the hero of Aeschylus. And yet
of course, in performing those gestures, he is, in a deep sense, reversing
their effects.

Prometheus, we never forget, is immortal. The desire for death in the
words "Oh, that he had hurled me below the earth" is ironical: he can
never be dead! The sentence really affirms his ultimate invulnerability.
There is a defiance in the wish itself, for Zeus cannot consign him to the
kingdom of Hades. All he can do is give his enemies occasion to gloat
over him. Here the injury that Prometheus complains of is to his *standing*
as a Titan. To be bound to a rock and made the victim of Zeus's torments
after he had helped Zeus to gain mastery of the world demeans him.
This is the blow of which Prometheus complains. The parallel expressions in Job are really ways of saying the opposite. Job is all too mortal. In
saying,

> Why is light given to him that is in misery,
> and life to the bitter in soul;
> who long for death, but it does not come . . .
>   (3:20–21)

he is saying in effect, "Since you could so easily destroy me, why do you
keep me alive?" That "Why" is the most persistent question in the book.
Why is life given to the bitter in soul, why are human beings, mortal as
they are, vulnerable and helpless as they are, given the burden of life? To
what must they witness, for what undisclosed purpose must they survive?

His yearning for death is sharpened by the thought that it is so tantalizingly close to him—he can almost touch it; he has the smell of it in his nostrils. "I say to the pit, Thou art my father; to the worm, Thou art my mother and my sister" (17:14). In a moment, if only God would release his hold, he will be able to rest, he will descend into darkness. Prometheus has neither the consolation nor the fear.

Job on his dunghill and Prometheus on his rock thus become type and antitype. The Greek hero triumphs in the magnificence of his heroic ordeal; Job cowers and weeps, laments and shrieks. His pain is real pain; it recalls all too vividly the precariousness of our hold on life. The wonder is that he still lives. It is that which must be understood. If Job's enemies strike him insolently on the cheek (16:10), it is because he is truly down-and-out, groveling on the earth. Not his pride is here threatened but the last shred of his human dignity. He is loathsome to himself, reduced to the condition of a mere wretch for whom death is better than life.

Varied as are the definitions of tragedy that we may cull from the critics, one feature derived from Aristotle seems to be constant: the tragic hero must be noble, or at least a little nobler and grander than we are, so that we can approach him with the necessary awe. Prometheus is the extreme example of this: Job, by the same token, is not really fitted for the role of tragic hero. He is a little more abased than we are even in our most dreadful abasements. If we imagine ourselves cast among the Untouchables in the dust of an Indian village, then Job is located just a little way below that:

> I have sewn sackcloth upon my skin,
> and have laid my strength in the dust.
> My face is scalded with weeping,
> and on my eyelids is the shadow of death.
> (16:15–16)

He pleads with his friends for their pity in a way that no tragic hero can ever plead. Orestes and Oedipus arouse our pity, but they do not actually beg for it—that is left for the Chorus. If the hero were to do so he would have to abandon that pride of life, that self-sufficiency which makes him a hero. For the same reason, Job's submission and repentance in 40:4 and 42:6 are entirely foreign to the heroes of Greek antiquity. As D. D. Raphael aptly remarks, "Prometheus defies Zeus; Job lays his hand upon his mouth."[14]

Job, of course, also has his pride, his streak of rebellion. It seems sometimes as though, in this, the Hebrew poet were trying to outgreek the Greeks, as though saying to his public, "Is it hubris you expect in the tragic hero? I will give you hubris!" And so he has his hero demand that God step down and declare what are the charges against him:

> Yet I would speak to the Almighty,
> and I desire to reason with God . . .
> Behold now, I have ordered my cause;
> I know that I shall be vindicated. . . .
> Then call thou, and I will answer;
> or let me speak, and thou answer me.
>
> (13:3, 18, 22)

It is as though Oedipus should demand that Apollo come down and explain himself to Oedipus. But Job is both more and less sure of himself than is the Greek hero. He is less sure because his hold on life is more precarious. He knows he is no king nor is he the son of kings or gods: he is only the dust of the earth who has said to the pit, You are my father, and to the worm, My mother and my sister. He is more sure of himself because he knows that he has one claim that God cannot ignore, namely his integrity. Here is the basis of a defiance more staggering than that of Prometheus: "Till I die I will not put away my integrity from me. / My righteousness I hold fast, and I will not let it go" (27:5–6). The combination of such utter helplessness and such extraordinary self-confidence is what constitutes the posture of Job. His rebellion is founded upon a confidence that God is bound to acknowledge the virtue of the righteous man. He calls God so to speak to testify against God, the God who has made a covenant with man founded on justice and law to testify against the God of the thunderstorm and the cataclysm. Here is the impudent claim of the Hebrew Bible; it would have been for the Greeks a matter of unimaginable presumption.

So that if, compared with Prometheus, Job is nought, a mere speck of dust, a tormented shred of human flesh, in another way he is elevated beyond the rank of tragic hero. In chapter 31, as many commentators have noted,[15] Job's defiance reaches a peak in his great oath of clearance. He now challenges God to appear and prove his case against him by calling upon himself the direst of penalties if he has at any time neglected his duty to God or his fellow men. It is for God to answer now or lose his case by default: "Here is my mark," says Job, "let the Almighty answer me" (31:35). And he continues, "Let my adversary pen his writ!" God, it is true, does not answer Job's specific question about why he is made to suffer, but he does *answer Job.*[16] He addresses his word to him and, what is more, he vindicates him (42:7). There is a trial at the end of the *Oresteia* also, in which Orestes is vindicated, but it is really the victory of Apollo more than that of Orestes. By contrast, Job tests and is tested. God not only tests him; he tests God, summons him to an interview—

and the interview is granted! Job could have said with the psalmist that he was a worm and no man (Ps. 22:6), but he was a worm to whom God was to grant an audience.

The appalling heights and depths that mark the status of such a hero imply categories of significance and insignificance unprovided for in ancient tragedy. We will find a key to the paradox only in the biblical doctrine of creation. Job is from this point of view a major document. The poetic exploration of the paradoxes of creation is conducted in many parts of the book, and nowhere more intensely than in chapter 10. We are here taken back not to Genesis 1, where man is a little less than the angels, given mastery over the rest of creation, but to Gen. 2:7, where man is conceived as no more than a handful of red earth, of clay in the potter's yard. He has no inherent dignity arising out of his rank as "crown of creation." God kneads him and forms him from the dust of the ground.[17] It is that image that Job here recalls:

> Thy hands have made me and fashioned me together round about;
> yet thou dost destroy me.
> Remember, I beseech thee, that thou has made me like clay;
> and wilt thou bring me back to dust?
>
> (10:8–9)

It is an image of radical dependence and also extraordinary intimacy. Job is always in the hands of God. He does not have to exercise a great leap of faith in order to meet his creator. He knows in whose hands he is mere dust and clay. In the continuation, the image of the potter and his clay gives way to the image of the growth of the embryo in the womb:

> Hast thou not poured me out like milk, and curdled me like cheese?
> Thou hast clothed me with skin and flesh,
> and hast knit me together with bones and sinews.
>
> (10:10–11)

Here there is a suggestion of nutrition and blessing and above all of love. Again radical dependence, but to it is added the elemental love, the womb-love, or *raḥămîm*, of the mother or father for an infant. On this love (or *ḥesed*) the creature may build his claim ("thou hast granted me life and *ḥesed*" in verse 12). But what kind of claim can he build? The form of the question in verse 9 contains the key to the claim that the creature can make of the creator: "Remember, I beseech thee, that thou hast made me like clay; / and wilt thou bring me back to dust?" The image of the artificer of man fashioning the clay or knitting the fetus together with bones and sinews is an image of purpose. To be taken out of the dust and fashioned into a human being is to be miraculously

converted from a nothing into a vessel invested with purpose and meaning. God who did it is called upon to remember that he did it. Not Job's
claim to consideration is here the issue but God's purposes as creator.
Total dependence goes together with an awareness of having been manifestly charged with a reason for being alive—a reason that lies hidden in
the will of God and the love of God. The rebel is that man who calls upon
God to remember what, as God, he was doing at the moment he made
man. It is again the reverse of the situation of Prometheus: Prometheus
reminds Zeus that he helped to make him Zeus; Job reminds God that he
made him Job. He needn't have made him at all and perhaps Job would
have been better off if he hadn't, or if, when fashioning him, he had
decided to return him to the condition of an unformed piece of clay. But
having fashioned him, he now has to answer for what he has done.

In the continuation (v. 18), Job puts the issue of God's purpose in
creating him in the form of a direct challenge: "Why then hast thou
brought me forth out of the womb?" The force of the question resides
not in any implied answer but in the question itself. The very power to
ask the question becomes itself a testimony to God's purposefulness. As
Job asks the question "Why hast thou brought me forth from the
womb?" he is saying in effect: You made me, and here I am, capable of
asking you questions about it. Job's questioning of God—and the book is
conducted largely in the form of such questions—implies its own answer.
The question appears in each case to be a presumptuous challenge to
God's wisdom and authority; but the challenge is itself made possible
only by the having been fashioned by a creator God in such a way as to be
able to ask such questions.

Does the clay say to the potter, What are you doing? asks the prophet
Isaiah (45:9). Clearly, the clay can do no such thing. The image of clay
and potter precludes any defiance, or even independence on the part of
the human vessel. And yet in these words, spoken by the prophet of a
rebellious generation, the clay is manifestly saying to the potter, What
are you doing? The sentence contradicts itself. To be able to say, "What
doest thou?" or "Why hast thou brought me forth out of the womb?" is to
demonstrate that man is more than dust, more than clay on the potter's
wheel, more even than embryo. These images dissolve at the moment
they are affirmed as argument. To say Why is to say that none of these
images adequately expresses the mystery of human creatureliness. The
clay cannot say to the potter, What are you doing, but man can and does.
The embryo cannot bid its father and mother remember, but man can
and does. All such images ask to be transcended. Ultimately, we return
from the model of Gen. 2:7 to Gen. 1:26f., where the relation between
creator and creature is founded not on the kneading of clay but on the
majesty of saying itself. "God said, Let us make man in our image." To

turn to God and ask him to remember is to challenge him with that mystery. A human creature may be no more than a shred of protoplasm, but he is endowed with the commanding power of saying and asking. To see God as artificer in accordance with the imagery of Gen. 2:7 gives us access to the realm of art, but to see God as a saying God and to see man as made in the image of a saying God takes us beyond art to the realm in which God and man address each other in their mutual independence. If mere creatureliness signifies total dependence, then being made in the divine image endows us with the power of radically questioning the creator himself. Such paradoxes do not merely take us beyond the categories of tragedy; they explode the frame of tragedy; they demolish the figure of the tragic hero.

II

In chapter 31, Job challenges God to produce his writ and in chapter 38, as we noted, God answers Job out of the stormwind. But in between there are the speeches of Elihu the Buzite, who comes on the scene at the beginning of chapter 32 and continues his speech until the end of chapter 37. He does not belong to the same group as the three "friends"—he has, we are told, been waiting in the background (32:4). The speech is a powerful poem on some of the main themes of the book, especially God's power in the creation, but it remains unanswered. Job does not react to it and God does not refer to it in the speech out of the stormwind. Mysteriously, Elihu is not included in the roster of the friends who seek Job's intercession in chapter 42. He disappears as mysteriously as he enters. What is he then doing in the book? We could of course take the easy way out and judge these chapters as extraneous additions that spoil the symmetry of the book. Even Otto Eissfeldt, who has, alone practically among the critics of the philological-historical school, defended the unity and integrity of Job in the received text, cannot find a place in his scheme for the Elihu chapters.[18] However, if we think of Job as a kind of Hebrew response to the genre of Greek tragedy, it would seem that we may have here a key to the function of Elihu also. Prometheus's final visitor before the storm breaks at the climax of the play of Aeschylus is Hermes, the messenger of the gods. Hermes is privileged, supercilious; he is not identified with the visitors who have so far appeared. He imperiously calls upon Prometheus to submit himself to the will of Zeus. Now if Elihu does not exactly claim to be God's messenger like Hermes, he does claim to be his confidant and privileged spokesman:

> Behold, now I have opened my mouth,
> my tongue has spoken in my mouth.

My words shall be of the uprightness of my heart:
and my lips shall utter knowledge in sincerity.
The spirit of God has made me,
and the breath of the Almighty has given me life.
                                        (33:2–4)

He is specifically animated by the breath of Shadday (32:8; 33:4), the
God of creation in its more demonic aspects. (No one else in Job, indeed
no one else in the Hebrew Bible is said to be made by Shadday.) As with
Hermes, who warns Prometheus of worse things to come, there is a
veiled threat in the words of Elihu as though he knows what is still in
store for Job if he does not submit (36:13–23). Elihu in short is the
Hebrew Hermes; his speeches (like that of Hermes) also prepare us for
the stormy theophany by speaking of God as the God of thunder and
lightning (36:29f.). But of course in the end he is there to show that there
is no place for Hermes in the Hebrew pantheon! As his words come to an
end, it is God himself who comes forward to speak to Job, sweeping aside
all the pretensions of Elihu and the others to speak in his name. Just as
Job rises higher in his "rebellion" and questioning than Prometheus, so
God descends closer to man, speaking his word to Job, choosing him for
a divine utterance, ignoring all mediation, and ignoring in particular the
self-appointed confidant who had just presented himself on the stage as
the would-be manager of the catastrophe. He is saying to Elihu-Hermes:
"I will manage the ending of this play in my own way. I need no help
from you or any other messenger. Unlike Zeus, I am not too busy to
come down and speak to Job and, unlike Prometheus, Job can summon
me to such an interview by merely reminding me of the claims of his
creaturely status. True, I am a God of thunder and lightning, but even
that will not be the last word. For I have a surprise in store for the
readers who expect this to end like *Prometheus Bound* or *Agamemnon*.[19]
The surprise is that I am going to make it up to Job. Not death, but
survival is the meaning of the drama of creation."

<hr>

III

Job is often compared with another primary text in the history of tragedy, Shakespeare's *King Lear*. Here if there is influence, it is the other
way round, for Shakespeare's play has been seen as a pantomime version
of Job.[20] We are by now in a literary culture deeply suffused by the Bible
so that we may expect the norms of tragedy to be different from those of
the age of Pericles. Lear is not Prometheus. There is, of course, much of
the Titan about him as he conducts the cosmic orchestra in Act III and
defies the powers of nature. He

Bids the wind blow the earth into the sea,
Or swell the curled waters 'bove the main,
That things might change or cease . . .
                          (III, i)

As he curses his daughters, he seems not merely to ally himself with cosmic forces but to become one of the gods of nature himself. And yet at the same time we are made conscious that he is nothing more than a "poor infirm, weak and despis'd old man." He is reduced to the lowest bounds of the human, reminding us in this much more of Job on his dunghill than of Prometheus fettered to the rock. Lear in the fourth act reduced to madness ("a sight most pitiful in the meanest wretch") has little of Promethean grandeur left. His kingliness has now been redefined in Christian terms; we see him learning a new humility, kneeling to beg his daughter Cordelia's forgiveness and repenting for the years of mindless despotism during which he had given no thought to the sufferings of his poorer subjects. Edgar the bedlam-beggar is the most obviously Joblike figure in the play—naked, helpless, and demanding our pity. In the critical central scene of the storm, Lear sees in Edgar a reflection of himself and tears off his clothes so as to share the fate of Edgar. As a matter of fact, the Job function is distributed among three characters: Gloucester, Lear, and Edgar. Gloucester's expressed desire for death (IV, vi, 36) reminds us of Job's opening speech in chapter 3; Lear raises acutely, like Job, the question of undeserved suffering ("I am a man more sinned against than sinning"); and Edgar's total abasement reminds us of the absolute abasement of Job. Above all the hero here, unlike the heroes of Aeschylus and Sophocles, has discovered the soul. "In the make-believe world of art . . . the self ever remains self, never becomes soul," says Franz Rosenzweig, speaking of the tragic hero of antiquity.[21] However, with modern tragedy (in which Rosenzweig included Shakespeare) the mute self becomes a soul: he speaks, he prays, he loves.[22]

All this helps to account for the phenomenological duality of Shakespeare's play. As a drama of salvation in which the saving event is the discovery of the soul, and with it the life of dialogue in which soul opens to soul, the true dénouement is reached in Act IV with the reunion of Lear and Cordelia, with Lear's repentance and their exchange of blessings—a biblical moment unknown to ancient tragedy. It is a moment in which, after his long estrangement from his daughter, Lear discovers a reason for living. We would expect him to express that discovery in a determination to affirm the bonds of life. And indeed he does that in his second and last meeting with Cordelia. "We'll live and pray and sing," he says, and he adds very pointedly,

we'll wear out
In a wall'd prison, packs and sects of great ones
That ebb and flow by the moon.

                                        (V, iii, 17–19)

Not the ritual cycle of death and rebirth as performed by "great ones," but the harder trial of survival and witness is what he promises to them both. And yet the laws of tragedy doom them; they must in the end perform the descent into Avernus, for this is the goal of tragedy. Rosenzweig very perceptively underlines the tragic hero's propensity for dying. "His whole existence," he tells us, "becomes the enduring of this one encounter." Death becomes the sovereign event. "He yearns for the solitude of death because there is no greater solitude than this. . . . For him, eternity is just good enough to echo his silence."[23] Shakespeare, therefore, who has his hero saved in Act IV, has him die in Act V. Lear has to act out the part of an Oedipus just as Cordelia has to act out the part of an Antigone. The ritual of dying is not an accidental ending for *King Lear;* it is part of the myth pattern on which tragedy is founded. In another play of Shakespeare's, Juliet, like Proserpine, is kept in the dark by Dis, the god of death, to be his paramour. Behind such images we have the inevitability, the beauty, indeed the seduction, of the cycle of nature. Lear too, as we have said, is a kind of nature god and he will be doomed by that same nature which he had made his goddess and in whose name he had uttered his magnificent oaths and curses.

There is something in us that obscurely desires the death of the hero—Aristotle said that tragedy affords us a *catharsis,* a purgation. But there is also something in us that resists this seduction. Not surprisingly, over the years spectators and readers of *King Lear* have found themselves unable to accept the way in which the hope of salvation kindled in the fourth act is frustrated by the cruel ending. Even the suggestion of a kind of crucifixion event in Lear's dying (for which there is also a textual basis)[24] does not satisfy them. Tolstoy found the deaths of Cordelia and Lear unbearable, indeed gratuitous; in the seventeenth century (before the text of Shakespeare was held to be quite as sacred as it is today) Nahum Tate rewrote the play leaving Cordelia and Lear alive at the end; his version held the stage for 150 years. It seems that just as there are those today who think that Job ought to end like *King Lear,* and that the happy ending is false, so there were many more in the eighteenth century who thought that *King Lear* ought to end like Job, with the sufferer granted restoration and ease in which to end his days! Powerful though the laws of tragedy are, human beings evidently yearn also for other patterns of significance. Job provides us with such a pattern: it is the biblical alternative to tragedy. It is this Joban model, communicating itself to the literature of the West, that helped to produce the mixed form of Shakespeare;

ultimately it helped to bring about the death of tragedy and the anti-tragic form of Goethe's *Faust*.

IV

Job is driven to ask himself the question "To be or not to be?" The answer forced out of him is that life, however unwelcome, has to be endured. To choose life becomes the supreme challenge, the near-impossible task for a hero as sorely tempted as Job is to curse God and die. When all the interpretations have been heard, this remains the irreducible core of Job's righteousness. Job, a worm and no man, reduced to a condition in which life is loathsome to him and death is the desired goal, nevertheless chooses life. It is life itself that is commanded, even life without comfort, hope, or honor. It is in his flesh, or even it may be when his flesh has been stripped from his bones, that he will see God. Here is the impossible claim of the Hebrew religion. "Therefore choose life" is the command of a creator God who has made us into a living soul, a *nepeš ḥayyâ*. We will not fathom his purpose in so doing, but in the very breath we breathe, in the pulse we feel still beating in our tormented flesh, we have the manifest command of that creative will. We may look again at Job's first cry of pain and despair in chapter 3. Here we have the tragic desire for death but we also have its precise antithesis. In the surface meaning of the words, Job is asking to be dead, but each question, as it is added to those which precede it, makes it ever clearer that the death option is closed:

> Why is light given to him that is in misery,
> and life to the bitter in soul;
> who long for death, but it does not come;
> and dig for it more than for hidden treasures;
> who rejoice exceedingly,
> and are glad, when they can find a grave?
> Why is light given to a man whose way is hidden,
> and whom God has hedged in?
>
> (3:20–23)

This is misunderstood if it is taken as a nihilistic demand; it is the very opposite of nihilism. The power of the longing for death expressed here is only exceeded by the strength of the conviction that that longing is not to be gratified. Light is given. Light and not darkness is the fundamental datum, much as we would desire it to be otherwise. Life is given even to the bitter in soul—and it obligates. Such perceptions are formulated as questions, but they are questions that contain their own answer. If death "does not come" and if light "is given," then the existence so extraor-

dinarily thrust upon us has its imperious claim. We must carry our light
and our breath to the end of the day. So Job remains on his dunghill,
when all that is left of human glory is the breathing human flesh, no
more.

The despair of Job is deeper, blacker than that of the tragic heroes of
antiquity. He digs for death more than for hidden treasures; if he could
attain it, that would be his happy ending. He would rejoice as much as
Romeo in Shakespeare's play as he "shakes the yoke of inauspicious
stars / From this world-wearied flesh," or as much as Cleopatra, who
embraces death like a lover or a babe sucking at her breast. Job's longing
is as great but, unlike theirs, it will not be gratified. Here the Hebrew
poet sets his face not only against *thanatos,* the dark desire for death, but
against the aesthetic form that it yields. The loss of responsibility in
death gives us the beauty of the marvelous downward curve of tragic
destiny as the hero descends in his nobility and grandeur, to assert his
ultimate freedom. Against this perfection of tragic form, Job gives us the
more untidy, less determined pattern of a test, an ongoing pilgrimage, a
trial. There is a violation here not only of an ethic that has powerfully
moved men from antiquity, through the stoicism of the Renaissance to
the present day, but the violation too of the aesthetic principle of coherence. No wonder that the ending of Job in chapter 42 has been a
scandal to critics. How can Job end with life and prosperity? Does not the
movement of the earlier chapters call for the opposite? What we desire is
the Passion of Job. This would not only make it consistent with the
Crucifixion, it would give it the roundedness of tragedy, the perfection
of an artistic masterpiece. This would give the book the shape of an
inverted U, which we are told is the proper shape of tragedy.[25] The
ending that gives us the survival of Job and the restoration of his fortunes must be the addition of some pious editor. The best thing to do is
to ignore it.[26]

Some critics have taken a different tack. They have wondered whether
perhaps the book is not to be treated as a comedy, that is to say, that it
has the structure of an uninverted U.[27] This makes the happy ending
integral, but it does so at the expense of making Job's repentance and
submission only half-serious or of making God's speeches from the storm
something neither we nor Job can take seriously.[28] Above all, such a
reading robs the book of its bitterness, its root of despair. If Job, as we
have argued, goes beyond tragedy, it is not because it is less tragic than
tragedy. To the contrary, its sense of the pain we endure is sharper than
that of the ancient tragedians, but it denies us the structural coherence,
the consistency of tragedy. By the same token it goes beyond comedy, in
spite of the happy ending.

The mistake is to look for coherence, unity, to insist on finding in or
behind the books of the Bible an artistic shape having a beginning, a

middle, and an end.[29] Such a principle requires us to be hunting for U's or inverted U's. Is it not possible that this is in itself a fundamental error? In a way such confidence in the symmetrical shape of things is the confidence of Job's friends. It is they who assure him that "though thy beginning was small, yet thy end will be very great" (8:7). That would make an excellent story, as would the opposite notion; Job's complaint is that life is not quite like that. His test is open-ended, undetermined; he is not in the region of myth, but in what we may term antimyth.[30] Herbert N. Schneidau is basically right it seems when he claims that the Bible "does not give us genres or archetypes," but that it "demands that we acknowledge how precarious is our grasp of any meaning in the world at all."[31] This is certainly true of Job, which is a work not only about the asymmetries of existence but also about the asymmetries that necessarily characterize any literary plot that would attempt to do justice to that existence. Tragedy is one magisterial attempt to encompass the nature of human suffering, to link our boundary experiences with our destiny. But tragedy is not enough. When our Hebrew poet sets his hand to it, he gives us an aborted tragedy, one that deliberately, it seems, swerves aside from the direction that tragedy leads us to anticipate, affirming at the end, absurdly, life instead of death.

Actually, the swerve begins before Job's repentance and the restoration of his fortunes. The great speeches of God out of the stormwind in chapters 38–40 are part of it. True, God does not give Job any answers regarding the moral economy of the universe; he does not reveal the reason for Job's unparalleled sufferings, but he nevertheless speaks to the main issue, that of life or death, "to be or not to be." The speeches celebrate the *vitality* of the universe: abundant life and creation are their theme. In this, God responds to Job's first speech in chapter 3: life, not death is given. Crude, barbaric, even chaotic the creation may seem, but it is bursting with energy and purpose. The creator God who breathed into Job and bid him live is the God who stretched his line upon the earth "when the morning stars sang together / and all the sons of God shouted for joy." There is terror in the universe here revealed—darkness, cloud, thunderbolts, unimaginable distances in which man is lost, but it is all vibrating with life and power and purpose:

> Do you know the time when the wild goats of the rock bring forth?
> or canst thou mark when the hinds do calve?
> Canst thou number the months that they fulfill?
>
> (39:1–2)

Job is asked. Again these questions are only seeming questions. The point is not that Job doesn't know, but that God does. The world is full of mind, ruled over not by a god of death, by Hades, but by a living god, the

God of the spirits of all flesh, *'ĕlōhê hārûḥōt lĕkol-bāśār*. Job in his life is linked with the sportive leviathan on the one hand and with the sons of God shouting for joy on the other. Wherever he looks there is an abundance of life, of creativity, and of beauty. He is bound up in the bond of that creativity.

No more extraordinary anticlimax to a would-be tragedy could be imagined. The tragic mood is radically undermined in this "carnival of animals."[32] The vision of Behemoth and Leviathan may not be strictly relevant to the questions raised by Job. But these chapters are utterly relevant to the artistic and structural questions that the book raises. They are part of the character of Job as antitragedy. Esther seemed to be shaping up as a romantic novel of the Persian court; it turns out to be that and something else. Likewise, when the audience of Job have settled in their seats expecting to see a Hebrew "tragedy," the author dashes their expectations with a "carnival of animals," a magnificent display of creative energy that dispels the tragic mood, destroying the expected curve that would lead us to the final demise of the hero. Suffer and live, says this God. Once the message has been received, life will be the last word of the book.

The near-unanimous view of the critics that the surprise ending is nonauthentic is bound up therefore with those myth patterns which still exercise a powerful compulsion on our minds. The same applies, as I have tried to show elsewhere, to the difficulty that readers have experienced with regard to Isaac's release from death with which the Binding, or *'ăqēdâ*, ends in Genesis 22.[33] There is something in us which obscurely expects, even desires that Isaac should die, just as Iphigenia dies at the hand of her father. In nineteenth-century literary versions of the *'ăqēdâ* the sacrifice is generally carried out—in Melville's *Billy Budd*, or in Ibsen's *Brand*, for instance. During the First World War Wilfred Owen wrote a poetic parable in which the angel calls out to "Abram" to offer a ram instead of his son, "But the old man would not so, but slew his son,— / And half the seed of Europe with him, one by one." Jewish midrash often takes the same line of "correcting" the biblical form;[34] in Christian typology the *'ăqēdâ* is linked with the Crucifixion (there is a hint of this already in Heb. 11:17–19). Isaac carrying the wood for his own sacrifice becomes the type of Jesus carrying the cross, and of course for the latter occasion there is going to be a real death and a real sacrifice. Roger L. Cox is right in claiming that the Gospels are not merely tragic, they are supertragic.[35] A single heroic individual sacrifices himself for the world. Isaac's Binding is in this sense no tragedy. It is a near-miss, circumcision rather than castration. The same applies to Job. Like Genesis 22, it denies us the *consummatum est* of the completed tragic pattern. Hence the need to "correct" the text in order that Job bear his cross to the end, or at least as far as the repentance "in dust and ashes" of 42:6. The scandal is Job restored to health and prosperity, with his brothers and sisters eating bread in his house. The question is not whether this is credible; if we are concerned with realism, then it is perfectly in line with our experience that even a man afflicted as Job is might one day recover his fortunes. The survivors of Auschwitz have been known to establish new families and set themselves up in business. This may not have the aesthetic tidiness of art, but human beings are resilient—and that in a way is what the book of Job is saying. Of course, the prose ending returns us, it is said, to the atmosphere of a folktale in contrast with the high poetry of the middle chapters with their powerful myth content, their images of primordial grandeur. There is a letdown. The argument of this chapter is that the letdown is part of the book's strategy. We touch the depths and heights, but life goes on. We do not remain in the world of myth or the world of art. The literary pattern—in this case the pattern of tragedy—is evoked, but there is a traitor in the house. In the end we confront not tragedy but something else.

I would also wish to argue that while critics and readers have aesthetic expectations, while they respond to those forms of art to which ancient models have accustomed us, the common reader is also responsive to the art-that-denies-art of the Bible. For that reason the book of Job as a whole—folk ending included—continues to speak to us if we let it. Actually, the notion of the ending as a folktale is misleading. The prose of 42:7–17 is more that of a historical record. The naming of his daughters, the account of his livestock, and the record of his death—all have a familiar ring. Such narrative takes us back to the patriarchal age, to the stories of Genesis. The clear force of these verses is that we are in the realm of historical writing. True, we are not talking about factual history but we are speaking of the kind of prose that claims a connection with history. These closing verses of the book, indeed, serve to anchor the high poetic invention of the earlier chapters in a world of men and women, marrying and giving in marriage, bearing children, establishing themselves economically, receiving and giving gifts, and finally, if they are lucky, dying "old and full of days." This is no more or less "legendary" in its impact on the reader than the stories of the generations preceding and following the Flood. Moses, according to a rabbinic tradition, was the author of Job just as he was the author of Genesis.[36] Perhaps what they were saying is that Job is, like Genesis, a great creation poem; it tells of a primordial world fresh from the hands of the creator. True, it is a different creation from Genesis: it has more in it of terror, more images of darkness; it has a vastness in which man is dwarfed. But it is creation nonetheless; as in Genesis, so here, man is formed of the dust of the earth and into his nostrils is breathed the breath of life. But we should remember that the visionary poetry of the first three chapters of Genesis, with its account of the Garden of Eden, the drama of the first human pair tempted to eat of "the tree of the knowledge of good and evil"—another tragic "fall"—gives way in chapter 4 to a more prosaic unfolding of the life of Adam. "Adam" is now not a generic but a personal name. Like Job in the last chapter of his book, he is no longer a figure in a cosmic drama or debate, but a man like ourselves, a kind of middle-class citizen, settling down to a life of domesticity, "knowing" his wife, begetting children, and having trouble with them as they grow up. In short, we move exactly as in the final chapter of Job into the world of historical doings, trials and comforts. The mix is peculiarly Hebraic. High literature lurches into low literature; the everyday world obtrudes with its practical demands. It is to this region that the poets of the Bible, however epic, however mythological, however tragic, will ultimately bring us back.

Nor is this lurch into history confined to the stories of Job and Adam. There are other candidates in the Bible for the role of tragic hero. The figure of Athaliah attracted Racine by its tragic force, but it is notable that there too Racine, instead of providing us with a cathartic ending of the Greek type, emphasizes instead the ongoing, covenantal history of the house of David under Joash. The dynastic theme overlays the tragic ending and in some sense subverts it. King Saul has likewise often been seen as a tragic hero and he has something of the pathos as well as the grandeur of such a hero, but he can only fully realize this role if his story is isolated from its context, which again emphasizes the history of the royal house to be founded by his rival, the young David. Saul's replacement by David rather than his tragic death in battle is what ultimately counts and it is on that that our attention ultimately focuses.[37] In sum, biblical stories of the "fall" of a hero lack the closure that tragedy seems to require; instead of fable rounded in upon itself, we have the undetermined movement of historical time, a witnessing to purposes still to be disclosed and by no means confined to the fate of the hero.

•4•

PROPHET AND AUDIENCE
A FAILED CONTRACT

Ezekiel describes the setting for his prophetic utterances in several different passages: 8:1, 14:1, 20:1, 33:31. We see the elders of the people sitting around him, perhaps in a circle, waiting for him to begin. Ezekiel needs his audience to witness his symbolic actions and to hear his oracles and yet we see him rebuking them for their eagerness. What, we may wonder, was the kind of gratification they expected and why do they merit rebuke? The clearest glimpse of the scene is given in chapter 33:

> As for thee, son of man, the children of thy people, who talk against thee by the walls and in the doors of the houses, speak one to another, everyone to his brother, saying, Come, I pray you, and hear what is the word that comes from the Lord. And they come to thee as the people come, and they sit before thee, my people, and they hear thy words, but they do not carry them out; for it is become love songs in their mouths, whilst their heart is set on unjust gain. And, lo, thou art to them like a love song [or perhaps: a flute song] by one who has a pleasant voice and can play the instrument well: for they hear thy words, but they do them not. (33:30–32)

In much the same spirit the prophet Amos had nearly two hundred years earlier condemned those who idly amused themselves with lute-singing and ignored the pursuit of justice (Amos 5:23, 6:5). But the exiles in Babylon whom Ezekiel is here addressing have a more sophisticated artistic taste: they react to the words of the prophet himself as a musical entertainment, a performance. At about this same time Homer's poetry would be chanted, if not to the flute then to the lyre or cythara, before a duly appreciative audience in Athens or Smyrna. The people around Ezekiel in Tel-Abib in the sixth century had similar expectations. They had settled down rather comfortably in Babylon and had acquired a taste for fine words and allegories. "Does he not speak in allegories?" (better, metaphors), they say of Ezekiel (20:49). The prophet is their bard and minstrel, and the beauty of his language only confirms them in their way of relating to him as to one who sings love songs. There is his

43

marvelous vision of the valley of dry bones (37), of the mighty armies of
Gog storming in epic style out of the land of Magog (38); there is his
romantic tale of the foundling girl who becomes the beautiful bride of
her foster father (16). Of course Ezekiel is claiming to speak of things
more important to them than the things spoken of in Homer's epics,
because he speaks the word of God, but if it is God himself who prompts
Ezekiel to tell the tale of "a great eagle with great wings and long pinions,
rich in plumage of many colors" (17:2), that does not make the telling of
such a tale a less powerful literary event.

The audience, we should remember, does help to determine the nature of the event or genre to which a particular piece of writing or
speaking belongs. Novels are novels because the reader agrees that that
is what they are. A different contract between reader and writer would
make *Robinson Crusoe,* for instance, something else—say a newspaper
account of a remarkable voyage, or a report to the Royal Society of
conditions in the South Atlantic, or a tract written to support the aims of
the Society for the Propagation of the Gospel. There is always such a
contract. A preacher in a church or synagogue knows he is there to
preach and the audience agrees to react according to the nature of the
occasion. Abstracted from that occasion and that agreement, the words
could add up to something different—a contribution to the gossip col-
umn of a weekly paper, or an exercise offered in partial fulfillment of the
requirements of a bachelor of divinity degree. In the case of Ezekiel we
seem to have a failed contract. He rejects with some violence the role of
minstrel that has been assigned to him—he will not be like one who
sings flute songs, he tells them—while the audience for their part reject
what he has determined as his mode of speech, i.e., the prophetic word
as command, for "they hear thy words, but they do them not." Or as we
might say in our modern jargon, "They read your words, but they write a
different text."[1]

But it is not only the reader who is enticed by the fascination of artistic
speech. The prophet himself has a struggle. Remember, he is a poet as
well as a prophet: that other kind of relation between text and reader,
text and author, viz., the artistic relation, cannot be avoided. The more
strongly Ezekiel protests against the role of poet, the richer does his
language become, the more vivid his imagery. He would banish his audience, and yet without their presence, his words will echo in the vacant
air. He needs to fascinate them with words. More than that, he himself
cannot escape the fascination of words. After saying with disgust, "Ah
Lord God! they say of me, Does he not speak in allegories?" (20:49)—he
proceeds to his great oracle about the sharpened sword:

> A sword, a sword is sharpened
> and also polished;

it is sharpened to make a sore slaughter:
it is polished that it may glitter.
                    (21:9–10)

And then he breaks off with the words "Or do we make mirth?" Perhaps he has noticed his audience nudging one another and smiling with pleasure at this "Song of the Sword," as some editors have termed these verses. And so he rebukes them by telling them that they had better stop enjoying the poetry, for the sword is intended for them! "Cry and howl, son of man, for it is against my people; / it is against all the princes of Israel" (21:12). Of course, if and when that sword manifests itself against the princes of the people, it will put a stop to the very *Sitz im Leben* of the prophecy itself, to this scene in which the people sit around him waiting for their entertainment. It is no wonder that the prophet is bidden to cry and howl; his prophecy is a self-destroying prophecy; it announces the doom of its own language, the coming of silence.

Earlier on, in chapter 20, Ezekiel had turned angrily on the elders and had said to them, "Are you come to inquire of me? As I live, says the Lord God, I will not be inquired of by you" (20:3). Is it oracles you want? he is saying. Well, there will be no more oracles. A passionate and moving speaker, Ezekiel here anathematizes the very art of speech itself. He enacts a drama in which he performs symbolic signs and explains them to a delighted audience come to observe him, but then, somewhat in the manner of the Cynic philosopher Diogenes, he excoriates them for having come to the play.

We may pause to consider the verb *dāraš* in the last-quoted passage, here translated "to inquire of." It is this inquiring of him as of seeking an oracle that Ezekiel spurns. But there is a further overtone of meaning. The term with its cognate noun *midraš*, as in 2 Chron. 13:22 and 24:27, suggests also "imaginative exposition" or "interpretive discourse."[2] It points evidently to the verbal aspect of prophecy. To be a prophet is to be a master of words that invite interpretation. The people come to *lidĕrōš* and he, by the power of his language, submits to *lĕhiddārēš*, i.e., to being inquired of or interpreted. At the heart of this mode of communication is the play of words, the use in particular of paronomasia for assonance, or explication, or antithesis. It is this transaction that the prophet is here savagely abjuring. No more *midraš*, he is saying. And yet the very verse that says this is, in its paratactic sequence of the two forms of *dāraš* ("Are you come to inquire of me? As I live . . . I will not be inquired of by you"), a perfect example of that verbal play which is here being proscribed.

The verse that follows introduces for contrast a different verbal double: "Wilt thou judge them, son of man, wilt thou judge them? Let them know the abominations of their fathers" (20:4). (Better perhaps with

Moffatt: "Arraign them, son of man, arraign them.") Instead of the *dāraš*, or verbal function of the prophet, here we have him in his judgmental role, that denoted by the verb *šāpaṭ*. No more words, he is saying: instead of that, you will get from me the sword of chastisement. I will be Moses, he seems to say; but not Moses who speaks to the rock, rather Moses who strikes the rock. The image, six times repeated, that governs the whole powerful discourse that follows (20:5–44) is that of the raised hand. God raises his hand to take Israel out of Egypt and to declare himself to the people (5, 6) and he raises his hand to punish them in the wilderness and scatter them among the nations (15, 23). The gesture suggests an oath but also a blow, thus ambiguously combining promise and punishment. Eventually, the raised hand is transmuted (v. 34) into the well-known figure of the mighty hand and outstretched arm of the God who judges both his people and their enemies.

A metonymic term for judgment, the uplifted arm of God (or of his prophetic messenger) had been originally introduced, as noted above, for a sign of the nonverbal (indeed, antiverbal) function of the prophet, but it has now become the focus of a sinuous play of language whereby all the various possibilities of the trope are explored. Instead of discourse, he says, you will have the arm, a kinesics of pure gesture. But even as the gesture is performed, it becomes an eloquent utterance, one made richer by the multiple repetition of the phrase and its variants. Anaphora constitutes the basic rhetoric of this chapter. In verses 35–36, the verb *šāpaṭ*, to judge or remonstrate, returns to be thrice repeated. Indeed, the accumulation of words by the device of anaphora is the very medium of this prophecy. But the prophet is saying, ironical though the claim is and defeated though it is in the very moment of saying it, that it is not words he offers but acts, judgments. In verse 37 that claim resolves itself into another image of violence, perhaps one associated with and suggested by the raised arm. It is the image of the rod: "I will cause you to pass under the rod, and I will bring you into the discipline of the covenant: and I will purge out from among you the rebels, and them that transgress against me" (20:37–38).[3] The punitive force of the "rod" is intensified by the sequel that speaks of the bond or discipline of the covenant by the term *māsōret*, suggesting binding or imprisoning but perhaps also chastising and perhaps also (as in later Hebrew) handing down (from the verb *māsōr*), i.e., the handing down of a verbal tradition.

The whole paradox we have been discussing is compressed in the three words bridging verses 37 and 38—*māsōret habbĕrît ûbārôtî*—"the discipline: the covenant: I will purge." The covenant, in its original essence a verbal exchange or contract, here becomes a physical bonding or chastisement (linked to the "rod" of the first half of verse 37). The verb *bĕrît* (covenant) then yields by paronomasia to the following word, *ûbārôtî,* here translated "I will purge"[4] but perhaps suggesting also the sharpening of an arrow (as in Isa. 49:2). A contract sealed in words changes into a cleansing agency or a sharpened arrow but does so actually through a play on words—that very same wordplay which is here supposed to be banished so as not to obtrude upon the direct judgmental role that the prophet has assumed. Language here undoes itself at the same time as it knits its marvelous web. The audience is held enchanted at the same time as all such enchantment is condemned as so much flute music to be cut off by the sword of judgment.

II

We may consider the special relationship between the prophet and his audience under this term "covenant." Clearly from the phrase just quoted the covenant or *bĕrît* suggests a bond or partnership but it also suggests a measure of constraint on both sides. "I will cause you to pass under the rod, and I will bring you into the discipline of the covenant: and I will purge out from among you the rebels, and them that transgress against me." As well as referring to the drama being played out between God and Israel, this sentence viewed metapoetically—as it demands to be viewed—also refers to the drama being played out between the prophet and his audience. They are bound together by a common destiny and common obligation and yet the audience is being coerced, the prophet in effect saying to them, "I will make you read the words my way." They in their turn are rebelling and insisting that they hear a different word, see a different vision; if you wish, they are writing a different text. "Covenant" signifies relationality, even a mode of relationality that neither side can abrogate—for they are bound to one another—and yet it is an uneasy, an antithetical relation, one full of tension, of recalcitrance on both sides. Chapters 3 and 4 of this prophet are full of dreadful images of constraint. In chapter 3 it is said that the people will put him in bonds; they will rebel against him, but to match their refusal to hear him, his own power of speech will be paralyzed—he will be struck dumb:

> But thou, O son of man, behold, they shall put cords upon thee, and shall bind thee with them, and thou shalt not go out among them: and I will make thy tongue cleave to the roof of thy mouth, that thou shalt be dumb, and shalt not be able to reprove them: for they are a rebellious house. (3:25–26)

If they will not obey the voice of command, they will not have fine words either—the prophet will become speechless. But the irony is that in the sequel the speechless acts become themselves an eloquent language of signs. The prophet acts out the drama of coercion: he lies on his side for forty days bound with cords "so that thou shalt not be able to turn thyself from one side to the other" (4:8). But no doubt the audience was as fascinated by that vivid performance as it was by his fine speeches. The audience is not eliminated: it is bound to him and he is bound to it, evidently by those very same ropes which bind him to his task!

The biblical text as a whole is founded in relationality. It demands an audience, actively participating not merely in understanding but even in constituting the text. This is of course classical Jewish doctrine. The written law, *tôrâ šebbiktāb*, cannot stand alone; it is validated by the *tôrâ šebbĕ'al-peh*, i.e., the oral Torah, or continuing tradition of interpretation. This is a "community of interpreters" from whom the written text receives its meaning and its generic character.[5] That is possibly also what is meant in Ezekiel's term *māsōret habbĕrît*—the bond or tradition of the covenant. Relationality continues, a living "bond" of continuing interpretation in which the text is constituted from age to age by the dialectical relation subsisting between the written and the unwritten scripture, between a community of interpreters and a text that is constantly reinterpreted by them. The "text" does not exist anywhere except in the tension-laden space between that community of interpreters and the words that they have received by tradition.

Such relationality is not an invention of rabbinic Judaism. It is already asserted in the most notable passages of scripture. "Hear O Israel: the Lord our God, the Lord is one" (Deut. 6:4). This is not a simple proclamation, a *kerygma,* nor is it simply a prescriptive statement; it is much rather an invitation, a summons to "Israel" to *hear,* to apprehend, to interpret. What it tells us is that the divine unity is realized only when there is a community of hearers to achieve that perception, to make that affirmation; it is a perception that has to be striven for, created in the act of reading, hearing, and understanding. Nor are the words *šĕma' yiśrā'ēl* a form of apostrophe, a mere rhetorical gesture: they imply rather a genuine partnership, the invocation, as a necessary presence, of a hearing ear and a perceiving intelligence in the constitution of meaning. We have in short a covenantal encounter in which the very mode of the utterance is governed by the categories of covenant. The willingness to hear, to understand, to cooperate is here declared to be a prior condition for the affirmation to which the sentence moves. And it is that willingness which the sentence solicits. Relationality, in short, precedes pronouncement and precedes command. And relationality—the presence within that discourse which we call Torah of the hearing ear and the perceiving mind—is the theme of this sentence.

A question also arises as to where to situate these words in the dramatic pattern of the relationship. Who speaks them to whom? In their deuteronomic context they seem to be words spoken by Moses to Israel in the name of God and are from this point of view parallel to the sentence that precedes them: "Hear therefore, O Israel, and take care to do them [i.e., the commandments]; that it may be well with thee . . ." (6:3). But this is not how they have been construed by the interpreting community in practice. The words "Hear, O Israel: the Lord our God, the Lord is one" have become much rather a passionate cry from the hearer to whom they are ostensibly addressed! In fact, their direction has been exactly reversed. In the daily repetition of that sentence it becomes the sign of "the acceptance of the yoke of the commandments." The interpreting community now takes the words that summoned it into existence and makes them its own. What had seemed to be in the original signification something, as I have said, between an invitation, a summons, and a command, now becomes a speech-act of a very different kind—a passionate acceptance of the hearer's own role in the discourse and a cry to the fellowship of Israel to share in his discovery and affirmation. There is thus an exchange of roles in the process of communication from speaker to reader. The reader himself becomes speaker accepting an active role as a full covenanting partner without whom the sentence cannot achieve its meaning. But we should not underestimate the strain involved, the sense of difficulties to be overcome—what I have previously termed recalcitrance on the part of the audience. The same verb *šĕmaʿ* occurs in the phrase *naʿăśeh wĕnišmaʿ*, "we will do and we will hear," in connection with the acceptance of the Law at Mount Sinai (Exod. 24:7). Commenting on that phrase, the rabbis say that the willingness to both do and hear—the latter implying also perceiving, obeying, and understanding, as in the present context of "Hear O Israel"—was only achieved after God had inverted the mountain of Sinai over the heads of the people like a great barrel and threatened them with destruction.[6] To accept the role of "hearer" in the sense understood by "Hear O Israel" is to accept an almost overpowering responsibility. It is not a simple act of response that is required of us as though we were readers of a novel called upon to assist in the creating of a fictional illusion; rather we are called upon to commit ourselves, to accept an obligation. For the word *šĕmaʿ* implies not only reading but also obeying; the text seizes us even against our will.

III

One element in that contract which determines the manner of reading biblical texts deserves to be emphasized. The words "Hear O Israel" do not only say something about relationality in the present; they affirm, as noted above, a continuing relationality—a community of interpreters that carries perceptions (in this case the perception of the divine unity) derived from the past into the present and future. Rashi following the Sifre links our sentence with Zech. 14:9—"And the Lord shall be king over all the earth; on that day the Lord shall be one, and his name one." There is according to this a time dimension, a future reference. The hearer in the *šĕmaʿ* affirms a continuity of which he is himself the guarantor. In other words, the verb *šĕmaʿ* implies not only hearing, perceiving, interpreting, but also *remembering*. Past occasions are linked by memory to present occasions—that is the true hermeneutic circle of interpretation. "Hear O Israel" in fact says something about history: the word that has been heard validates itself in the historical present as it did in the past; it continues to resound. The words "Hear O Israel" can thus be glossed, "*Continue* to hear, O Israel; a living word is carried into the future by a living people constituting an undying community of auditors. I declare myself to be part of that community."

Such historical continuity must, accordingly, be distinguished from the relativism that some modern theorists have maintained, according to which the hearer or reader, situated in his own historical context, can never reach the same perception of the text as his predecessor or successor. There is no essential continuity of meaning.[7] This is not the position taken by the sentence we are considering, nor can it be supported by biblical poetics. "Hear, O Israel: The Lord our God, the Lord is one" may further be glossed: "Hear, O Israel at all times and you will hear that the same Lord is still our God, the same one Lord." The hearing itself becomes, in short, the affirmation of a unity of perception, a covenantal bonding of the generations. Each reader becomes a witness to that continuity, firmly placing himself in a context that includes the witnesses who have gone before him and those who will come after him. Again, this unifying perception has to be striven for, recalcitrance has to be overcome. It is so much easier to slip into total relativism, to assume that the generations of readers are not bound each to each. But we are enjoined not to let this happen.

The demand made of the reader that he become a witness, a guarantor of continuity, is central to the Bible's own definition of poetry. It is that definition which I now wish briefly to consider. It occurs in Deuteronomy, chapter 31. There Moses is instructed to write a poem before he dies, a poem that will live unforgotten in the mouths and minds of the people. The poem itself, usually known by its opening word *haʾăzînû*, is given in chapter 32. Here from chapter 31 is part of the programmatic introduction (or instruction):

> Now therefore, write you this poem, and teach it to the children of
> Israel; put it in their mouths, that this poem may be a witness for me

against the children of Israel. For when I shall have brought them into the land of which I swore to their fathers, one flowing with milk and honey; and they shall have eaten and filled themselves, and are grown fat; then will they turn to other gods, and serve them, and provoke me, and break my covenant. And it shall come to pass, when many evils and troubles have befallen them, that this poem shall answer them as a witness, for it shall not be forgotten out of the mouths of their seed: for I know their inclination, and what they do, even now, before I have brought them into the land of which I swore. (Deut. 31:19–21)

There is a rather complex time scheme. The poem takes us back to a time of origins, to the sojourn in the wilderness "before I have brought them into the land of which I swore," but it is designed for a future time, after the land has been settled and has become flourishing and fertile ("a land flowing with milk and honey"). It will then act as a mnemonic, an aid to memory, because during the intervening period it will have lived unforgotten in the mouth of the reader or hearer, ready to come to mind when the troubles arrive. Poetry is thus a kind of time bomb; it awaits its hour and then springs forward into harsh remembrance. If the sequence of the sentences in the quoted passage is attended to, it will be seen that the poem will come as a warning, even a kind of punishment, to a people that has broken the covenant. It will live in their minds and mouths, bringing them back, whether they like it or not, to the harsh memory of the desert sojourn. Once learned it will not easily be forgotten. The words will stick, they will be importunate, they will not let us alone.

It is worth pausing on this word 'ēd, "witness"—a key word twice repeated in the quoted passage and twice again in the continuation (vv. 26, 28). As in Lam. 2:13 it seems to connote the actual process of poetic imagining. It is evidently related to a root 'ûd with the sense of *persistent repetition*. It enters into the definition here as an aspect of the process of learning, of lodging the words in the memory ("teach it to the people . . . put it in their mouths, that this poem may be an 'ēd [witness]"). But it also seems to refer to the process of the poem's evocation in the future time; it will then become *a nagging presence*, returning upon those who have learned it with a disturbing constancy like a revenant ("this poem shall answer them as a *witness*, for it shall not be forgotten out of the mouths of their seed").

The poem as a revenant is a concept not easily accommodated to modern poetics. It calls to mind the romantic poets' interest in the action of memory, but memory was for them on the whole not painful or, if it was, the poem would help to ease that pain. The 'ēdût or witness function of the poem of which we are here speaking has nothing to do with the easing of pain. We have instead a disturbing shock of recognition as a remembered text comes to us charged with a new historical urgency. The 'ēd function means that texts from the past do not simply echo; they invade us, they demand attention. We discover that ʿēdût is a covenant word, a synonym for bĕrît itself, as in the phrase ʾărôn hāʿēdût (meaning the "ark of the covenant"). It signifies a dynamic of relationships, a bond between hearer and utterer constantly reimposed, sometimes even on an unwilling hearer. It takes him back to earlier sayings, earlier encounters, reminding him of obligations he would rather forget. Like a revenant, it arrests him as though to say, "You know me, I come to remind you of what you know." Within the Song of Moses, i.e., the poem that follows in chapter 32 of Deuteronomy, there is a call to remember—

> Remember the days of old,
> consider the years of many generations:
> ask thy father, and he will recount it to thee;
> thy elders, and they will tell thee.
>
> (32:7)

—and also a condemnation of forgetfulness: "Thou hast forgotten God that formed thee" (v. 18). The memory forced upon the reader is not exactly pleasurable; it is the memory of an encounter in the wilderness— "He found him in a desert land, and in the waste howling wilderness" (v. 10)—that was the setting for the fundamental exchange of words on which the covenant was founded. It is that scene to which future poems will bear witness, or rather to which the reader of those future poems will himself have to bear witness.

There is one further implication of the notion of the reader as witness. A relationality between text and reader founded on the term ʿēd or ʿēdût suggests the relationship of litigants in a lawsuit. The reader is cast in the role alternately of witness and defendant; he is called upon to "respond" in the special sense of a witness or litigant responding to a charge or a piece of evidence in a court of law. There are many images relating to the justice and the administration of justice in the Haʾăzînû poem itself that follows. In verse 4, we are told that "all his ways are justice." In verse 36 we are told that God will judge his people; in verse 41 his hand "takes hold on judgment"—there he is, as it were, giving sentence. Some modern students of the form-critical school have in fact related the opening verse of the poem to the literary type or *Gattung* of the lawsuit.[8] In the formula with which the poem opens, heaven and earth are called upon to bear witness against the people of Israel: "Give ear, O heavens, and I will speak; and hear, O earth, the words of my mouth" (32:1). "Hear" in the second half of that verse gives us the same stem šĕmaʿ that we have already considered. The antithetical relation of text and audience is gathered again into the root šmʿ, with a strong additional sense here of "bearing witness against." To hear or read is to be confronted with such testimony. Actually *witnessing against* had already been announced as part of the poem's function in the programmatic chapter 31 that we considered earlier, where Moses is told to write a poem as a witness. The continuation of that passage reads: "Gather to me all the elders of your tribes, and your officers, that I may speak these words in their ears, and call heaven and earth to witness against them" (31:28). The first verse of the poem represents the fulfillment of that announcement. Heaven and earth bear witness against Israel.[9] One is required to "respond" to that. The reading of the poem thus becomes a struggle for vindication. The notion of a trial or a court of law is not here a pleasing trope as in Shakespeare's sonnet—"When to the sessions of sweet silent thought, / I summon up remembrance of things past"—but rather a *Gattung*, a way of structuring the relationship between the text and the reader, or more correctly, between the reader and the God who is seen to stand behind the words of the text. The *Ha'ăzînû* poem, from this point of view, "puts the reader on the spot." He is attacked, challenged. But here again there is an exchange of roles. To adapt a phrase of Milton's (also spoken with reference to the covenanting God of the Old Testament) the reader "judges and is judged."[10] He is a defendant, but he is also, as the poem proceeds, a "witness for the Crown." He is not only rebuked; he is also caught up in the majesty of the impeachment itself. He becomes as it were God's witness (as in Isa. 43:10), as the poem mounts to its triumphant conclusion:

> See now that I, even I, am he,
> and there is no god with me;
> I kill, and I make alive;
> I wound, and I heal;
> neither is there any that can deliver out of my hand.
> For I lift up my hand to heaven,
> and swear, as I live for ever,
> if I whet my glittering sword,
> and my hand take hold on judgment;
> I will render vengeance to my enemies,
> and will reward those who hate me. . . .
>
> (32:39–41)

It will be seen that in these final sentences we have not left behind the *Gattung* of the lawsuit. God is here seen raising his hand to take an oath. The reader has become a witness to that oath-taking. In the oath, judgment is promised on "my enemies"—the enemies of the people who have also become God's enemies. The reader is promised that (as with Job) his judge will become his vindicator, bearing witness on his behalf in a future that is "laid up in store with me, sealed up among my treasures" (v. 34). And the reader for his part will testify to the oath that he has witnessed. The poem has now become a testimony in the sense of a saving word, an affidavit, to which the reader is himself the witness. This is the sense that the verb *ʿûd,* "to testify," finally comes to bear. It occurs for the last time in the short prose passage that follows the song at the end of chapter 32. There Moses says to the people:

> Set your hearts to all the words which I testify *[mēʿîd]* among you today . . . for it is not a vain thing for you; because it is your life: and through this word you shall prolong your days in the land, which you are going over the Jordan to possess. (32:46–47)

·5·

THE SONG OF MOSES
PASTORAL IN REVERSE

The verses of Deuteronomy 31 that introduce the Song of Moses seem to hold out the promise of the pastoral. We are told that the poem will have reference to a time when the people will have arrived in "the land of which I swore to their fathers, one flowing with milk and honey." There is here a momentary vision of a Hebrew Arcadia. But the poem, we are told, will not celebrate milk and honey but rather the bad effects of milk and honey. It is when the day of evil comes and milk and honey are at an end that "this poem shall answer them as a witness" (v. 21).[1] We shall not, it seems, be granted the delights of the pastoral with its shepherds and happy milkmaids—we shall be given something more like an antipastoral.

The *Ha'ăzînû* poem itself, which follows in chapter 32, has a similar opening promise. Again the pastoral note is struck:

> Give ear O heavens, and I will speak;
> and hear, O earth, the words of my mouth.
> My doctrine shall drop as the rain,
> my speech shall distil as the dew,
> as the small rain upon the tender grass,
> and as the showers upon the herb.
> (Deut. 32:1–2)

Moses said the poem would be remembered on a future day. He was right—as it happens, it was remembered by Shakespeare, who somewhat perversely echoed it in the words of Portia to Shylock in condemnation of the supposed grimness of Old Testament justice! "The quality of mercy is not strained," she said, "It droppeth as the gentle rain from heaven / Upon the place beneath." But the Hebrew author of *Ha'ăzînû* does not remain for long in the pastoral mode. He moves quickly as we noted earlier to his remembrance of the past with the announcement:

> Remember the days of old,
> consider the years of many generations;

> ask thy father, and he will recount it to thee;
> thy elders, and they will tell thee.
>
>   (32:7)

The "days of old" take us to the primal scene of Israel's historical memory, namely the desert experience:

> He found him in a desert land,
> and in the waste howling wilderness;
> he led him about, he instructed him;
> he kept him as the apple of his eye.
>
>   (32:10)

The desert is the scene of the love affair between God and Israel ("he kept him as the apple of his eye"), but it is not a place where we sport with Amaryllis in the shade. There is no shade, for the sun beats and the dead tree gives no shelter and the dry stone no sound of water.

Ha'ăzînû offers us a kind of condensed history of Israel. We are told how after he had found Israel in the desert land, God had carried the people aloft like an eagle carrying its young and had transported them to a place where they had enjoyed a paradisal fertility. We have Arcadia again:

> Butter of kine, and milk of sheep,
> with fat of lambs,
> and rams of the breed of Bashan, and goats,
> with the fat kidneys of wheat;
> and thou didst drink wine of the pure blood of the grape.
>
>   (32:14)

But there in Bashan and Samaria Jeshurun had waxed fat and kicked (v. 15) and, as a result, had been brought back to the desert to be punished and purged. The great central image of this poem of Moses is the image of the burning heat of the desert. That, rather than the charm of the pastoral, is what would be remembered from the past. That too is what would be laid up in memory for the future:

> And I will heap mischiefs upon them;
> I will spend my arrows on them.
> They shall be sucked empty by hunger,
> and devoured with burning heat,
> and with bitter destruction:
> and I will send the teeth of beasts upon them,
> with the poison of crawling things of the dust.
>
>   (32:23–24)

This vision of a wasteland culminates in a central memory from the past, which will henceforth function as a root image in the biblical poetry of lament. It is the remembrance of the overthrow of *Sĕdōm* and *ʿĂmōrâ* (Genesis 19). Speaking ambiguously of both Israel and of the enemies of Israel who come to punish it for its wrongdoings, the poet continues:

> For their vine is of the vine of Sodom,
> and of the fields of Gomorrah:
> their grapes are grapes of gall,
> their clusters are bitter;
> their wine is the fierceness of crocodiles,
> and the cruel venom of asps.
>
> (32:32–33)

Milton was to remember the bitter fruit of Sodom in his account of the punishment of the fallen angels in Book X of *Paradise Lost* when the wicked angels, transformed into venomous serpents, chew bitter ashes instead of the fair fruit of Eden. So this poem lived unforgotten in the mouth of Milton!

II

However, if we are to speak of Milton or indeed any other major poet of the Western literary tradition, we will note that the accent of lament or joy is much more likely to be evoked by the scenery of Arcadia than by that of Sodom and Gomorrah. The bitter ashes of Sodom are good enough for the fallen angels, but when Adam, Milton's human hero, falls, he does so in a forest glade, "where highest woods impenetrable / To star or sunlight, spread their umbrage broad, / And brown as evening" (*Paradise Lost* IX, 1086–88). There Adam would not see the face of god or angel; he would lament his fate in the musical softness and "umbrage" of a remembered paradise: "Cover me ye Pines / Ye cedars with innumerable boughs, / Hide me where I may never see them more. . . ." We are reminded of Moeris going into exile in Virgil's ninth eclogue, the sadness of his loss emphasized by the inserted poem on the sad demise of Daphnis—"Graft the pear trees, Daphnis. Descendants will pick your fruits."[2] Indeed, behind Adam's lament is the lament for all the heroes of the pastoral, for Daphnis in Theocritus's first idyll, for Adonis in Bion's first idyll, and the sad self-mourning of Gallus, victim of unrequited love, in Virgil's tenth eclogue. They all remember the sunsets spent in pasturing their goats by the spring amid the shade of the forest trees, the cedars and the pines. To such memories they turn nostalgically. The heroes of the pastoral had lived in a golden world and it is that which they recall in their laments: "Lay him down on the soft vestments in which he was wont to pass the night: in which with thee along the night he would take his holy sleep, on a couch all-of-gold; yearn thou for Adonis, sad-visaged though he be now; and lay him amid chaplets and flowers."[3]

What does such memory have in common with the action of the memory called for in Deuteronomy, chapter 31? Surely very little. Nostalgia for the Golden Age is not what Moses means by "witness," but rather memory weighted with obligation. Nostalgia does not obligate; it fills the mind with a rosy image tinged with sadness. In that sadness we take a kind of consolation; we hide ourselves in "the soft vestments." The image of hiding is primary in the lines quoted above from Milton—"Hide me where I may never see them more." He wishes to be safely hidden. It may be argued that this is not memory at all, but the closing of the mind to what is unpleasant in the past or the future. While seeming to indulge in a sad dream of loss, the pastoral elegy really scatters flowers over the dead, enabling us to forget, rather than to remember, to lose ourselves in a myth of the eternally revolving seasons. In one of the most elaborate pastoral elegies in English, "In Memoriam," Tennyson makes the point that the words of the poem actually serve to conceal the jagged outlines of grief and loss:

> In words like weeds, I'll wrap me o'er,
> Like coarsest clothes against the cold;
> But that large grief which these enfold
> Is given in outline and no more.
>   (Section 5)

Laurence Lerner, discussing the "uses of nostalgia" by pastoral poets, finds here the basic difference between the Greek vision and that of the Hebrew prophets. "Isaiah's paradise is different from Hesiod's. It belongs not at the beginning of time but at the end."[4] The Greeks looked back to a Golden Age, the Hebrews look forward. The remembering of which Moses speaks in his song ("Remember the days of old") assumes responsibility also for a future. The poetry that such remembering produces will be laid up by the people to explode on them at some future time; it is dynamic, active memory. "One speaks an elegy, the other a call to action."[5]

But the situation is a little more complex than this. If persistent repetition is characteristic of the ʿēdût function of the poem—the text as a nagging presence to return upon us in the future like a revenant—then repetition also belongs to the essence of the pastoral elegy as we may trace it back to the Greeks. But it is the repetition of the cycle of the seasons rather than the conning of an urgent historical task. Tennyson gives us the classical spirit almost in cliché form. At his friend's death, he

says, the seasons always return and they bring with them the comfort of
regularity:

> The season brings the flower again,
> And brings the firstlings of the flock;
> And in the dusk of thee, the clock
> Beats out the little lives of men.
>
> (Section 2)

Especially does the season of Christmas come round again and again in
the poem and, as it does, so sorrow is assuaged in a dream of eternal
recurrence in which the individual and his losses "remerge in the general
soul" (46). Annual recurrence not only takes the edge off the sadness of
loss but turns death into a kind of triumph. The death of Daphnis celebrated annually by shepherds and farmers becomes in Virgil's fifth
eclogue a source of religious exaltation:

> As long as boar loves mountain ridge, and fish loves stream,
> as long as thyme is food for bees, and dew for crickets,
> always will your fame, your name, your praises flourish.
> As to Bacchus, as to Ceres, so each year to you,
> the farmers will make vows; you too will see vows paid.
>
> (1.76–80)

The mention here of Bacchus (Dionysus) and Ceres reminds us that the
mourning for the shepherd's death in the traditional pastoral elegy is
associated with the ritual of the vegetation deities (specifically Tammuz
and Adonis), who died in the autumn and were annually reborn in the
spring (or as in the case of Tammuz, with the coming of the autumn
rains). The pattern lives on as a major element in the literary culture of
the West. In Shakespeare's *A Winter's Tale*, Perdita is the lost one who will
be found and so will her mother Hermione. All sad far-off lost things are
marvelously renewed in the ever-returning spring. In such poetry man
blends with nature in a cyclical movement in which the self is caught up
with that which lies beyond the self, and death is annulled. Lycidas, we
are told in Milton's poem, is not really dead, he merely sinks like the sun
in the west:

> And yet anon repairs his drooping head,
> And tricks his beams, and with new spangled ore,
> Flames in the forehead of the morning sky.

This sense of being rolled round in earth's diurnal course with the sun
and the planets can yield many moods, from languor to ecstasy. To be
aware of oneself as continuous with nature and as ruled by its rhythm is

to gain access to a world of primal simplicities. The power and attractiveness of such a mythological sense of time and existence should not be underestimated, nor can we ignore the richness of the poetic patterns to which it gives rise. It is not merely a particular poetic structure we are here talking about but a key to a whole poetic universe.

The pastoral, we may say, represents the Western literary tradition at its most characteristic and its most triumphant. It seems to speak out of the very heart of nature and this gives it a wonderful strength. Poetry measures itself against death and loss and emerges triumphant. We recall Walt Whitman's poem on the death of Lincoln. It is redolent with memories of earlier pastorals, Milton's "Lycidas," Shelley's "Adonais," Virgil's tenth eclogue:

> When lilacs last in the dooryard Bloom'd,
> and the great star early droop'd in the western sky in the night,
> I mourn'd and yet shall mourn with ever-returning spring.
> Ever-returning spring, trinity sure to me you bring,
> Lilac blooming perennial and drooping star in the west,
> And thought of him I love.

The sweetness of this eclogue consoles us for the worst of losses. The incredible beauty of the lilacs—in the metalanguage of Whitman's elegy, simply the words of the poem itself—is potent to console us for the death of Lincoln! No less. It is the highest reach, in a way, of Western art. And yet the Hebrew poet and legislator (and in this case he is also the legislator for Hebrew poetics) sets his face against this solace. He does not allow us that sweet indulgence. The Hebrew poet will strip death and disaster naked. He throws away the flowers, he abhors the pastoral. We remember Ezekiel's wrath at the women sitting weeping for the vegetation god Tammuz at the northern gate of the temple (Ezek. 8:14). Memory is something else, not the ever-returning spring, coming to us again with the perennially blooming lilac, but a naked confrontation with a past that is terribly present in spite of the passage of the years. We see the nakedness of Sodom and Gomorrah behind the bloom of Samaria. One wonders whether Theocritus or Virgil would have recognized this as poetry at all—this transparent language of witness that does nothing at all to hide us from the terrible things that lie buried in our memories, but brings them fiercely into the light. The concept of ʿēdût stands, as we have said, for recurrence but it is the opposite of that sort of recurrence that belongs to the cycle of nature. Oneness with that cycle implies the loss of responsibility, ultimately the loss of individuality; ʿēdût by contrast implies the recurrent awareness of a responsibility that comes from the individual's isolation from nature. Genesis dramatizes this break in a fundamental paradigm: Adam and his wife following their natural instinct try to hide among the trees of the Garden, but the voice that cries out, "Where art thou?" summons them from the pastoral glade to a more strenuous task. That task is what biblical poetry is about.

This point, however, needs to be modified. For Hebrew poetry does not abolish the rhythm of the natural world. *Ha'ăzînû* celebrates in its opening verses the presence of heaven and earth as actors in the poem. The rain and dew are brought into organic relation with the "teaching" that is nothing other than the poem itself seen as the distillation of Torah. Conversely, the Greek and Latin pastoral does not really achieve oneness with nature. It is in an important sense the most artificial, the least natural of poetic forms. True, it proclaims itself to be the song of the shepherd who has access to the very heart of nature; the poet is said to draw his inspiration from the spring at the wayside or from the sound of the Hybla bees. But all this too is part of the essential nostalgia of such poetry. It seems to say all the time, "if only"—if only the life of the poet were as simple as the shepherd's piping, but sadly it is not so simple. The very yearning for simplicity becomes indeed the substance of the poem and that yearning depends on the tension between a desire for oneness with nature and a knowledge that the desired oneness is unattainable. The element of distance, of isolation is, as Empson has shown, at the heart of this poetic genre.[6] Pastoral puts the complex into the simple[7] and in so doing betrays its own subject matter. The poet in Virgil's tenth eclogue declares that the Arcadian shepherds singing verses to their mountains "alone are skilled in song." But we know that shepherds are not skilled in song and those who are, are not shepherds. To assume that they are is a trope for expressing nostalgia itself. If only poets could take their inheritance from nature like shepherds; but merely to say so is to declare that such simplicities are impossible. For the shepherd is, by definition, one who does not need to wish he was a shepherd; nostalgia for the shepherd's life is precisely what he does not have. The poet, who has such nostalgia, is by that very token denied access to the simplicities. The fruits he gathers are poetic fruits; the wine he drinks at the wayside is the wine of poetry; the sheep and goats he tends are the poems he nurtures.

But is this reflexive self-consciousness of the pastoral a triumph or a defeat? For the modern critic such self-involvement of the poet in poetry is a recognized and commendable norm and, from this point of view, the great pastoral poets of antiquity are seen as having grasped, long before others, the very essence of poetry. The pastorals of Theocritus and Virgil represent, according to William Berg, "an intensified experience of poetic inspiration."[8] Theocritus's seventh idyll is, he remarks, a poem about poetry and as such is a prototype not only for later pastoral but for Western poetry as we know it; it is "the first conscious evocation of the

pastoral landscape as a garden of the poet's mind."[9] There is here an
obvious link with the symbolists nearer our own time. We may suggest,
for instance, that Rilke's elegies are from this point of view the modern
and ultimate distillation of the pastoral mode. The wanderer, he tells us,
brings no earth to the valley but only the word. The poet's gift is to *say*
and, through that saying, to transform the world, for the world wishes
for an invisible rebirth as poetry:

> Are we, perhaps, *here*, only to say; House.
> Bridge. Fountain. Gate. Jug. Fruit-tree. Window.—
> at most: Pillar. Tower. . . . But to *say*,—you understand,
> O to *say*, with an intensity the things themselves never
> hoped to achieve.[10]

Language, and specifically poetic language, says things with an intensity that things themselves could not hope to achieve. We have arrived
here at the apotheosis of art; the poet is no longer the servant of the
myth; rather he nurtures the rare fruit of poetry and in that nurturing
assumes a new and special nature.[11] Poetry becomes for the first time a
thing complete in itself, a perfection of words and sentiments not requir-
ing legitimation from things—from house, bridge, fountain, gate, fruit-
tree, or window. But those critics who rightly perceive this purity of
poetic self-involvement as the peculiar achievement of the pastoral have
failed to note that the poetry often bears witness to the frustration and
loneliness that such an achievement yields. Rilke's triumph has its
shadow side, for the "holiest inspiration" that the poet finally wins is
"friendly death." The sense of loss, of death, or of unrequited love is no
incidental feature of the pastoral; it lies at the very heart of such poetry.
And ultimately what is lamented is not the loss of a loved one or an
estate, but the fleetingness of the poetic word itself, which, even as we
grasp its fragile perfection, seems to evaporate, to vanish as its echo dies:

> Show him how joyous a thing can be, how innocent, and ours;
> how the wailing lament clearly unfolds into form,
> serves as a thing, or dies in a thing—and fades in the beyond
> like the melody of a violin. And these living things
> that are departing, understand when you praise them fleeting,
> they believe they will be saved by us, the most fleeting of all.[12]

Moeris in Virgil's ninth eclogue had caught just this same accent:

> Age takes all away, the mind as well: oft, I recall,
> I laid long days to rest with song when but a boy.

Now I've forgotten just as many songs, and Moeris' voice
itself is going. . . .

(Lines 51–54)

What we have here is the pathos of the poetic voice itself, which has
become the sole possession of the poet, his only space. And that voice is
itself fading, vanishing. One suspects that many pastoral elegies, while
seemingly addressed to dead poets, are really concerned with their own
insubstantiality. Their pathos is that of a poetry which celebrates its own
essence and, knowing itself, knows that it can make nothing happen. It is
left with the echo of its own voice, a voice that declares its own manifest
presence and at the same time disappears into vacancy.

The pastoral is thus endlessly self-referential. It is a poem about a poet
and his poems; those poems in their turn celebrate other poetic moments. This is not some modern sublimation of the pastoral mode but is
already a feature of Theocritus's first idyll, a poem presenting us with an
image of a poet, Thyrsis, who sings a lament for the dead poet Daphnis;
as a reward for the song Thyrsis receives a marvelous drinking cup that is
itself "a cunning work of divine art" and on which are fashioned the
themes of pastoral poetry. The poem of Theocritus is thus an endless
reflection of itself and its own poetic activity. But there is a further
dimension. This self-echoing and self-reflection are not merely an internal feature of these poems, they also govern the intertextual relations set
up among the works of different poets. Theocritus's lament for Daphnis
(or rather, the lament by Thyrsis for Daphnis in the poem of Theocritus)
is echoed in Bion's lament for Adonis; Bion's lament in its turn is echoed
by the lament of Moschus for Bion himself, and later, all three are
echoed in Shelley's "Adonais"—a lament for Keats. Imitation and mutual reflection and echoing are in a way the very substance of these
poems, for the evocation of the poetic voice as fading and yet as mysteriously alive is essential to the pastoral genre. The dead poet who is
echoed testifies by the very echoing to his survival in the timeless world
of poetry. Intertextuality here is not merely a matter of relationships
between poems; it constitutes the poem, providing its very *raison d'être*.
We noted earlier that Whitman's "When lilacs last in the dooryard
bloom'd" was heavy with memories of earlier pastoral laments. But this is
not just a matter of Whitman's provenance, of literary "influence" in the
ordinary sense. Whitman is offering his dead leader a poetic tribute, a
mourning procession of poets, a gift of lilacs. The lilacs as we have noted
are the fading echoes of the poem, for what can be more transient than
the beauty of lilacs? But by rooting them, so to say, in past and future
lilacs, he gives them a kind of permanence. Those self-same lilacs will

reappear in the first section of T. S. Eliot's "The Waste Land" as part of a miniature pastoral eclogue:

> April is the cruellest month, breeding
> Lilacs out of the dead land, mixing
> Memory and desire, stirring
> Dull roots with spring rain.

Later in that same section, the "hyacinth girl," her arms full of flowers, will express the essence of that same nostalgia. For Eliot too imitation of earlier poets becomes in an important sense the matter of the poem. In "The Waste Land" the technique of echoing other poetic voices, Spenser, Webster, Baudelaire, Dante, etc., is brought to a pitch of unparalleled sophistication. By it, Eliot perfectly resolves the dialectic of presence and absence. Even as the past becomes a heap of broken images, existing only as a sad and ironic memory, so it is recovered in the words of earlier poets. It lives again.

Thus, through the echoing of the poetic voice, loss and absence are transcended. This strategy goes back through Milton's "Lycidas" to the ancients. Lycidas is dead and he is not dead; similarly Adonais is dead and not dead.[13] But it is only the breath of the poet that makes such transcendence possible, just as it is only the praise of Menalcas that makes Daphnis live eternally. In such an eternity time is abolished, for we are talking not about historical persistence but about poetry surviving as poetry in its own timeless realm. By contrast, Moses was promised that *Ha'ăzînû* would have a more than poetic survival: it would live in the mouths of the people, a people living, sinning, and struggling in the dust of history. That is a measure of the distance between such poetry and the fragile, melancholy grace of the pastoral. The Song of Moses seems to be again in this respect a kind of answer to the pastoral.

III

We need to look a little more closely at this notion of poetic survival, for, if Hebrew poetics looks to history and to the survival of a people, it would also be true to say that it is the word that bears the people, enabling it to survive. According to Deuteronomy 31, it is not because the people is undying that the word survives; it is rather the other way around. The poem that Moses was about to pronounce would, he says, live unforgotten, ready to come to life again at a future time, enabling the people to endure the many evils and troubles that would befall them. Poetry is in an important sense that which makes historical endurance possible. In spite of the lapse of time and the decay of memory, the words remain potent. Moreover—and here is a point to be emphasized—it is by literary imitation that the past voice would be recovered. If Whitman's lilacs bloom again for Eliot, then likewise we taste the bitter fruit of Sodom in other poems too, not just in Milton, but in the Bible itself:

> They are all of them become to me like Sodom,
> and its inhabitants like Gomorrah.
> Therefore, thus says the Lord of hosts concerning the prophets:
> Behold I will feed them with wormwood . . .
>
> (Jer. 23:14–15)

Imitation and echo are here likewise of the essence. The poem is not forgotten. The Song of Moses echoes endlessly throughout the Psalms and the Prophets.[14] We may say that the continuity of the covenant as that which binds the generations each to each is guaranteed by the survival of such a poem in other poems. That is, among other things, what is meant by saying that the poem is a witness. It is a presence evoked and re-evoked in other times and settings and in other poems.

Literary echoing is as fundamental a category for biblical poetry as for the pastoral. Poems are constantly remembered in other poems; we pursue the meaning of biblical texts via their intertextual relationships. But we have only to put it this way to see that there must be a fundamental difference. For what we have here is not a poetic universe complete in itself, not the sad withdrawing note of a lost world and a lost voice, now fleetingly recovered, not the uses of nostalgia, but something else. And that something else needs to be defined. To arrive at a notion of literary imitation as it might apply to biblical poetry, we may consider in this section some of the intertextual relations of *Ha'ăzînû*, including the by-now well-established link between Deuteronomy 32 and the vision of Isaiah the son of Amoz in Isaiah 1.[15]

The opening verse of Isaiah's prophecy with its angry "Hear, O heavens, and give ear, O earth" immediately brings to mind the opening verse of Moses' song with its slower movement: "Give ear, O heavens, and I will speak; / and let the earth hear the words of my mouth." The talmudic rabbis had already noted the echoing of the verbs *šimě'û* . . . *ha'ăzînî* but in a reverse order from the Song of Moses. The reason, they said, is that Moses was nearer to heaven than Isaiah and therefore applied the more intimate *ha'ăzînû*, "give ear," to the heavens, while Isaiah, who was farther away from heaven, employed the more distant *šimě'û*, "hear," when speaking of heaven and the more intimate *ha'ăzînî* when speaking of the earth.[16] But what strikes us is not so much the reversal of the order of the verbs as the echo itself: we have the identical two verbs and the identical two nouns—in fact, the same sentence compressed and used as a weapon against the rebellious sons who are the object of this opening verse of Isaiah:

> Hear, O heavens, and give ear, O earth;
> for the Lord has spoken:
> I have reared and brought up children,
> and they have rebelled against me.
> (Isa. 1:2)

The RSV translators place quotation marks before the words "Sons have I reared . . ." and close them at the end of verse 3, assuming that the words *kî YHWH dibbēr*, "for the Lord has spoken," refer to the words that follow. However, A. Kaminka, in an early study of Isaiah 1 in relation to Deuteronomy 32, read the expression *kî YHWH dibbēr* as referring to the *preceding* words, *šimě'û šāmayim wěha'ăzînî 'ereṣ*, "Hear, O heavens, and give ear, O earth." Those are the words that "the Lord has spoken," and he has spoken them in Deuteronomy 32![17] A similar use of the same formula occurs further down in Isaiah's vision at verse 20:

> But if you refuse and rebel,
> You shall be devoured by the sword;
> for the mouth of the Lord has spoken it.

Clearly there the phrase *kî pî YHWH dibbēr* refers to what precedes, and that too turns out to be an echo of *Ha'ăzînû*, taking us back to verse 25 of that song with its reference to the bereaving sword that shall lay waste young and old among the disobedient children of Israel, in a context that speaks of the devouring action of fire and animals. Kaminka notices a similar example of the same phrase *kî pî YHWH dibbēr* at Isa. 58:14, and there too there is evident echoing of the Song of Moses. The prophet in that place foretells the joys of an obedient people restored to prosperity, and says:

> And I will cause thee to ride upon the high places of the earth;
> and feed thee with the heritage of Jacob thy father,
> for the mouth of the Lord has spoken it.

The whole cluster of terms in that verse, *hirkabtîkā . . . bāmo(w)tê 'āreṣ . . . ha'ăkaltîkā . . . naḥălat ya'ăqōb*, "ride . . . heights of the earth . . . feed . . . heritage of Jacob," are drawn from Deut. 32:9, 13. Thus when the prophet wishes to enforce a warning of imminent disaster he does so by recalling the *ipsissima verba* of the Song of Moses, snarling them at the people and, so that there should be no mistake, adding the words *kî (pî) YHWH dibbēr*, "for the (mouth of the) Lord has spoken." Likewise, when he wishes to make real the promise of blessing, he echoes the precise words of the same song, adding for assurance the phrase *kî YHWH dibbēr*, "the mouth of the Lord has already said this and you know it!"

This is precisely what was meant by saying the poem would be an *'ēd*, a witness. It is summoned in evidence at critical moments, i.e., when danger threatens as a punishment for recalcitrance, or when a repentant generation may expect the rewards of its rightdoing. These situations had already been foretold, and the words, still living in the "mouth" (and spoken by God's "mouth"), can be called to do their task of reminding, of coming to life. They are in truth a revenant. But it will be seen at once that this mode of echoing and recall has a far more dynamic function than the linking of texts by imitation that we noted among the poets of the pastoral. What we have here is not merely the incantation of a voice and a melody, as the descendants of Daphnis pick the fruits of poetry from the tree he had grafted long before. It is not the voice of the Deuteronomist that lives again in the breath of Isaiah, the word answering the word within the enchanted circle of the poem. Hebrew poetry resists such complete interiorization. Instead, we have the disturbing shock of recognition as a remembered text comes at us charged with a new historical urgency. The *'ēd* function means that texts from the past do not simply echo; they invade us, they demand attention. Moreover, they point outwards, beyond themselves; they remind us of duties, perils that likewise invade the poem. World and word bear witness to each other. It is precisely this gesture of reaching out to a world or, rather, of a world ominously reaching in to us, which the opening words of both the Song of Moses and the vision of Isaiah enact: "Give ear, O heavens and I will speak; / and hear, O earth, the words of my mouth." Earth and sky are here included in the witness function of the poem. They assert themselves as an active presence. When the pastoral poet calls upon the woods to answer and their echo ring, he is using a trope—the poem really echoes back upon itself. It would be true to say that when, in Virgil's fifth eclogue, Menalcas announces that the cliffs and orchards resound the songs of Daphnis, there is no mutual activity of witness and response as between the cliffs and the song. It is an "as if" statement—a lovely conceit. For essentially the song echoes itself, resounds back upon itself. For this reason the notion of echo is a fundamental category in pastoral poetry. The poetry itself is the reality, nature a mere sounding-box. In the two biblical passages we are considering, however, heaven and earth are summoned not as echo or audience but, as noted earlier, as witnesses to a lawsuit.[18]

It is misleading, however, to speak of the witness of the "outer world" as something opposed to the witness of the "word." "Heaven and earth" as spoken of in Deut. 31:28 and in Isa. 1:2 are not *things* merely, a cosmos of mass and extension. They too are parts of a verbalized, poetic universe. They can listen and "give ear" because they too are bound by the "words of my mouth" and the "doctrine" mentioned in the continuation. *Šāmayim wā'āreṣ*, "heaven and earth," are in fact remembered from Gen. 1:1–10, where they were constituted by language, indeed by the same *'imrâ* or "saying" spoken of by Moses in Deut. 32:1. They can listen and respond because they occupy the same space as the "words" and the "doctrine" by which the poet and his audience are bound. If they are going to listen to "the words of my mouth," it will not be the first time they have so listened. The first time was when they were created by a word and became forever inseparable from a poetic system of words. But we are talking about words of a special kind, words that bind and command, that have reference to a covenantal reality. Heaven and earth are thus bound. If the teaching is heeded, we are told elsewhere, there will be gentle rain indeed, but if Israel transgresses the covenant, then "he will shut up the heavens, that there be no rain" (Deut. 11:14, 17). To be created by a saying, a command, means to be the kind of witnesses who have a dynamic role in seeing that the covenant is carried out. It means that heaven and earth in the Hebrew imagination are significantly different from the Greek cosmos; they are part of "a contractual history."[19]

It has been shown that the verses of *Ha'ăzînû*, starting from this first verse, follow the thread of the story of creation beginning with the first chapter of Genesis.[20] A whole group of signifiers links Deuteronomy 32 with the early chapters of Genesis. There are not only "the heaven and the earth" from Gen. 1:1; the "grass" and the "herb" from the beginning of the Song of Moses are likewise from the continuation of the same chapter of Genesis (Gen. 1:11), which speaks of the same *dese'* and *'ēseb* as having been created on the third day. Moreover, this thread linking the Song of Moses with Genesis also links the former with Isaiah 1 and other oracles, giving us a whole intertextual network of verbal echoing. For instance, reference to the sons who "have dealt corruptly" (*šiḥēt . . . bānāyw*) from Deut. 32:5 is picked up in Isaiah's vision (*bānîm mašḥîtîm*, 1:4) and goes back to the story of the Flood, where we are told that "all flesh had corrupted [*hišḥît*] their way upon the earth" (Gen. 6:12). The stem *šḥt* in its different constructions, signifying both corruption and the punishment for corruption, occurs six times in relation to the Flood (Gen. 6:11–13; 9:11, 15). It becomes the fundamental sign for the sin of the generation of the Flood as well as for the punishment that overtook them. Its resonance in the Song of Moses and in Isaiah 1 is unmistakable (see Table 1).

Echoes of Genesis continue. As the Song of Moses proceeds, we seem

TABLE 1

The Song of Moses and Some Other Places of Scripture: The Intertextual Weave

The Flood Genesis 6–10	The Overthrow of Sodom and Gomorrah Gen. 13:9–11; 18:20–19:38	The Song of Moses Deuteronomy 32	The Vision of Isaiah Isaiah 1
1.		"*Give ear*, O heavens, and I will speak; and *hear*, O *earth*, the words of my mouth" (haʾăzînû haššāmayîm . . . wĕtišmaʿ hāʾāreṣ) 32:1	"*Hear*, O heavens, and *give ear*, O *earth*" (šimĕʿû šā-mayim wĕhaʾăzînî ʾereṣ) 1:2 "*Hear* the word of the Lord, rulers of *Sodom*; *give ear* to the Torah of our God, you people of *Gomorrah*" (šimĕʿû . . . sĕdōm haʾăzînû . . . ʿămōrâ) 1:10
2.	"Because the cry of *Sodom* and *Gomorrah* is great . . . their sin is very grievous" (zaʿăqat sĕdōm waʿămōrâ) 18:20	"For their vine is of the vine of *Sodom*, and of the fields of *Gomorrah*" 32:32	"If the Lord of hosts had not left us a very small remnant, we should have been like *Sodom*, we should have resembled *Gomorrah*" 1:9

TABLE 1 (*Continued*)

The Flood Genesis 6–10	The Overthrow of Sodom and Gomorrah Gen. 13:9–11; 18:20–19:38	The Song of Moses Deuteronomy 32	The Vision of Isaiah Isaiah 1
3. "for all flesh had *corrupted*" (hišḥît) 6:12 "I will *destroy them*" (mašḥîtām) 6:13 "to *destroy* all flesh" (lĕšaḥēt) 6:17	"the Lord is about to *destroy* the city" (mašḥit) 19:14 "when God *destroyed* the cities" (bĕšaḥēt) 19:29	"Not his *corruption*, but the blemish of his *sons*" (šiḥēt . . . bānāyw) 32:5	"*sons that deal corruptly*" (bānîm mašḥîtîm) 1:4
4.	"Then the Lord rained upon *Sodom* and upon *Gomorrah* brimstone and *fire* . . ." (himṭîr . . . goprît wāʾēš) 19:24	"for a *fire* is kindled by my anger" (ʾēš) 32:22	"your cities are burned with *fire*" (śĕrūpôt ʾēš) 1:7 (and compare Deut. 29:22)
5.	"and he *overthrew* those cities" (wayahăpōk) 19:25 "that I will not *overthrow* this city" (lĕbiltî hopkî) 19:21	"for they are a *perverse generation*" (dôr tahpūkôt) 32:20	"it is desolate, *as though overthrown by aliens*" (kĕmahpēkat zārîm) 1:7

70

6.	"And God remembered Noah" (wayyizkōr) 8:1 "and [he] sent forth the raven" "Then he sent forth the dove from him" (wayešallaḥ) 8:7, 8	"God remembered Abraham and sent Lot out of the midst of the overthrow" (wayyizkōr . . . wayešallaḥ . . .) 19:29	
7.	"he drank of the wine, and was drunk" (yayin) 9:21	"let us make our father drink wine" (yayin) 19:32	"their wine is the fierceness of crocodiles" (yênām) 32:33
8.	"From these were the isles of the nations separated out . . . the boundary of the Canaanite" (niprĕdû . . . haggôyim . . . gĕbûl) 10:5, 19	"separate thyself, I pray thee from me . . . and they separated themselves one from the other" (hippāred nāʾ mēʿālāy . . . wayyippāredû) 13:9, 11	"when he separated the sons of Adam, he set the bounds of the peoples" (behaprîdô . . . gĕbulōt ʿammîm) 32:8
9.		"a sword shall bereave" (tĕšakkel-hereb) 32:25 "my sword shall devour flesh" (wĕharbî tōʾkal bāśār) 32:42	"You shall be devoured by the sword for the mouth of the Lord has spoken it" (hereb tĕʾukkĕlû kî pî YHWH dibbēr) 1:20

to move chronologically through the early chapters of Genesis. In the light of this, special significance attaches to the words "Remember the days of old, / consider the years of many generations" (Deut. 32:7). These "days of old" evidently point back to the primeval record of the creation of heaven and earth, to the story of the Flood and what follows. And immediately in verse 8, we move to another item in the same record of antiquity:

> When the most High divided to the *nations* their inheritance,
> when he *separated* the sons of Adam,
> he set the *bounds* of the peoples . . .

This takes us back to the immediate aftermath of the Flood story in Gen. 10:5, 19, where we learn that the islands of the nations *(gôyim)* separated out *(niprĕdû)* after the Flood "everyone after his tongue, after their families," and thereby the boundary *(gĕbûl)* of the Canaanites was established. The three key terms from this record reappear in this verse from the Song of Moses.

From verse 22 that song is now dominated by the memory of the next great disaster in the Genesis record, namely the overthrow of Sodom and Gomorrah, of which we have spoken earlier. The first signal for the entry of the record of Sodom and Gomorrah into our poem is in verse 20:

> And he said, I will hide my face from them,
> I will see what their end shall be,
> for they are *a perverse generation,*
> children in whom is no faith.

The term "perverse" *(tahpūkôt)* is from the stem *hpk,* usually rendered "overthrow," a central term for defining the ruin that overtook the cities of the Plain (Gen. 19:21, 25, 29). The "perverse generation" is already being likened by association to the inhabitants of Sodom and Gomorrah. We might render *tahpūkôt* more correctly as turbulent, riotous, or unruly. They are inclined in their unfaithfulness to overthrow all rule and order, and the implication is that God could likewise overthrow *(hpk)* the order of their world. To confirm this, images of fire and overthrow, hunger and waste, in which the vegetation would be consumed and the very foundations of the mountains would be ignited, now come to the fore—

> For a fire is kindled in my anger,
> and shall burn to the depths of Sheol,
> and shall consume the earth with its produce,
> and set on fire the foundations of the mountains.
> (32:22)

Finally the dreaded names of Sodom and Gomorrah are uttered and the memory is made explicit:

> For their vine is of the vine of Sodom,
> and of the fields of Gomorrah;
> their grapes are grapes of gall,
> their clusters are bitter;
> their wine is the fierceness of crocodiles,
> and the cruel venom of asps.
>
> (32:32–33)

We are now at the center of a crisscross pattern of verbal echoes and allusions. *Ha'ăzînû* takes us back to Genesis 19 and related accounts of the overthrow of the cities of the Plain, and forward to other prophetic passages such as Isaiah's great opening oracle. That poem, as already noted, is linked by its opening apostrophe to *Ha'ăzînû;* we may now add that it is also linked to it by its powerful evocation of the memory of the great overthrow of Sodom and Gomorrah. Isaiah 1 early on moves to its fierce climax in the vision of a land laid waste:

> Your country is desolate,
> your cities are burnt with fire *[śĕrūpot 'ēš]*:
> as for your land, strangers devour it in your presence,
> and it is desolate as though overthrown by strangers *[kĕmahpēkat zārîm]*.
> And the daughter of Zion is left
> like a shelter in a vineyard,
> like a lodge in a garden of cucumbers,
> like a besieged city.
> If the Lord of hosts
> had not left us a very small remnant,
> we should have been like Sodom;
> we should have resembled Gomorrah.
> Hear the word of the Lord
> you rulers of Sodom!
> give ear to the Torah of our God
> you people of Gomorrah!
>
> (Isa. 1:7–10)

The words "as though overthrown by strangers" *(kĕmahpēkat zārîm)* in verse 7 are often thought of as due to a faulty text that should read: "like the overthrow of Sodom" *(kĕmahpēkat sĕdōm)*. This would make the Sodom reference explicit already in verse 7. But there is no need for such emendation. It is more than likely that the poet is here trying to resist the ugly word "Sodom," which is practically required by the contiguous term "overthrow" *(mahpēkâ)*. Instead he clutches at the euphemism "strangers" *(zārîm)*, picked up rather awkwardly from the previous phrase. But it doesn't work for more than a moment. In verse 9, Sodom and Gomorrah

invade the poem, asserting themselves as an inescapable memory. And
then comes the crowning, bitter taunt:

> *Hear* the word of the Lord,
> you rulers of Sodom!
> *give ear* to the Torah of our God,
> you people of Gomorrah!

Here the grave opening formula of *Ha'ăzînû* echoes again in the verbal
couple "Hear . . . give ear" *(šimĕʿû . . . haʾăzînû)*. But it is not heaven and
earth that are now called upon to hear and witness; instead, the witness is
drawn from the ancient and terrifying record of disaster, a disaster so
closely bound up with the sin of the inhabitants of those cities that the
names Sodom and Gomorrah are simultaneously and indistinguishably
the sign for archetypal iniquity and for archetypal disaster. The language of the record *(hpk . . . šḥt)* firmly brings the two together—viz., the
aspects of moral enormity and of utter ruin. That is the special significance of this witness. Such memories leveled at the people have little in
common with the melancholy but pleasurable sadness of the pastoral.
The fascination is as great—the auditors we may suppose are held by the
power of Isaiah's fierce eloquence—but in the end such memory shocks,
violently disturbs, disrupts. What Isaiah seeks to bring about is, literally,
an overthrow. If the term "overthrow" is central here, it is because the
poem is designed to bring about an upheaval in the mind as powerful as
the upheaval it records. Here the word of the Lord, the *dĕbar YHWH* that
they are to hear, is nothing like showers on the herbs. It is more like the
brimstone that rained on Sodom. But the grim irony involved in using
the same *šimĕʿû . . . haʾăzînû* formula would not have escaped Isaiah's
auditors.

IV

It is worth observing that the intertextual weave of which we are speaking not only serves to link Deuteronomy 32 and Isaiah 1 with the Genesis
record but also seems to connect the Genesis stories with one another.
There is in fact a sustained parallelism between the story of the Flood
(Genesis 6–9) and that of the overthrow of Sodom and Gomorrah (Genesis 19) (see Table 1). The same stem *šḥt*, already mentioned, meaning
"to be corrupted" and, in the intensive form, "to ruin utterly," dominates
both narratives. Just as God determined to ruin *(lĕšaḥēt)* the whole world
at the time of the Flood because the people were corrupt *(hišḥît)*, so he
determined to destroy *(bĕšaḥēt)* the cities of the Plain. But the two stories

are also bound together by the pointed references to Elohim "remembering." He remembers Noah and all the creatures that were with him in the ark (Gen. 8:1), and, in Gen. 19:29, he remembers Abraham and as a consequence reminds himself to save his nephew, Lot, from the overthrow of the doomed cities: "So it came to pass, when God destroyed *[běšaḥēt]* the cities of the valley, that God remembered *[wayyizkōr]* Abraham, and sent Lot out of the midst of the overthrow *[hahăpēkâ]*, when he overthrew *[bahăpōk]* the cities in which Lot dwelt." There is also a link between the sending out *(wayěšallaḥ)* of the raven and the dove from the confines of the ark to freedom and the sending out *(wayěšallaḥ)* of Lot from doomed cities. Finally, there is a curious parallel in the situation of the two survivors after their rescue: both Noah and Lot get drunk and do so with scandalous consequences. The one episode is meant to give us an insight into the background of Canaan and the Canaanites; the other accounts for the births of Ammon and Moab.

It is as though we were being offered two alternative records of primordial disaster, both of which have a similar moral tendency and meaning, as some later writers sensed.[21] Of the two, it would seem that the Flood is the more universal tale of disaster, one conceived as engulfing mankind as a whole. It is not the individual aberrations of a group but that of "all flesh" which is here the issue; and the punishment, on a universal scale, is commensurate with the scope of the sin that gives rise to it.

Oddly, however, when the two chapters of lament and warning that we are discussing, viz., the Song of Moses and the Vision of Isaiah, are placed alongside these two stories from Genesis and the parallels are noted, it will be seen that the story of the overthrow of the doomed cities is incomparably the more important of the two. While the story of the Flood was evidently known and remembered by both authors, the story of the destruction of Sodom and Gomorrah had clearly made the greater impact. In both chapters explicit mention is made of Sodom and Gomorrah in close association with key terms drawn from that record, in particular the stem *hpk*, signifying overthrow or riot, as well as the stem *šḥt*, signifying corruption and ruin. In both chapters of warning and vision, images of fire and desolation are prominent; the cities burnt with fire of Isa. 1:7 immediately suggesting overthrow *(mahpēkâ)*, and then we have the actual naming of Sodom and Gomorrah in both texts (see Table 1). Indeed the memory of Sodom and Gomorrah turns out to be a more fundamental memory than that of the Flood. In both stories God remembers; but men remember the one story more vividly than the other. The author of Isaiah 1 may also have been remembering another text about Sodom and Gomorrah, viz., Deut. 29:23, which also cites it as a warning to a sinful generation. All the key terms relating to the overthrow had there been concentrated in a single verse: "the whole land is brimstone, and salt, and burning *[śĕrēpâ kol-'arṣâ]*, that is not sown, nor bears, nor does any grass grow on it, like the overthrow *[kĕmahpēkat]* of Sodom and Gomorrah, Admah and Zeboim, which the Lord overthrew *[hāpak]* in his anger, and in his wrath." Nor is the emphasis to be found only in these places. If we take the Hebrew Scriptures as a whole (as distinct from the New Testament) we shall see that explicit references to Noah's Flood are rare—there is virtually only Isa. 54:9, Ps. 29:10, and a doubtful reference in Job 12:15—while allusions to the overthrow of Sodom and Gomorrah abound in the prophets Isaiah, Ezekiel, and Jeremiah, and they occur also in Zephaniah (2:9) and in Lamentations (4:6).[22] Why should this be and why, on the other hand, should the Western imagination find itself more attracted by stories of the Flood? Stories of Noah's Flood and of the rainbow that guarantees that it has ended had a deep fascination for the authors of the medieval miracle plays; it is a motif of some importance in Shakespeare's *As You Like It* and in the poetry of Wordsworth; it still makes its appeal to the modern imagination of André Obey and D. H. Lawrence and it helped Archibald MacLeish to find a way of ending his Job play on a suitable note of salvation.

We are here of course back again with our central distinction, i.e., pastoral versus antipastoral. The death by water of the generation of Noah, we may say, fits the pastoral mode. Edward King died by water and slept by the fable of Bellerus old. The thought of a drowned man ("those are pearls that were his eyes") from Shakespeare's *The Tempest* echoes in Eliot's *The Waste Land*. Abraham Lincoln, who wasn't drowned, becomes associated for the purpose of Whitman's poem with a lost ocean voyager—the poet himself becomes identified with such a figure: "Lost in the loving floating ocean of thee / Laved in the flood of thy bliss O death." Imagery of flood and ocean appears to be essential to the Western imagination, perhaps because the ocean lulls us to death in its maternal embrace.[23] Such a death wish and such a maternal embrace seem to be less important to the Hebrew imagination. As between the memory of Noah's Flood and that of the overthrow of Sodom and Gomorrah, it is the latter that becomes normative for the Hebrew imagination. There is perhaps another reason for this preference. Both are stories of survivors and survival is a major theme throughout the Hebrew scriptures. In the greatest survival story of all, Isaac escapes the knife, the wood, and the fire, but only just. The postbiblical imagination of the rabbis brooded over that near-death until it seemed to become a death indeed. Lot's survival is of that kind; it is a grudging and bitter survival; no rainbow spans the sky after that disaster promising that ruin of that kind will never be visited again on the human race. Any promise that it contains is darkly hidden. The ashen taste remains with us, reminding us of ever-present possibilities of recurrence:

> If the Lord of hosts
> had not left us a very small remnant,
> we should have been like Sodom,
> we should have resembled Gomorrah.
> (Isa. 1:9)

The first phrase, "if the Lord of hosts had not left us a very small remnant," conveys the sense of a doom that is all but total, and that leaves with us a sense of our continuing vulnerability to such ruin. It overthrows all structures of charm and order and becomes in that sense the prototype for all future disasters that share its terminal quality. The author of Lamentations, writing probably in the immediate aftermath of the fall of Jerusalem in the sixth century, can find no more appropriate analogy for the state of his country:

> For the doom of the daughter of
> my people is greater
> than the sin of Sodom,
> that was overthrown in a moment,
> no hands being laid upon her.
> (Lam. 4:6)

The continuation of that passage reads like a veritable confrontation between pastoral and antipastoral. The heroes and the heroines of the pastoral are introduced in verse 7—their skin whiter than milk, their bodies ruddy like rubies, the beauty of their form like sapphires. But in the next verse they have become blackened and shriveled out of recognition in the dark destruction of this wasteland:

> Now their visage is blacker than coal,
> they are not known in the streets;
> their skin is shrivelled upon their bones;
> it is become dry like wood.
> (4:8)

What makes such poetry endurable? More than endurable. What makes these terrible phrases cling to us when more charming elegies fade from remembrance? We are nearer somehow, at the end of this terrible twentieth century of ours, to the blackened faces of the victims of the destruction of Jerusalem in the sixth century than we are to the dead of the Flood, or to Arthur Hallam gone to his reward and recalled ever more faintly as Christmas comes round each year. Perhaps it is that the language that exposes wounds in this way proves stronger than the language that covers up wounds, wrapping up the large grief in words like weeds. There is perhaps also another reason for the hold this poetry exercises on us. The poet of Lamentations indicates the unique horror as well as the fascination of the Sodom model in the phrase quoted above, "that was overthrown in a moment" *(hahăpûkâ kĕmô-rāgaʿ)*. We have once again the inevitable stem *hpk*, signifying a violent overthrow, but the added phrase "in a moment" *(kĕmô-rāgaʿ)* provides a special insight. It suggests a version of history as proceeding by sudden catastrophe rather than by gradual change or development. Not the seasons of the year ever returning, but the unanticipated and catastrophic about-face of circumstances marks the Sodom model. The story of Noah's Flood, we remember, ended with the assurance that the cycle of nature would continue; the seasons would make their annual return giving continuity and stability to our existence. "While the earth remains, seedtime and harvest, and cold and heat, and summer and winter, and day and night, shall not cease" (Gen. 8:22). But this does not exhaust the Hebraic sense of time and history. As against the rhythm of the natural world, we have a different rhythm, one that carries with it the ever-present potentiality of sudden divine interventions. In a moment the world is transformed. And this dictates a different poetic from the pastoral, committed as it is to the rhythms of nature. The memory by which the Song of Moses kept its power was one of sudden overthrow, turning gladness into mourning. But sudden overthrow can work both ways. The Song of Moses itself ends with a good miracle—a shout of praise goes up from the nations as God takes vengeance on his enemies, making his arrows drunk with blood and thus the evil done in the Land is made good (Deut. 32:41–43). That is the real meaning of *hpk*: it signifies not only overthrow but the overthrow of overthrow. Sodom, the garden of the Lord (as it was termed in Genesis 13), was suddenly turned into a wasteland. The good miracle is when, with almost equal suddenness, desolation is turned into a paradise. Jeremiah 31 celebrates such a turnabout: the wasteland is transformed into a garden world as the imagery of the pastoral returns:

> Therefore they shall come and sing in the height of Zion,
> and they shall be delighted at the bounty of the Lord,
> at the wheat, and at the wine, and at the oil,
> and at the young of the flock, and of the herd:
> and their soul shall be like a watered garden;
> and they shall not languish in sorrow any more.
> Then shall the virgin rejoice in the dance,
> and young men and old together:
> for I will turn their mourning into joy.
>
> (Jer. 31:12–13)

Here in the last phrase we have the stem *hpk* once again, but now signifying the turnabout from mourning to gladness, for *hpk* can itself be turned about—that is its virtue. Paradoxically, the prophet discovers the key of promise in the very language of the disaster of Sodom. To remember that overthrow is to remember that it can be itself overthrown.

We have then a poetics of violence as against the placidities of natural, biological process. But we would be wrong to see the poet of *Ha'ăzînû* or of the other Hebrew texts we have been considering as seeking a region of historical cataclysm removed from the world of nature. The opening words of *Ha'ăzînû*, "Give ear, O heavens . . . and hear, O earth," remain valid. Nature is a prime witness, but it has become a witness to revolutionary change. This is not the universe of eternal forms that the Greeks knew, but a created universe, created suddenly by a word of power, and as such it is a place of extraordinary surprises. Not the gradual change but the sudden cataclysm is its mark. When the psalmist wants to convey what the restoration of Zion would be like, he uses a natural image: it would be like the filling-up of the dried-out wadis in the Negeb (Ps. 126:4)—as the first downpour of autumn rains bursts over the mountains, they suddenly become rushing torrents. Blessing can be as violent and sudden as disaster—in fact it can be disastrous too for those who are not prepared for it. Such a notion of catastrophe suggests a duality at the very heart of salvation history. The desert is a place of burning but also of the burning bush. That burning bush too is a natural phenomenon, like the sudden torrents in the Negeb; but it challenges us differently from the way that we are challenged by Arcadia or the forests of Arden. To attend to such witnesses is to be denied the comforts of the pastoral, but there are compensations for that as we wait, booted, our loins girded and staff in hand for the next unanticipated stage of the journey.

·6·

SONG OF SOLOMON
THE ALLEGORICAL IMPERATIVE

A good way of rebutting nearly everything that has been said in the previous chapter would be to take a cursory look at the Song of Solomon. There it would seem we have not an antipastoral but rather an unclouded idyll celebrating the love of a shepherd and shepherdess amid the hills of Galilee and Lebanon. Milk and spices are in abundance, as the lovers pasture their goats and ewes beside springs of water: "I have eaten my honeycomb with my honey; / I have drunk my wine with my milk" (5:1), declares the happy lover in a paean of praise to his beloved. Her response is no less enraptured and no less in harmony with the rural world she inhabits: "I am my beloved's, and my beloved is mine; / He feeds his flock among the lilies" (6:3).

It is not surprising that a strong group of critics have found here a pastoral impulse comparable with what was to emerge later in Greek poetry.[1] The Shulammite maiden is of course not unambiguously of the countryside; she is also associated with artifacts that have their place in the court or city—a goblet, an ivory tower, a jeweled necklace—for she is a *bat-nādîb,* "a noble lady," and as such would properly be adorned with jewels and perfumed with costly spices. But this again is sufficiently like the pastoral poetry of Virgil, which projects the aristocratic culture into the country.[2] There are also more particular analogues. The lover's comparison of the Shulammite to "a mare of the chariots of Pharaoh" (1:9) anticipates, or was anticipated by (depending on the date one assigns to the Song), Theocritus's eighteenth idyll, where Helen, the bride of Menelaus, is praised in similar terms:

> As of a field or garden ornament,
> The lofty cypress shoots up eminent;
> As of the chariot the Thessalian steed,
> So rosy Helen of the Spartan breed
> Is ornament and grace.[3]

Walter Woodburn Hyde offers it as his view that the author of the Song had read and been influenced by Theocritus's twenty-seventh idyll, where Daphnis and Chloe, after a certain amount of love banter and discussion of marriage settlements, proceed at once to nuptialities.[4] The most intriguing parallel, however, is to be found in the fifth idyll of Theocritus. There, in the spiteful exchange between the two shepherds Comatas and Lacon, Comatas remarks that he "hates the bush-tailed foxes which are ever going and gathering the grapes of Micon at evening." There is a similar remark in the first idyll about the ravages caused by foxes in vineyards. All this reminds us of the beloved's complaint in the Song:

> Take us the foxes,
> the little foxes,
> that spoil the vineyards,
> for our vineyards are in blossom.
> (2:15)

In both cases the foxes seem to be an image for the jealousy from without that threatens the smooth course of love. Robert Graves concludes from such analogues that the Canticles were written "under the strong influence of Greek pastoral poetry."[5]

It is tempting to agree. But leaving aside the question of dating, we must first stand back from the Song of Solomon and consider how little its overall effect resembles that of the pastoral either in its Greek or Roman form. The Hebrew poet has really little or nothing of the artificiality, the posing, the playfulness of Theocritus. We are not being offered the idle diversion of a summer's day as the shepherd-poet alternately pipes to his sheep and snatches a kiss from the nearest pretty girl (or boy). We do not associate the *dôd* of the Song with the shepherds of pastorals who amuse themselves and us on their pipes of straw or flutes to while away the long hours as "During the noontide of the summer heat, / They by a fountain sung their ditties sweet."[6] This is not the mood of *šîr haššîrîm*. Love for the Shulammite and the *dôd* is not a lighthearted game but a consuming fire:

> For love is strong as death,
> jealousy is cruel as Sheol:
> the coals thereof are coals of fire,
> which has a most vehement flame.
> (8:6)

The little foxes of chapter 2 may suggest the little world of the pastoral with its minor annoyances, but by the time we reach the intensity of *'azzâ kammāwet 'ahăbâ*, "for love is strong as death," we have left the charm of the pastoral far behind.

One other Middle Eastern poetic form that has been seen as offering

similarities to one of the poetic procedures of the Song is the Arabic *wasf*.
This consists of an elaborate and detailed praise of the bride's (and less
frequently, the bridegroom's) beauty from head to toe; it was still heard,
it seems, until recently in village weddings in Syria.[7] This subgenre,
wherein the lady's beauties are systematically catalogued, persists in *The
Thousand and One Nights*;[8] it was taken up in the Renaissance in the
poetry of Petrarch and Spenser—in the case of Spenser, the mode was
evidently inspired by its use in the Song of Solomon.[9] The Song provides
us in fact with as many as five examples of such catalogues (4:1–7; 4:11–
15; 5:10–16; 6:4–9; 7:2–8). The most elaborate of them is the first:

> Behold, thou art fair, my love,
> behold, thou art fair;
> Thou hast doves' eyes
> behind thy veil:
> thy hair is like a flock of goats,
> that stream down from mount Gilead.
> Thy teeth are like a flock of shorn ewes,
> which came up from the washing;
> all of which bear twins,
> and not one of them miscarries.
> Thy lips are like a thread of scarlet,
> and thy mouth is comely:
> thy cheek is like a piece of a pomegranate
> behind thy veil.
> Thy neck is like the tower of David,
> built with turrets,
> on which there hang a thousand bucklers,
> all shields of mighty men.
> Thy two breasts are like two fawns,
> twins of a gazelle,
> which feed among the lilies.
> Before the day cools,
> and the shadows flee,
> I will get me to the mountain of myrrh
> and the hill of frankincense.
> Thou art all fair, my love;
> there is no blemish in thee.
>
>   (4:1–7)

Here we have the elaborateness and formality of a well-established
literary convention. The obsessive return to the same strategy shows us
the poet again and again seeking to catch the meaning of his love by this
exhaustive summary of the physical and sensuous items that make up
the beauty of the loved one, choosing every time more extravagant images. It is rather like the Persian display of detail—the detail of the
banqueting hall for instance—in the Book of Esther. But just as we saw
in that case that the style contains its own antithesis, so it is with the *wasf*.

As the poet seeks repeatedly and with a feverish and mounting intensity to base the unique and transforming nature of his experience of love upon the sensuous catalogue, so he reveals at the same time how doomed to inadequacy such a catalogue is. Having achieved all the magnificent wealth and ostentation that the genre affords, he falls back at the end of the passage quoted on those simpler words *kullāk yāpâ ra'yātî,* "thou art all fair, my love," which, like the phrase *'ănî lĕdôdî wĕdôdî lî,* "I am my beloved's and my beloved is mine" (6:3), seem to dismiss the ceremonial of love as a feast of sense. Such phrases seem to say, in contradiction to the elaborateness of the *wasf,* that the beauty of the beloved is more than the sum of its parts. He speaks now in these simpler phrases of a whole person *(kullāk yāpâ)*—"thou art all fair"—and of a relationship that cannot be localized or itemized. The phrase "I am my beloved's and my beloved is mine" expresses from this point of view the meaning of the whole song as a witness to a transforming encounter between two persons who know one another with a knowledge that the account of nose, eyes, and breasts taken separately can never achieve. "I am my beloved's and his desire is for me" (7:10) is in one sense a summary of the elaborate account of the Shulammite's beauty that has gone before (7:2–8), but in another sense it is a negation of that account as inadequate to convey the reality of what has been revealed.

The clearest example of this retreat into primal simplicity as the language of extravagant praise exhausts itself, is in chapter 6. After a particularly bold and striking opening, the middle verses continue with the praise of hair, teeth, and cheeks in exactly the same terms as in the previously quoted passage from chapter 4. The passage ends with a pointed gesture of renunciation as the catalogue is, so to speak, deconstructed:

> Thou art beautiful, O my love, as Tirzah,
> comely as Jerusalem, terrible as an army with banners.
> Turn away thy eyes from me,
> for they have overcome me:
> thy hair is like a flock of goats,
> streaming down from Gilead.
> Thy teeth are like a flock of sheep,
> which go up from the washing,
> all of which bear twins,
> and not one of them miscarries.
> As a piece of pomegranate is thy cheek
> within thy veil.
> There are sixty queens and eighty concubines,
> and maidens without number.
> My dove, my unadorned, is but one;
> she is the only one of her mother,
> the choice one of her that bore her.

$$(6:4–9)$$

We may note the utter simplicity of the repeated phrase in verse 9, *'aḥat hî' . . . 'aḥat hî' lĕ'immâ;* it could be rendered *"the one is she,* my dove my unadorned, *the one is she* for her mother." In contrast to the statistical account of the ladies of the court ("sixty queens and eighty concubines") and the tale of the "maidens without number"—all of them we may suppose capable of being listed according to the charms revealed when appropriate attention is given to cheeks, hair, teeth, etc.—we have here in this phrase *'aḥat hî' lĕ'immă* the exhaustion of all summaries. She is, as we would say, the one and only. We have gone beyond the beauty principle to an affirmation of the absolute uniqueness of the other. The words *'aḥat hî'* express or seek to express—for ultimately uniqueness is inexpressible—the irreducible quality of that uniqueness. The only word that helps to define or explicate it is the word *tammātî,* rendered here "my unadorned." But in fact the Hebrew term is not a negative of anything else but denotes such unqualified positives as "wholeness," "simplicity," "perfection." The effect is to reduce the bride's personality to its primal essence, where all charms have become vain and all that is left is the perfection and wholeness of a unique individual person as that uniqueness is discovered in the direct, dialogic relationship of the lovers to one another. The *wasf,* we may say, gives us a love language that is essentially transferable.[10] All that we need to do is to change the name of the addressee and the catalogue will do just as well for any one of the sixty queens and eighty concubines; *'aḥat hî'* gives us something else—a kind of transcendent oneness. It is not surprising that the rabbis were driven to relate the love of the *dôd* and the maiden to that of God and Israel. In reference to that mystery too we are ultimately left with the simple affirmation of unity. As seen by Israel, God is simply One as in Deut. 6:4 (*YHWH 'eḥād*), and, as seen by God, Israel too is "a singular nation" as in 2 Sam. 7:23 (*gôy 'eḥād bā'āreṣ*).

The repeated *'aḥat hî'* of 6:9 therefore not only constitutes a precise and explicit antithesis to the "sixty queens and eighty concubines and the maidens without number" of verse 8; it represents the reversal and denial of the poetic strategy of the preceding catalogue and of all the other catalogues in the poem, for that which can be separated into its parts and defined by neat and appropriate images drawn from topography, from flora and fauna, is not "whole" or "one." Wholeness or oneness points us eventually to a mode of love that has nothing left in it of things that can be perceived, counted, or measured. It is this mystery which the poem ultimately meditates:

> Many waters cannot quench love,
> nor can the floods drown it:
> if a man would give all the substance of his house for love,
> it would be utterly scorned.
>
> (8:7)

And we might add that if a poet offered for love all the wealth of the poetic catalogue as the tribute to a supreme and triumphant beauty, that too would be scorned. It is this dialectic which the poem enacts.

II

Another important and persistent feature that distinguishes this poem from the other models of love poetry we have considered is its dramatic tension. Love is something to be struggled and striven for more than it is something to be celebrated. The terror of loss and emptiness, the longing for fulfillment are more central to the poem than fulfillment itself or descriptions of beauty. There is an agony of yearning or, to give it the more exact metaphor provided by the Song itself, an unremitting *search* as the lover, or more specifically, the *beloved,* i.e., the Shulammite, seeks him whom her soul loves, seeks him and does not find him:

> By night on my bed,
> I sought him whom my soul loves,
> I sought him but I found him not . . .
> (3:1)

The incremental repetition in these last two lines is typical of the Song.[11] Another example would be, "A garden enclosed is my sister, my bride; / a spring shut up, a fountain sealed"(4:12). A phrase is repeated like the refrain in a pastoral but, unlike the pastoral, the idea is carried a stage further the second time around. This movement forward in the passage cited above—"I sought him whom my soul loves, / I sought him but I found him not"—suggests the unremittingness of the search, a longing ever increasing, an intensity of devotion seeking but never quite finding its embodiment in language. Greek and Roman pastoral knows desire (usually of the swain), but the yearning of the loved one whose lover is absent and whose soul is empty of content is something different. A parallel has been noted in the Tamil poetry of South India of the Solomonic period, where the lovesick bride utters her longing for her absent lover in passionate terms.[12] And there are suggestions of similar states of mind in ancient Egyptian love poetry.[13] But when all the parallels have been noted, the Song really stands out as unique. It touches heights and depths that are unknown in love poetry of the ancient Middle East, indeed in love poetry of any time. Shelley comes near it in some of his shorter lyrics, as for instance, in his famous "Indian Serenade."

> I arise from dreams of thee
> In the first sweet sleep of night,
> When the winds are breathing low,

> And the stars are shining bright:
> I arise from dreams of thee,
> And a spirit in my feet
> Hath led me—who knows how?
> To thy chamber window, Sweet!

This has something of the passion and the longing we are seeking to define; it is also marked by incremental repetition. The second use of the phrase "I arise from dreams of thee" literally carries the action forward—the lover is seen first to arise from his slumbers and, when the phrase occurs a second time, it leads him, "who knows how," to the chamber window of the beloved. But the poem from which this stanza is taken is essentially a short lyric; it gives us an intense moment of devotion and complaint, it catches yearning in motion, fixes it in a gesture. The Song of Solomon, by contrast, is a long poem of sustained lyric force, unified and powered by this very quality of yearning. The poem circles around certain fixed centers of description (such as we saw in relation to the model of the *wasf*) and certain repeated states of feeling (such as we saw in the pastoral), but it does not rest content with them; there is also a restless onward search, a longing not merely of the lover denied the presence of the loved one but of the poem itself seeking its final meaning, its epiphany. There is a dynamic movement of longing that becomes a structural principle in the poem as it moves forward incrementally from one stage of yearning to the next.

The phrase "I sought him but I found him not" in 3:1, quoted above, is repeated again in the next verse as the maiden now calls upon the watchmen to assist her in her search:

> I will rise now, and go about the city,
> in the streets, and in the broad ways
> I *will seek* him whom my soul loves:
> *I sought him but I found him not.*
> The watchmen that go about the city found me: to whom I said,
> Have you seen him whom my soul loves?
>
> (3:2–3)

In a parallel episode later in chapter 5, the same phrase, "I sought him but I found him not," is repeated and the same watchmen appear, but there is a further incremental movement forward as they beat her and wound her:

> *I sought him but I found him not:*
> *I called him, but he gave me no answer.*
> The watchmen who went about the city found me,
> they struck me, they wounded me,

they took away my mantle,
those keepers of the walls.
I charge you, O daughters of Jerusalem,
if you find my beloved,
that you tell him,
that I am sick with love.

(5:6–8)

The phrase signifies longing, and that longing expresses itself in an ever-moving horizon of deferred gratification, as the object of the search constantly eludes the speaker. "I sought him but I found him not" thus comes to mean: I seek the meaning implied in this seeking, I seek it by constantly moving forward, never finding a point of rest, but I still seek in spite of pain and rebuffs. The term *biqqaštîhû*, "I sought (or seek) him" takes on an almost transcendental character, becoming a focus for the total meaning of the poem, and it comes as no surprise to learn that the same verb, indeed virtually the same phrase, occurs in Hosea, where it signifies Israel's vain pursuit of false lovers:

And she shall follow after her lovers,
but she shall not catch them;
and she shall seek them,
but shall not find them:
then she shall say, I will go
and return to my first husband;
for it was better with me then than now.
(Hos. 2:7)

In the deep structure of the sentences we have the same tension and the same search: only the referent is different, as Hosea explicitly directs us to the identity of the *true* lover and husband as the God of Israel, whom Israel should have sought had she known the true meaning of her search. In Deut. 4:29 the same combination of words occurs in a more frankly didactic context. "And if from there [i.e., from the place of exile] thou shalt seek the Lord thy God, thou shalt find him, if thou seek him with all thy heart and with all thy soul."

It would be hardly an exaggeration to say that this seeking and finding (or not finding) are a major theme of the Hebrew scriptures. There may be a shifting of predicates but the purposive gesture itself, the ever-defeated longing and search are the deep core of Israel's story, its phenomenological essence. The greatness of the Song of Solomon is that it expresses this phenomenological essence in its intensest form, almost, one might say, as pure lyric, without a didactic spelling out of historical referents or contexts. It is pure signification, almost one might say, pure poetry. Perhaps that is why it is called the "song of songs." Rabbi Akiba gave it another title based on the same linguistic model: the rest of the writings were, he said, holy, but *šîr haššîrîm* was the "holy of holies."[14]

We are not of course talking about allegory in the commonly accepted sense; we are talking about a poetic language that, when it reaches a certain pitch of intensity, becomes foregrounded as pure image, pure gesture, pure sign. "I sought him but I found him not" is a pure sign of that kind. It asks us not to rest with one particular referent—for instance, the *dôd* or lover in a pastoral romance, but rather to *seek* and *find* its meaning in other texts and contexts. Through such pure signification, it becomes a key to the understanding of Hosea and Deuteronomy just as those texts become a key to the understanding of the Song. It is in that sense the "Song of Songs."

III

We could approach the same conclusion by another route. The two scenes in which the repeated phrase "I sought him but I found him not" occurs are dream episodes. They are in fact parts of a recurring dream of which we have three instances in the Song; namely, 2:9–14, 3:1–5, and 5:2–8. In the first instance, the *dôd* seems to be gazing in at the window as the Shulammite rests on her couch and he invites her to arise and join him; the second is a more troubled dream—the bridegroom is absent and the Shulammite rises in her slumber from her "bed at night" to seek him about the streets and squares, for the scene has changed from country to city; as we noted, she calls upon the watchmen to help her in the search until finally she finds "him whom [her] soul loves" and imagines herself bringing him home to her mother's house (3:4). The third dream (5:2–8), introduced by the phrase "I sleep, but my heart wakes," is the most disturbing of the three. The lover seems to be again, as in chapter 2, behind the wall or at the door of her room and now he calls upon her to admit him but, as so often happens in a dream, she cannot easily manage to stir and dress herself, so that by the time she reaches the "handles of the bolt" to admit him, he has turned and gone. In her pain, frustration, and longing she turns for help again to the watchmen. In chapter 3 these watchmen had been indifferent, not answering her appeal; now they have become hostile, beating and wounding her. The scenes are parallel, with linking phrases and episodes, but there is also, we may note, an intensification of the search until, in the third dream episode, she declares herself "sick with love." We do not need Freud to tell us that dreams have their own language and that its symbolism is multivalent, not necessarily confined to one realm of experience. The soiled feet, the handles of the lock, the fingers dripping with myrrh, the watchmen who go about the city—all have the importunacy of dream symbols—they draw maximum attention to themselves—but as symbols, not as events or details to be taken in their straightforward, representational sense.[15] There is, strictly speaking, no "literal meaning" of a dream, no *peshat*. You may see a horse in a dream—and it may mean many things, but of one thing you may be sure: it does not simply mean a horse! If we think of the language and imagery of the Song of Solomon as a whole in terms of dream symbolism as the text, I think, requires us to—then the search for the so-called literal meaning, a search that has so much exercised the commentators, becomes very questionable indeed.

Though there are only three identifiable dream sequences, these are very centrally located and the mood and imagery of these scenes merge with the rest of the poem. There is no clear division between the waking and dreaming portions of the poem, no announcement by the lady that she is now quite wide awake and that we are to take her account of events from now on in a different, more everyday sense. The whole poem is dominated by a heightened dreamy atmosphere. It is this in fact which bestows on the poem the remarkable unity of tone and style that the more perceptive critics have noted.[16] We do not have anything resembling an Aristotelian unity of action; in formal terms the poem seems to be a jumble of different lyrics and snatches of story. But this is precisely the incoherence of the dream and it is that quality which seizes and holds our attention throughout and which establishes continuity.

Many problems of understanding disappear once we recognize in the poem the free flow of images and the shifting kaleidoscope of a dream. We move unexpectedly from the rocky cliffs to the nut garden, from the realistic vineyard to the more fantastic and exotic garden of spices (6:2), from the Lebanon in the north to Engedi by the Dead Sea and to the great desert in the east; we have alternations of invitation and alarm, of intimacy and distance; there are the sudden disappearances of the lover, the anguished searches, the unexplained reappearances (6:12). The recognition that here we have to do with a dream syntax also explains the undetermined identity of the *dôd* himself; sometimes he is a king and sometimes he is a shepherd and sometimes he seems to be both together—so much so, that a group of critics have proposed to understand the poem as a drama involving three figures, the two lovers and the king who desires the Shulammite for his harem. We are to suppose that eventually the lovers win and the king accepts defeat.[17] But there are manifold difficulties about fitting all the parts of the poem to such a story line: they disappear when we accept the fact that there is no story line at all but rather the shifting iridescent movement of a dream where stories merge into one another and identities change and combine.

Unexpectedness is the mark of events in a dream and yet it is an unexpectedness that never seems to take us by surprise. If the horse mentioned above appeared in the middle of a railway journey, we would accept it as perfectly natural, just as it would be natural for us to find ourselves in the palace talking to the king or for the king to visit us at home. That is in fact what happens in the poem. The sudden materialization of the palanquin of Solomon with its sixty armed guards (3:7) is of that kind. The king is about to be married and so the figure of Solomon merges with that of the *dôd* and we cannot be quite sure who speaks the praises of the Shulammite in the sequel (4:1–7). Is it Solomon or is it the shepherd? Or has the shepherd become Solomon? Among the unexpected events that we accept quite naturally is the appearance of the "friends" at what seems to be a private assignation of the lovers and the invitation then extended to them to eat and drink deeply (5:1), or the appearance of the "little sister" as a main character at the end of the poem. There is nothing to lead us to anticipate her arrival and yet, as every reader knows, when she appears, she becomes significant, she assumes momentousness and power. Perhaps she is the Shulammite herself seen in some kind of early retrospect, merging with her and then disengaging from her as the Shulammite attains the majesty of full adulthood. The key to the imagery that accompanies the little sister eludes us—she is a wall or a door enclosed with boards of cedar (8:9). And yet the phrases, strange as they are, cling to us with a certain intensity, as does the earlier phrase relating to the Shulammite herself, who is, we are told, "terrible as an army with banners." This is the nature of dream symbolism.

What do such images portend? Do we simply ignore the question of meaning and treat them as a kind of free-flowing stream of consciousness? Certainly, the Song is a riot of images; it has a greater abundance and confusion of similes and metaphors than any other book of the Hebrew scriptures. But this does not mean that they have no structure or meaning, or, more correctly, that they do not challenge us to fathom their meaning.[18] The images in the poem peremptorily demand to be interpreted. They also seem to guide us along the path of interpretation.

The Song itself, let it be said, has not only an abundance of similes and metaphors; it also has an abundance of terms that draw attention to these imaginative functions. And these terms, used to announce the presence of similes and metaphors, are themselves foregrounded, as in the following:

> This thy stature is like a palm tree,
> and thy breasts are like clusters of grapes.
> I said, I will go up into the palm tree,
> I will take hold of its boughs. . . .
>
> (7:7–8)

The verb *dāmĕtâ*, rendered here as "is like," is really more emphatic than that and should be rendered "is comparable to" or "resembles," as though the text is saying to us: "read me as simile." A similar use of the stem *dmh* in the intensive *piʿēl* form occurs at 1:9—"I compare thee, O my love, / to a mare of the chariots of Pharaoh." Again the emphatic announcement has the effect of: "pay attention, this is a simile and it has to be understood as such." In the first quoted passage, we move from the announced simile ("This thy stature *is like* a palm tree") to the other kind of trope, viz., metaphor—"I said, I will go up into the palm tree, / I will take hold of its boughs." Here too the transition from simile to metaphor is announced by the deictic *ʾāmartî*, "I said" or "I am now saying." In effect, the lover is making an announcement; he is saying to us: "I take what seemed to be a 'mere' simile and I turn it around into metaphor. You are not merely to be compared with a palm; I will enact the very process of climbing the palm tree; I will turn that trope around and you will see how difficult it will be to keep the two sides of the comparison separate from one another."

Leo Krinetzki in his literary study of the Song of Solomon follows Kayser and others in making a distinction between simile and metaphor. "Das Vergleichswort distanziert, legt Bild und Sache auseinander, die Metapher sieht beides ineinander."[19] Simile distances tenor and vehicle, metaphor approximates them. But Krinetzki treats the two kinds of images in the poem as constants—we are confronted either with metaphors or with similes at any one point. What I would like to suggest is that there is a constant interchange between the two modes, a constant collapsing of that distance or, alternately, an expansion of the distance between the two parts of an image. Such a strategy occurs at the beginning of chapter 2:

> I am the tulip of the Sharon,
> the lily of the valleys.
> Like the lily among thorns,
> so is my love among the daughters.
> (2:1-2)

Here the maiden relates herself first by metaphor to a wild flower—she is as passive and untroubled as the lily, with nothing to do except grow and be herself. Beauty, charm, an organic relation to the world of nature are assumed by that metaphor—there is a close but passive relationship between tenor and vehicle, as close as can be between the human and the inanimate world. The reply of the *dôd*, which turns the metaphor emphatically into simile (through the connective *kĕ*), animates the image, makes it dynamic by the distancing of tenor and vehicle. The lily metaphor now becomes available as argument, almost as parable. "You speak of yourself as a wild flower," he seems to say. "Well, wild flowers are often isolated and surrounded by thorns; you stand out from your surroundings *like such a flower*." Through this distancing, the tulip, the lily, and in subsequent verses, the apple tree, become part of an "allegory of love," just as the eating of the fruit (v. 3) takes on a clear symbolic meaning, inviting us further along the path of interpretation.

This constant commerce between the two sides of the image in the course of which the distance between them is constantly changing also has the effect sometimes of confusing the two. It is not always clear whether A is being compared to B or B to A. The vehicle can take charge. E. M. Good has noted that in 4:12–15 the garden image takes over.[20] It becomes a poem about a garden rather than about a girl. The girl becomes the reflection of the beauty of the garden. When we reach verse 15, the focus is on the garden fountain, which suggests by association the flowing mountain streams. The vehicle still has the dominant role. This takeover by the image is particularly noticeable in the many topographical references in the poem. It has been well said that "nowhere else in the Bible has the Palestinian landscape been so presented to us as a world reborn, as a land so completely enwrapped in grace, as it has in this song."[21] The sights and sounds of the land are lovingly recorded as nowhere else in the Bible. You see the dark Bedouin tents, the fish pools of Heshbon, the tree-covered height of the Carmel; you hear the springs of water tumbling down from Lebanon and you glimpse the snow-capped peak of the Hermon. Above all there is Jerusalem with its streets and squares and, somewhere within, the curtained enclosure of King Solomon himself. The Shulammite is compared for her beauty to Jerusalem and Tirzah—"Thou art beautiful, O my love, as Tirzah, / comely as Jerusalem" (6:4). The effect of such a verse is as much to declare that Jerusalem is so beautiful that she is like a beloved woman as it is to say that the Shulammite is so lovely, she is like Jerusalem. We can read 7:5 as saying that the wooded slopes of the Carmel are like the head of a beautiful maiden. There is a kind of imaginative overspill, as the rapture of the lovers overflows into the sphere of geography, transforming the whole land into an object of love.

In the dynamic free-flow of images of which we are speaking, there is thus a certain ambiguity as to what the poem is about. It is a love poem, to be sure, but it is possible to read it as a love poem addressed to a beloved land. Now this very ambiguity is fundamentally biblical. In Isaiah 62 we hear of a land that shall no more be termed Desolate but shall be called instead Espoused; the poet concludes with the image of a passionate union between bride and bridegroom:

> For as a young man takes to himself a virgin,
> so shall thy sons take thee to themselves,

and as the bridegroom rejoices over the bride,
so shall thy God rejoice over thee.

(62:5)

This is deliberate, "planned" imagery, not the dreamy "stream-of-con-sciousness" of the Song, but it has similar components. What is more it introduces a further ambiguity that likewise helps us with our interpreta-tion of the Song. As well as speaking of the love of a land in terms of bride and bridegroom, it also speaks of the people of the land. If the first "thee" in the above-cited passage refers to a chosen land, then the second "thee" refers to a chosen people. The two are inextricably related by the system of parallelism in the preceding verse:

Thou shalt no more be termed Forsaken;
neither shall thy land any more be termed Desolate:
but thou shalt be called My Delight is in Her,
and thy land, Espoused.

(62:4)

It cannot be doubted that the Song of Solomon contains hints of this same parallelism. The bride is "comely *[nā'wâ]* as Jerusalem, terrible as an army with banners." The first phrase links her with the beauty of the land; the second, more startling, phrase introduces surely the dimension of peoplehood and sovereignty. In Hab. 1:7 the same adjective *'āyōm* (terrible) is used of the Chaldeans, an impetous nation marching in warlike array across the countryside. The *ra'yâ* of the Song is herself a symbol of a warlike people—a conclusion that should not surprise us in relation to a poem composed throughout in multivalent symbols. We are not talking of literal attributes; we are not saying that the *ra'yâ* is warlike, but she has become the symbol of a warlike people. Britannia may wear a most peaceful, amiable, even tender expression, but she rules the waves nevertheless. The Shulammite rules over a people terrible with banners. The royal or national overtone is strengthened by another phrase that has puzzled the commentators. 6:12 is rendered literally by RSV as "Be-fore I was aware, my fancy set me / in a chariot beside my prince." The words are obscure—the sentence is in fact a major crux—but the tal-mudic rabbis explain it by means of a helpful parable:

R. Hiyyah taught: To what may this be compared? To a king's daugh-ter who was gleaning in the fields. The king happened to pass by and recognized her as his daughter. He took her and seated her beside him in his carriage. Her companions were amazed and said: Yesterday you were gleaning among the stubble and today you are sitting in a carriage beside the king. She said to them: Just as you are astonished at me, so I am astonished at myself and she applied to herself the verse: "I knew it not, my soul set me in a chariot beside my prince." This refers to Israel in Egypt when they were subject to bondage, [working] with slime and bricks and were rejected and despised in the eyes of the Egyptians. And then, when they were set free and redeemed and were raised high above all others, the nations of the world were amazed and said: Yesterday you were laboring with slime and bricks and today you are set free and are raised high above all the world. And Israel said to them: Just as you are astonished at me, so I am astonished at myself, and she applied to herself the verse: "I knew it not, my soul set me in a chariot beside my prince."[22]

This midrash turns poetic symbolism into a parable about Israel's release from Egyptian bondage when she achieved peoplehood and dignity; to that extent it may seem to go beyond the limits of simple textual interpretation. Nevertheless, its sense of the direction in which the text is pointing is sound, for it is based on an accurate exegesis of the three words *markĕbôt ʿammî nādîb* (chariots, my people, prince), which are taken as signifying respectively power, peoplehood, nobility. These are the categories that the Shulammite has come to symbolize. And this same dimension is recaptured two verses later, in 7:1 in the phrase *bat-nādîb*, signifying "a noble (or queenly) maiden." We have here the suggestion of a girl belonging to what we would nowadays term "the ruling class." *Nĕdîbîm* elsewhere in the scriptures is a term applied to "rulers of the people" (Prov. 8:16; Ps. 113:8, 47:9, etc.). In the two last examples from Psalms, *nādîb* is placed in immediate conjunction with *ʿam* (nation). The *raʿyâ* is thus not just the daughter of a noble family; she is related by this language to the very categories of nationhood and royalty. In the dream symbolism of the poem she is both people and land.

But there is a further ambiguity. If we return to our explicatory model in Isaiah 62, we shall see that in the triangle of intimate relationships between God:land:people, the people has a dual or mediatory role— they are both bride and bridegroom:

> For as a young man takes to himself a virgin,
> so shall thy sons take thee to themselves,
> and as the bridegroom rejoices over the bride,
> so shall thy God rejoice over thee.

As we noted earlier, the first "thee" refers to the land, which will no longer be Desolate. The "young man" (or the "sons") who is the subject of the sentence is the people. In relation to land, the people act as male partner, as *baʿal* who will physically possess (*yibʿālûk*) the land. In the second clause, however, God is the bridegroom and the people assumes a feminine role in the sacred union that is the subject of this prophecy. Now, the allegorizers of the Song of Solomon have tended to interpret it in a fairly straightforward one-to-one fashion, according to which the *dôd* occupies the position of divine, male partner and the *ra'yâ*, or female partner, represents the people of Israel.[23] The poem relates the drama of their union, their estrangements, the "house" that they build to dwell in (i.e., the Temple), and the troubles that befall them until their reunion at the end of days. But this does less than justice to the fluidity of the image system. What I would like to suggest is that the *dôd* too, like the Shulammite, changes his role in the shifting kaleidoscope of the poem. As well as being the divine lover, he is also, at times, a persona for the people. He is more mobile, less passive, less organically related to the soil and what grows in the soil than is the *ra'yâ*, but he personifies the people just as she does. We see him bounding like a gazelle on the rugged mountains (2:17, 8:14), like Israel enjoying the gift of freedom in its land. He is in short the male aspect of peoplehood. The *ṣĕbî* or gazelle seems to be elsewhere emblematic for the Israelite nation. Its homonym (*ṣĕbî* meaning "beauty" or "glory") is regularly used for Israel; the land of Israel is the land of the *ṣĕbî* in Dan. 11:16. When Saul and Jonathan die, it is not only that the "beauty" of Israel is slain on the high places (2 Sam. 1:19); the other meaning of *ṣĕbî* seems also to be present.[24] It is the "gazelle" that is slain on the high hills. The nation mourns because its nationhood, symbolized by the gazelle, is diminished. The lover of the Song, linked as he is to the gazelle, is thus, among his other functions, Israel visualized as the owner and lover of the land just as the beloved is the land itself. But when the Shulammite functions as the female emblem of peoplehood—what the Targum calls *kĕništā' dĕyiśrā'ēl*—the *dôd* functions as the divine Lord of history who has entered into a covenant with his people, a covenant in which of course the promise of the land is central. To see such enfolded meanings in the Song is not to import some extraneous element: it is to seek out the meanings that the poem invites us to find in it, to operate with the language and the symbolism that the poem manifestly and abundantly calls to our attention.

IV

It seems that there is no way to avoid interpretation and that interpretation—especially in a poem so dreamlike in its symbolism—will tend to partake of the nature of allegory. This is true of all poetry and of all interpretations of poems.[25] It is more compellingly true of the Song of Solomon. If the ancients had not already taken this path, modern literary critics would certainly have felt obliged to do so. The typologists have turned the more straightforward earthy narratives of Chaucer's *Canterbury Tales* into typological renderings of such Christian mysteries as the nature of the Trinity. The same has been done for Shakespeare's comedies; *Twelfth Night,* we are told, has its hidden key: the twins, Viola and Sebastian, represent the dual nature of Christ as divine love, and Sebastian's timely appearance at the end of the play has something of the character of an epiphany or a Second Coming—all this without prejudice to the concretely human, indeed comic character of the plot.[26] It is a possible notion. The Song of Solomon, linked by so many phrases to other parts of the Old Testament Scripture where the "theological" sense is not in doubt and exhibiting a mode of imagery far more enigmatic than Shakespeare's comedies or Chaucer's *Tales,* is an obvious candidate for figural or allegorical interpretation.

As a matter of fact, many modern critics who would impatiently dismiss the Targum, the rabbis, and the church fathers as naïve allegorists have adopted allegorical readings more improbable than that which sees the poem as the story of the covenant drama between God and Israel. A substantial number of modern students, for instance, following the lead of T. J. Meek, have seen the poem as a cult liturgy connected with the rituals of Tammuz and Adonis. *Dôd* or *dôdî* is taken as the Palestinian equivalent of Tammuz, and the Shulammite is no other than his consort Shala or Shulmanitu, another name for Ishtar, the Palestinian goddess of vegetation who brings the life-giving rains. In 1:6, says Meek, "we have a clear reference to the drying-up of the vegetation under the scorching rays of the sun"—as the lady languishes from sunburn! Then there is the descent of the god into the underworld—the anguished search of the *ra'yâ* for the *dôd* is part of this fertility motif. The concluding chapter, in which we are told that "love is strong as death, / jealousy is cruel as Sheol," was "in its original context manifestly a reference to the power of the love of the goddess to win the god back from the netherworld."[27] Nearly all the different spices mentioned in the Song as well as the various flora and fauna are, we are told, related to the Ishtar cult.[28] Now all this is high fantastical, especially as the list of cultic *realia* is so exhaustive that one wonders which plants and animals the poet could have mentioned had he wanted to exclude the slightest suggestion of Ishtarism. But such a reading nevertheless is a tribute to what may be termed the allegorical imperative. A text so obviously symbolical, so rich in imaginative suggestions and reference, also so mysterious, calls out peremptorily for interpretation. Critics will be driven by the text itself to construct allegorical schemes of greater or lesser validity that will account for the hold that its strange and compelling language has upon us, to account also for the ineffable longing that this love song of a shepherd and a shepherdess calls forth. When so much metaphorical energy is expended on a shepherd and a shepherdess, they themselves become metaphor.[29]

It is often claimed that the allegorical reading of the Song was devised by the rabbis in order to justify its inclusion in the canon of holy writ, for otherwise, as a mere secular love song, it would have been in danger of being suppressed and thus lost.[30] The interpretation of the Song as shadowing forth the covenant love of God and Israel would thus be comparable to the allegorizing of Homer's poetry by the Stoics; that was done to give Homer philosophical legitimacy. Similarly, allegory was a means of giving the Song legitimacy within a scheme of dogmatic theology. The trouble with this notion is that, however far back we go, we cannot discern any traces of an earlier "literal" interpretation of the Song such as we can with Homer. Gerson D. Cohen has indeed argued very plausibly that "allegorizing activity took place not long after the Song itself was compiled."[31] It is the notion of the poem as a simple song of lovers that comes late—with Theodore of Mopsuestia in the fourth Christian century and, among Jews, much later. It may have provided material for songs at "banquets" in the early rabbinic period,[32] but this merely testifies to its popularity; it by no means justifies us in assuming that it was understood only in a secular sense. It may also be that the whole notion of a clear-cut canon of Scripture as existing in the pre-Christian period is something of an anachronism. Certainly, there were authoritative texts, chiefly the Torah and the Prophets. But the status of many of the "Writings" remained fluid down to the period of the Mishnah and beyond. In his day, Josephus knew of only twenty-two official books of Scripture. At the Council of Jamniah in the year 90, i.e., after the fall of Jerusalem, the status of both the Song of Solomon and Ecclesiastes was a matter of discussion.[33] And elsewhere in the Talmud, a third-century teacher, Samuel, expressed doubts about the status of the Book of Esther.[34] But this does not mean that such books were not known, treasured, and above all interpreted. Indeed Samuel himself devoted his exegetical efforts to the midrashic interpretation of Esther even though he was of the opinion that it did not "defile the hands," i.e., that the Esther scroll should not be kept in the same bookcase with indubitably sacred writings.

It does not seem that the felt need to *interpret* a text, even to interpret it allegorically, is bound up with any formal decision to "canonize" it. It is the text itself, even, we may suppose, its popularity, that calls attention to the possibility of further meanings. The compulsion exercised by the poem on its readers is what leads to the overdetermining of its meaning in the form of allegory. In the long run this may well lead to the work being regarded as sacred. But it was evidently not to justify such sanctity that the Song of Solomon was allegorized from the earliest period known to us, but because of the need to explain the extraordinary hold that it exercised on the imagination of its readers. Allegory was a way of accounting for the resonance of such a phrase as "I sought him but I found him not," for the intensity of such a phrase as "the one is she, my dove, my unadorned, the one is she . . . ," or for the unconditional, absolute devotion intimated by "set me as a seal upon thy heart, as a seal upon thy arm." The power of such images propels us beyond the limits of a marriage song, however exalted.

We are, in short, speaking of the pressure of the text itself, not of some imaginary canon, and of the vibrations that it sets up in the minds of its readers. Nor was the need to interpret by way of allegory, or something very like it, only felt by readers of the poem in the Middle Ages and earlier. It is evidently felt as an undiminished need by many modern readers and commentators. They find themselves as powerfully compelled to "allegorize"—witness the cultic theories of Meek, Schoff, and others. If it is a marriage that is being celebrated, then it must be a marriage between a god and a goddess! As a matter of fact, many modern readers have paid their tribute, sometimes unconsciously, to the traditional Jewish reading. The translation of 8:6 adopted by Robert Graves is: "Wear me like a charm on your breast, / or like a phylactery on your arm. . . ." The phylacteries are of course bound on head and arm in token of the covenant between God and Israel (Deut. 6:8, 11:18)! The same reading is mooted by Robert Gordis and Marvin Pope.[35]

There can be overspill also in the other direction. Rashi, who adheres to the allegorical reading, nevertheless pays his tribute frequently to the human level of meaning. On 8:5—"I roused thee under the apple tree"—he comments: "Thus she [Israel] declares: Remember that beneath Mount Sinai which formed itself over my head like an apple, there I stirred your love. The language is that of the love of a wife for the husband of her youth; she stirs her beloved in the night as they slumber, holds him in her embrace and kisses him." This is the short-circuit effect once again. Robert Graves would say that his mention of phylacteries is merely figure—the poem is not about phylacteries. Rashi would say that his mention of the intimate embrace of the wife and husband in their slumbers is again "merely" figure; the poem is about something different. The truth is that in this poem there is no mere figure, for metaphor and matter-in-hand have a way of moving into each other's territory. Vineyard stands for land, people, and loved one, but equally, loved one stands for vineyard and land. The "flowing streams from Lebanon" flow into the bounteous "garden," which is the maiden's love, but equally, her love makes real the bounty and grace of the land, gives force to those very streams.

As already noted, the only way to account for the amazing richness of the poem's imagery and also for the effect of this imaginative overspill is to see it as composed in the manner of a dream. This does not mean that the author had dreamed it or that it is susceptible to psychoanalytic testing, as one modern reader has suggested,[36] but that in its free-floating movement, its imaginative autonomy, it belongs to the literary genre of dream vision like *Finnegans Wake* or like Coleridge's "Kubla Khan." But here some care is needed. *Finnegans Wake* ends where it begins—it is a circular composition, its closing words completing the sentence with which the book begins. It is dreamy in the sense that it circles around certain unchanging nodes of consciousness. There is, strictly speaking, no advance, no purpose to be fulfilled. The same may be said of "Kubla Khan." The sunny pleasure dome and the caves of ice, the poem's two major symbols, reappear toward the poem's close; the shadow of the dome of pleasure still floats on the waves. The movement, if there is any, is toward a greater interiorization of that same vision. The symbols are self-fulfilling; the yearning expressed at the poem's close is for a more complete possession of those same symbols.

The dream work of the Song of Solomon is of a more active kind; it is, we may almost say, an anti-dream. The images of the garden and of the streams suggest still, tranquil nodes of vision, like Coleridge's dome and caves of ice, but working against these is the sense of what may be termed historical constraint. "I sought him but found him not." That search continues through the poem, underlined as we have seen by the forward movement of the incremental repetition. There are moments of seemingly gratified longing when the lovers seem to be united, eating the choice fruits of their garden, but these moments are overlaid by the struggle and the search, by the tension of a historical program, by memories that weigh us down with responsibility.

> Who is that, coming up from the wilderness,
> leaning upon her beloved?
> I roused thee under the apple tree:
> there thy mother was in travail with thee:
> there she who bore thee was in travail.
>
> (8:5)

The wilderness is not only a great expanse of rock and sand stretching out to the south and east; it is the land from which the loved one—interpreted to mean the collectivity of Israel—emerged at the beginning of its history, following her beloved as in Jer. 2:2. If allegory relates these verses of the Song too precisely to the birth of the Israelite nation, its wanderings in the wilderness and the great covenantal assembly at Mount Sinai, the overtones that lead to such a reading are surely there—they are almost required by the brooding sense in the poem of purposes announced in the past, frustrated often in the present, but weighing on us to the end. According to this reading, the Song takes us back to ancient beginnings; it takes us back also to nearer memories, to the dark night of the exile, when the Shulammite seeks her lover and finds him not and the watchmen wound and beat her. But the triumphant close is not the close of history, it is rather the reaffirmation of a faith that makes history endurable:

> Set me as a seal upon thy heart,
> as a seal upon thy arm;
> for love is strong as death,
> jealousy is cruel as Sheol.

If Job is an aborted tragedy because it gives way to a sense of historical purpose, and if *Ha'ăzînû* is likewise an aborted pastoral, then the Song of Solomon is, by the same token, an aborted dream poem. It is a dream poem invaded by the sense of historical time. The best analogy from this point of view is with some of the tales of the Israeli novelist S. Y. Agnon, and these are particularly relevant for many of them were inspired by a reading of the Song of Solomon. In one short novel, from a collection entitled *On the Handles of the Bolt,* the lovers enact the drama of estrangement and reunion, of bewildered search and longing. It is, as its title insists, "A Simple Tale"; it tells a realistic story of tragic misalliance and of the long struggle, through madness and grief, to repair it and achieve happiness. But there is a symbolic level to the story. We are told of a ruined synagogue, one wall of which is bent over in grief; according to local belief, on the ninth of the month of Ab, the date of the destruction of the Temple, it sheds tears. On Synagogue Street is the window of a house through which Herschel, the lover of the story, nightly seeks his beloved, but seeks her in vain. Both at its literal and symbolic levels, "A Simple Tale" is a story of the exile. It tells of the age-old, sad, and hopeless love of Israel for that divine presence which once dwelt in the Temple. If it tells of dream and delirium, it is thus a dream of history. Elsewhere in Agnon's writings, notably in his *Sepher HaMaasim,* we have an emphatically dreamlike mode of fiction, remarkable for its seeming incoherence and seeming confusion of times and places, but brooding over all these tales is a sense of responsibility, of tasks needing to be fulfilled and the difficulty of fulfilling them in the time available.[37] All this is surely not unlike the Song of Solomon, which, in spite of its dreamlike circling movement, also has a more determined incremental progression as well. At the beginning of the poem the maiden complains of not having tended her own vineyard; by the time we reach the close of the poem, she seems to have regained possession of it: "My vineyard is my own." History is not in vain. If there is separation and longing, there is also the sense of a promised reunion at the end of the long day of search and struggle. It is no wonder that this poem has been understood as an account of the troth plighted between a divine bridegroom and his chosen people. The wonder would have been if it had not been so understood. But one can go further than that; the fact is that the poem has had a role in maintaining and actively strengthening that bond. Its reading week by week has served as a confirmation of age-old vows and loyalties. Such an ongoing response of readers is also a dimension of literary understanding.

V

The Bible seeks through numerous systems of imagery to apprehend the mystery of the relation between God and man that is at the center of its meaning. There is the image of the vineyard and its keeper, of king and subject, father and child, mother and child (as in Isa. 66:12–13), master and servant, man and beast, the potter and his clay. Each of these has its richness and power, its mode of apprehending creatureliness and obligation. But none of these images proves ultimately satisfactory. The relations between the covenanting partners as signified by those images tend to be too fixed, too static, and also, too unequal. Dialogue is inhibited. There can be no true dialogue between man and beast, between an owner and a vineyard (or, as we nowadays might say, an automobile), close and even loving though such relationships may be. There are echoes of all these image systems in the Song of Solomon. We have the song of the vineyard (directly echoing, it seems, Isa. 5:1–7), images of royalty, of family authority, of animals—the maiden compared to a dove, the bridegroom to a gazelle, and of course there are the shepherd and his flock. Through all these we seek a language for defining the indefinable. We seek it but we find it not. The unappeased search of the ra'yâ in the poem is perhaps at bottom this search for an image that works. And the frustrations and difficulties are bound up with the knowledge that such a language is ultimately unattainable. The profusion of metaphor and simile in psalm and prophecy is a sign of the intensity of this search, but ultimately we reach the point where poetic language fails. "To whom then will you compare me, that I should be like him?—says the Holy One" (Isa. 40:25). If the Bible points to poetic imagery as in a way the only path of knowledge, it also points just as surely to the limits of art, the impotence of poetry. That has been the argument of this book. There is, however, one image that seems to have a better chance than the others. It is the image of bride and bridegroom, man and wife. It is easy to see why. In this relation we have the possibility of true dialogue between the covenanting parties and also something nearer to a genuine equality. It is the bride who in the Song actively seeks out her beloved, stirs him under the apple tree, bids him make haste to come to her, just as in Jer. 2:2 it is the bride, Israel, who, at great hazard, follows her lover into the wilderness. It is this capacity for independent action on the part of both partners which gives to that image a genuinely reciprocal character that is absent from that of master and slave or even parent and child. It also affords it an intensely dramatic quality. A vineyard can disappoint its owner by growing wild grapes, but it cannot really rebel. When it disappoints, the dialogue will be not between the owner and the vineyard but between the owner and the men of Judah who are asked to "judge between me and my vineyard" (Isa. 5:3). By contrast, a wife and husband can enact a true and agonizing drama of estrangement and the renewal of ties. This is the story of the prophet Hosea and his wife Gomer. There is always the potential for dramatic change in a relationship that is never static, a balance that is always shifting.

It has been well said that the conjugal trope is indispensable for expressing the reality of the covenant because it is invincibly historical.[38] It is weighted with a sense of responsibility, with the urgency of historical time. Tasks have to be undertaken in common, a house has to be built, a future has to be forged. Memory and responsibility are its mark, the memory of vows undertaken in one's youth, to be fulfilled and carried out to the end of the day—"before the day cools and the shadows flee away" (2:17, 4:6). Above all, in contrast to the other tropes that the Bible makes use of, the love of man and woman provides us with a means of understanding chosenness. Or perhaps it would be more correct to say that other tropes might give us the notion of choosing—after all, a man might choose an attractive automobile, or vineyard, or animal—but the corresponding awareness by the chosen one of his or her uniqueness and the discovery in that relation of the fullness of one's humanity—these belong to the symbol of espousal, it would seem, and to that alone. We have here an indispensable ground for the covenant relation as known in the Old Testament scripture. It is more than allegory. "I am my beloved's, and my beloved is mine" gives us access to the mystery of divine love because it is itself an incarnate mystery, a testimony to a transforming encounter, a means of transcending the merely natural.

But even that trope in the end declares itself to be merely trope, and, in the exhaustion of images, the divine love remains without words and without similitudes. The last two verses of the "Song of Songs" speak of the importunate need of poetry; there is, it seems, no substitute for poetry; it is man's highest reach. And so the Shulammite is bidden to raise her voice in song:

> Thou that dwellest in the gardens,
> The companions hearken for thy voice:
> cause me to hear it.
> (8:13)

But when the song is heard, it will be a mere similitude, for we strive to encompass that which cannot in the end be encompassed:

> Make haste, my beloved,
> and be thou like a gazelle
> or a young hart
> upon the mountains of spices.
> (8:14)

Again we have the urgency, the sense of a compelling need, as of a task still to be fulfilled, a race still to be run. And again we have the fore-grounding of the terms for poetic imagining. "Make haste," says the verse, and *dĕmēh-lĕkā*, "be a similitude." Be the similitude of a gazelle, of a hart. Indeed be the similitude of a lover, a *dôd*, for that too is a similitude, the greatest and the truest of them all. But even that is but a trope. Of God himself, of his choice of a people and of the mystery of that choos-ing, even this poem of poems will not directly speak. It will offer us instead a riot of images, but it will take care to tell us that these are but images and it will implicitly ask us to weigh the question that Isaiah three times propounds: "To what will you compare me and liken me and make of me a metaphor, that we may be comparable?" (Isa. 46:5).[39] In the end we are left with comparisons, with the beauty of poetic metaphor, but of God himself, whom all metaphors merely conceal, we shall only say what the prophet says of him in the verse preceding, *'anî hû'*, "I am he" (46:4), or again, later, "I am he, I am the first, / and I am the last"(48:12). Before all images are heard and after all images have worked their magic, we are left with just those two pronouns. According to the midrash, all that the people of Israel actually heard at Sinai were the first words of the great pronouncement: "I am the Lord thy God." The rest, we may say, is poetry.

·7·

PSALMS: THE LIMITS
OF SUBJECTIVITY

A striking feature of the Song of Solomon has misled critics as to the genre to which it belongs: I refer to its dialogic character. The lover addresses the Shulammite and she responds or fails to respond. There is a tension-laden space between the two, created by the mutuality of their cries to each other, their unappeased longing, their search. The object of the search is the other person, addressed in the directness of an I/Thou dialogue. This has led many to think of the Song in terms of drama. Milton, as we recall, thought of it as "a divine pastoral drama" and scholars nearer our own time have been attracted by the same notion.[1] And yet the poem manifestly lacks the shape of a drama. We have noted the undetermined nature of the figures, of their situation and the scene in which they are placed. What we have really are impassioned voices rather than characters. There is dialogue to be sure, but it is dialogue that gives us the maximum of relationality, the minimum of personality or setting. From this point of view, a book such as Esther or Ruth is very much more dramatic. If we need a genre for the Song of Solomon it will have to be the lyric. It also has, as we have noted, the associative rhythm of the dream and this, as Northrop Frye maintains, is distinctive to the lyric.[2]

And yet here another difficulty confronts us. Precisely the dialogic character of the Song sets it apart from the lyrical tradition as we know it in the West. The lyric knows of impassioned voices, of "the spontaneous overflow of powerful feelings"; it knows less of what I have termed the tension-laden space between voices, the mutuality of cry and response created in the I/Thou relationship. Its essential foundation is "the individual communing with himself."[3] This is particularly the case in the romantic phase of the European lyric in Germany and England. Wordsworth wanders lonely as a cloud, he calls on us to behold the solitary figure of the Reaper "reaping and singing by herself." The valley overflows with the sound, its thrilling beauty a function of her isolation from the "other." The speaker of the poem is there, but he plays no part in relation to the Reaper: he merely listens, notes, and moves on. The reader does the same. It may be that the song of the skylark in Shelley's poem of that title is a mating call, but there is no mate in sight or in hearing. The bird—who becomes a persona for the voice of lyric poetry itself—is separated from the world and from the other in a triumphant apartness. "The Indian Serenade" quoted earlier, in spite of its seeming to feature two actors, would lead us to the same conclusion:

> I arise from dreams of thee
> In the first sweet sleep of night,
> When the winds are breathing low,
> And the stars are shining bright:
> I arise from dreams of thee,
> And a spirit in my feet
> Hath led me—who knows how?
> To thy chamber window, Sweet!
>
> The wandering airs they faint
> On the dark, the silent stream—
> The Champak odours fail
> Like sweet thoughts in a dream;
> The nightingale's complaint,
> It dies upon her heart;—
> As I must on thine,
> Oh, beloved as thou art!
>
> Of lift me from the grass!
> I die! I faint! I fail!
> Let thy love in kisses rain
> On my pale lips and eyelids pale.
> My cheek is cold and white, alas!
> My heart beats loud and fast;—
> Oh! press it to thine own again,
> Where it will break at last.

There is (as in the Song of Solomon) a dreamer: there is a movement of longing, a turning toward the beloved; but we are struck by the essential passivity of the person addressed in the first two stanzas—she will do her part by allowing the lover to die on her heart. This is sufficiently unlike the Song of Solomon. In the last stanza there is a switching of roles: the beloved becomes the active partner, seeming to lift the speaker from the grass and rain kisses on his pale eyelids. But we see that this is merely a wished-for response, an echo or reflex of the longing expressed in the first two stanzas. The speaker for his part has now taken over the role of passive partner in a pose suggestive of death or sleep. There is, in sum, no genuine dramatic activity of responsiveness: what we have here is a defeated dialogue, the note again of lyrical subjectivity.

Viewed from another angle, however, lyrical subjectivity is not a defeat but a discovery within the self of new and rich inner sources of power. This is how it appeared to many of the romantic poets themselves. Coleridge discerned it in Milton, the biblically inspired poet of the seventeenth century. "The egotism of such a man," he said, "is a revelation of spirit" (*Table-Talk* for August 18, 1833). It is egotism in this sense that the romantic lyric achieved, a meditative inwardness for which the symbols were the lamp and the fountain.[4] It may be that one could no longer turn to Milton's God as a partner in dialogue, but the inspired subjectivity remained, "a revelation of spirit." The pagan gods too had withdrawn; for Keats it is "too late for antique vows"; the god who now rules is Psyche, the soul itself—"I see and sing by my own eyes inspired," he declares ("Ode to Psyche"). Hölderlin achieves a similar perception: The gods have disappeared but poetry remains and the poets are the holy priests of the wine god who wander from land to land in holy night ("Bread and Wine"). Living as they do "in dürftiger Zeit"—as Hölderlin termed it—the poets draw their strength from an autonomous region of selfhood, an inner world of the poetic imagination itself. Coleridge again sums it up: "I may not hope from outward forms to win / The passion and the life, whose fountains are within" ("Dejection: An Ode").

We may now add that such "revelation of spirit" often presented itself to the poets themselves in the form of biblical imagery. The "inland waters" of Wordsworth's subjective vision are biblical, taking us back to the story of Creation;[5] the fountain as an image of the spiritual powers is everywhere to be found in the Bible, and the lamp takes us back, via the Cambridge Platonists, to Prov. 20:27—"the spirit of man is the candle of the Lord." Such images could be drawn intermediately from Milton and from seventeenth-century divinity, with its stress on the evidences of the Spirit in the experience of Grace; but their ultimate source and authority was the Bible itself.

The one book of the Bible that, more than any other, more certainly than the Song of Solomon, seems to offer itself as a model of lyrical subjectivity and has generally been seen as such is the book of Psalms. There more than anywhere else we are given access to the inward zone of the spirit with its alternations of joy and dejection, nearness and distance. It is the most introspective book of the Bible, the prototype for all those spiritual confessions which from Augustine on have formed so important an ingredient in the development of our modern self-awareness, especially that mode of self-awareness which reached its intensest phase among the Puritans and later among the romantic poets. We may take two verses from Psalm 63 as an example:

> my mouth praises thee with joyful lips:
> When I remember thee upon my bed,

and meditate on thee in the night watches.
Because thou hast been my help,
therefore in the shadow of thy wings I will rejoice.
                              (5b–7)

We could take this passage as the Hebrew equivalent of that private communion with his muse which Milton referred to under the image of the song of the nightingale:

> Then feed on thoughts, that voluntary move
> Harmonious numbers; as the wakeful Bird
> Sings darkling, and in shadiest Covert hid
> Tunes her nocturnal Note.
> (*Paradise Lost* III, 37–40)

The activity and mood of the passage from Psalm 63 are remarkably like those implied in the scene from Milton. The psalmist too meditates in the "night watches," sheltered in the secret covert of "thy wings." There is the same inwardness, almost, one might say, the same romantic self-consciousness, that were later to make the image of the nightingale so crucially important for the poets of the romantic period.

We may pause over the word "meditate" in the third line of the passage quoted from Psalm 63. The verb, from two Hebrew stems (*hgh* and *śyḥ*), occurs fourteen times in the King James version of the Bible, and nine of these are in Psalms. The noun "meditation" from the same two stems occurs six times and all six are in Psalms! The Psalter, it would seem, is the special locus for the soul in meditation. It is worth noting that meditation was practiced as a formal art in the seventeenth century, shaping a great body of writing both in prose and poetry.[6] While there were contemporary manuals giving guidance in the practice of meditation, all of them leaned heavily on the examples of the psalmist, and the writers themselves, such as Henry Vaughan and George Herbert, clearly had the Psalms in mind.[7] As in Psalm 19 or 63 or 121 there is a remembered outdoor scene that is described in greater or lesser detail, but there is no interest in the scene for its own sake, for as the poem proceeds the scene is interiorized and the emphasis is on the meditating consciousness of the speaker, his spiritual struggles and insights. These verse and prose compositions generally end with an expression of hope or a prayer. Interestingly enough, this model passes into the romantic period to form the basis of what M. H. Abrams has termed "the Greater Romantic Lyric"—odelike compositions shaped in a similar fashion. Examples are Coleridge's "Dejection," Wordsworth's "Tintern Abbey," and perhaps some of the odes of Hölderlin and later, Rilke.[8] Many passages in Wordsworth's "The Prelude" are in fact meditations.

But to return to the Psalms themselves. The terms for "meditation" (*higgāyôn, śîḥâ, hāgîg*) come to refer to mental activity and are focused on the process of poetic composition itself. In Ps. 5:1 "consider my meditation" occurs as a kind of superscription announcing the nature of the poem to follow; in 19:14 "Let the words of my mouth and the meditation of my heart be acceptable in thy sight" is likewise a way of referring to the display of imaginative virtuosity that has just ended;[9] in 49:3 "my mouth shall speak wisdom; and the meditation of my heart shall be understanding" is in exact apposition to the sentence that follows, viz., "I will incline my ear to a metaphor: I will open my riddle to the lyre." It is in short an announcement of lyrical intent. In 104:34 "may my meditation of him be sweet" is a way of wishing that the poem just concluded shall be acceptable. Meditation in short and the related verbs point reflexively to the process of composition, in particular to the mental activity of the individual poet who presents himself to us as the source of the meditation. In this the two stems *hgh* and *śyḥ* are distinct from *zmr* or *šyr* (from which we get *šîr haššîrîm*, "the Song of Songs"). The *šîr* is the completed artifact, the song as produced or performed; it does not show us the mind brooding over its own activity or deliberating on the matter of the poem, as it weaves its imagery and cunningly contrives the pattern of its language. The *higgāyôn* or meditation of the psalmist gives us access to that zone.

II

Can we therefore conclude that the Hebrew term "meditation" suggests something like romantic self-consciousness—a self-consciousness that expresses itself essentially in monologue? The answer is that the Psalms are not monologues but insistently and at all times dialogue-poems, poems of the self but of the self in the mutuality of relationship with the other. They are in fact no less dialogic than the Song of Solomon, but here in the Psalms we have to do with a more whispered inner dialogue, what Joseph Hall in the seventeenth century was to call a *susurrium cum deo*, a whispering with God. The brief example from Psalm 63 will help us here again:

> my mouth praises *thee* with joyful lips:
> when I remember *thee* upon my bed,
> and meditate on *thee* in the night watches.
> Because *thou* hast been my help,
> therefore in the shadow of *thy* wings I will rejoice.
> (5b–7)

Here the self in meditation is immediately confronted with a "Thou." The first-person singular pronoun (or the corresponding suffix or prefix) occurs in each line of this passage but in each line it seeks a partner. The whole force of the poem is behind that search. This makes the passage more intensely dramatic than the passage from Milton where the blind poet broods introspectively in the company of his muse. That is a communion far less tension-laden than that intimated for us in this psalm. Here the speaker rejoices and sings, his joyful lips utter sounds, his need is the occasion of the poem, his mind and memory are the source of its meaning, but his "meditation" is not the introspective brooding of the "self" in monologue. He meditates "on thee" and that encounter between the subjective consciousness and the "thou [who] hast been my help" governs the nature of the poem. In fact we do not have here an autonomous ego at all: the "I" of the poem is in a real sense constituted by the dialogue with the "Thou." There is no "person" behind the "I" whose existence can be separated from that relationship. Psalm 63 is more autobiographical than most of the poems in the Psalter, with its image of the "dry and thirsty land" in which the speaker is exiled, but even that personal situation only exists to give force to the more unparticularized expression of relationality in the phrases "my soul thirsts for thee, my flesh longs for thee" (v. 1).

To speak of relationality pure and simple is, however, misleading. The Psalms are not exercises in existential philosophy; we are not speaking of an encounter for the sake of merely discovering the existence of the other and of the self in relation to the other. The "Thou" *answers* the plea of the "I" and that answer signals a change in the opening situation. The Psalms are in this sense dynamic, they involve action, purpose. W. H. Auden said in his elegy on the death of Yeats, "For poetry makes nothing happen." This is not true of the Psalms. In nearly every psalm something does happen. The encounter between the "I" and the "Thou" is the signal for a change not merely in the inner realm of consciousness but in the realm of outer events. To match the process of interiorization that we have noted, there is also a process of exteriorization, as the psalm shifts the focus from the historical to the psychological and then from the psychological back to the historical. Psalm 13 provides a simple example:

1. How long wilt thou forget me, O Lord? forever?
   How long wilt thou hide thy face from me?
2. How long shall I take counsel in my soul,
   having sorrow in my heart daily?
   how long shall my enemy be exalted over me?
3. Look and answer me, O lord my God:
   enlighten my eyes, lest I sleep the sleep of death;
4. lest my enemy say, I have prevailed against him;
   and those who trouble me rejoice when I am moved.
5. But I have trusted in thy mercy;
   my heart shall rejoice in thy salvation.
6. I sing to the Lord, for he has dealt bountifully with me.

It will be seen at once that the situation at the end of the psalm is not the same as that at the beginning.[10] The opening situation here as in many other psalms is the experience of personal hostility, hatred. The "enemy" is explicitly referred to in verses 2 and 4. Dahood's mythological reading according to which the adversary is Mot,[11] the god of death, should I think be rejected. The psalm does not refer to the antagonism of YHWH and Mot in the world of myth but to the speaker's political enemies in the world of history. Verses 1 and 3 give us the inward spiritual correlative, God's face is hidden; reacting to this, the speaker turns to God to "look and answer." We are in the realm of primary relations and primary images—the light of the eyes is invoked to counter the sleep of death (v. 3). The response to the plea of verse 3 comes in the last two verses. Paronomasia links *yāgôn bilbābî* (sorrow in my heart) from verse 2 with *yāgēl libbî* (my heart shall rejoice) in verse 5, underlining the alternation from sorrow to joy that the poem celebrates. But just as the initial sorrow had arisen from an external cause, so the joyous outcome of the crisis firmly links that joy with "thy salvation"—*yěšûʿâ* here as always signifying triumph in the realm of physical action. The final verse, "I sing to the Lord for he has dealt bountifully with me," is based on a formulaic pattern found also in the Song at the Red Sea—"I sing to the Lord for he has triumphed gloriously" (Exod. 15:1). Here as there we are emphatically in the realm of political and historical experience. The situation at the end of the psalm is not the same as that at the beginning. If at its opening the psalm takes us from the "world" into the inner realm of consciousness, it likewise and with an equally determined movement takes us back at the end into a realm of outer events. The psalmist knows "the passion and the life whose fountains are within," but he does not remain in that zone, for the God who meets us in the interior drama of the soul is the same God who acts mightily in history. This is a scandal to the many Bible critics who offer purely "psychological" readings of this psalm and others, seeking to preserve the purity of religion from the contamination of history and politics. Eerdmans reads the ending as a "confession of faith." Weiser finds the victory purely "religious"; "the worshipper," he says, "is assured of the grace of God."[12] Psalm 13 and others like it are a scandal also to those who, reading the Psalms as literature, specifically as lyric, strive to preserve the purity of the poetic "word" from the "world" of change. This becomes an article of faith for D. Robertson, who declares that "the Israelite community knows what Shelley knows, that no petition from them is going to lead God to make human life basically different."[13] This is *not* what the Israelite community knows: it knows that, mysterious though the ways of God are, there is still a potency in prayer, a power not to be rigidly separated from outer events in the "world"—"this poor man cried and the Lord heard, and saved him out of all his troubles" (34:6). Precisely here is the cutting edge dividing Western aesthetics from the implicit claims of biblical poetry. John Crowe Ransom insisted with no little dogmatic stridency that "over every poem which looks like a poem is a sign which reads: This road does not go through to action; fictitious. Art always sets out to create an 'aesthetic distance' between the object and the subject, and art takes pains to announce that it is not history."[14]

If Ransom is right we would have to conclude that the Psalms are not poetry and not art. The road *does* go through to action, for these are not fictions but testimonies. The crossing of the Red Sea, the "salvation" by which a bountiful God saves one from a boastful enemy as in Psalm 13— these are events that connect the subjective and objective realms. There are limits to subjectivity as the self emerges from its shady covert to behold a world that has changed. Extraordinary though it may seem, the change is seen to occur as an effect of the poetry, for the psalms are not only testimonies to past and present events; they are testimonies to the future as well. Having established or reestablished his bond with the "Thou" who "hast been my help," he already sees his enemy vanquished; he has no more to fear. Poetry has made something happen. No matter how deeply interior the meditation, the psalmist does not let go his hold on the historical and concrete, where the "word" or *dābār* is felt to be as active as it is in the inner realm of consciousness. "I await his *dābār*," declares one poet, and his earnest expectation is "a plenteous deliverance" (130:5, 7). The author of another psalm finds the same *dābār* at work in saving the faithful from various causes of distress, including storm at sea, sickness, and hunger (107:20, and passim).

This is the pattern in many psalms. In Psalm 3 subjectivity is breached in a similar fashion, but here there are added dimensions. The psalm takes its rise again from a condition of physical danger and menace ("how many are mine enemies become! Many are they who rise up against me"); again there is the interior dialogue as the speaker cries to YHWH and YHWH answers him (v. 4). And again there is the movement back from the "spiritual" to the "political" level as the Lord is seen to rise and smite the speaker's enemies upon the cheek, breaking the teeth of the wicked (v. 7). But we note that subjectivity is also breached in another way. In verse 4 God answers "out of his holy hill." Against the purity of the inner dialogue, or rather in addition to it, we have the emphasis repeated here, as in many other psalms, on the comforts of the Temple worship, where the well-tried and well-established forms of ritual observance bring to the dialogue with God an institutional basis and framework. Among the untold thousands who find a personal meaning in the august images and phrases of the Twenty-third Psalm there must be very few who give their attention to the final verse with its emphatic affirmation of the undiminished significance of the cult: "Surely good-ness and mercy shall follow me all the days of my life: / and *I will dwell in the house of the Lord* forever."

There is no substitute for the communal forms in which faith ul-timately finds its expression. This may not be the kind of message that seventeenth-century Protestant poets found in the Psalms and be-queathed to their successors among the poets of the romantic age (Mil-ton addressed himself to the Spirit that "dost prefer / Before all Temples th' upright heart and pure"), but it is too pervasive an aspect of Hebrew lyric poetry to be ignored. Critical writing on the Psalms from the time of Gunkel at the beginning of this century has stressed this aspect.[15] Weiser goes so far as to head his discussion of this topic "The Cultic Foundations of Psalmody."[16] It cannot be doubted that a preoccupation with the Temple worship is marked in poetry of the psalm type. The prayer of Jonah (Jon. 2:2–9) is really a psalm of thanksgiving, which, like the thanksgiving psalms in the Psalter, exhibits this same pattern. Jonah cries out from the deep, from the belly of Sheol; as the flood waters close over him he calls out to the Lord in the extremity of his anguish and God answers him, not only by rescuing him from danger, but by restoring him to his presence, as that presence is manifested in the Temple ritual: "When my soul fainted within me, I remembered the Lord: / and my prayer came into thee, into thy holy temple" (7). The speaker ends by announcing that he will fulfill his vows and offer a due sacrifice of thanksgiving in that same Temple.

Where does this leave the lyric, with its "anatomy of the parts of the human soul"?[17] Perhaps all these references to the Temple worship are no more than some archaic cultic residue that should not be permitted to jeopardize the purity of the lyric proper, which, as in Shelley's poetry, gives us the soul of the soul as it mounts with plumes of fire into the region of transcendence. The truth is again, however, that from this point of view the Psalms are and are not lyric poems, just as Job is and is not tragedy. The undeniable emphasis on the collective experience of worship radically compromises the subjective, lyric quality of the Psalms, for the implication of such an emphasis is that the I/Thou becomes the We/Thou. The final verse of Psalm 3 reads: "Salvation belongs to the Lord: thy blessing be upon thy people." It is not merely a question of institutionalizing the inner dialogue by transferring it to the context of the Temple worship; the people rather than the individual suppliant becomes the speaker. What we have is a collective cry and a response directed to a collectivity. This dimension is too conspicuous to be ig-nored. Nor is this a mere formal distinction. Mowinckel correctly dis-cerns that this significantly affects the nature of the discourse itself:

> The creating of the psalms differs . . . from what we moderns instinctively expect from poetry. The experiences and emotions to which the psalms give expression were not those of an individual, but such common events, general experiences and feelings as custom demanded in the particular situation. The poet who wrote a psalm for use, for instance at the purification rites, placed himself in a common situation and expressed what all were expected to feel and accordingly say.

And later on he insists even more strongly that the psalmist "is himself only when he is one with his family, his tribe, his people. He has no wish to be 'original.'"[18] If this is true then the "I" of the Psalms stands at a great distance from the autonomous ego that figures so largely in European poetry of the nineteenth century and earlier. George Herbert in the seventeenth century took a deep imprint from the dialogic poetry of the Psalter—more so it sometimes seems than any other Western poet of his time or since. The Psalms are a constant presence in his poetry. Nevertheless, Herbert presents himself to us as a *person*: we see him as a priest going about his duties, we see him as a poet sitting at his desk "often blot[ting] what I had begun." In "The Flower" we hear something of his spiritual history, how at one point he experienced the drying-up of his powers and how "now in age I bud again. / After so many deaths I live and write." Like the Puritan diarists, Herbert opens for us a window into his private world. He is autobiographical in a way that the psalmists never are. Only Jeremiah and Ecclesiastes offer comparable instances from time to time. We could put this another way. Herbert's emphasis on the inner struggle for Grace (like that of George Fox or John Bunyan) and the alternating phases of light and darkness is due to the conviction that the individual soul is the supreme locus of the religious life. There and there alone the signs of Grace and Justification are to be sought. For the Protestant believer the ideal state is in a deep sense the state of aloneness: when one is alone the greatest victories will be achieved, the greatest defeats will be suffered. It is a step from this to the solitary reaper or the lonely leech-gatherer of Wordsworth's poetry. That all-important solitude is what gives the lyric voice its pathos, its special resonance and power. Such song will have no ending.

Now, the Hebrew poet of the Psalms never looks upon his loneliness as a blessing, a source of benefits. Psalm 3 is the poem of a lonely fugitive "when he fled from Absalom his son." But he looks forward to the joy of no longer being alone, of being joined in fact to the collectivity of Israel—it is that state to which the poem aspires and which it finally reaches. That will be the state of spiritual fulfillment. Ringgren correctly notes that for the psalmist "solitude or isolation is an evil, since it is

primarily in the congregation that he experiences fellowship."[19] Psalm
22 is in this respect very explicit. In a verse that has become almost a
motto for the individual sufferer in his anguish, the poem starts with the
cry from the depths:

> My God, my God, why hast thou forsaken me?
> Why art thou so far from helping me,
> from the words of my loud complaint?
> I cry in the daytime, but thou hearest not;
> and in the night season, and I have no rest.
>
> (22:1–2)

It is there in the depths that he has encountered his God, in the intensity
of dialogue, but it is not in that encounter that he wishes to rest. The
sequel makes it clear that such loneliness must be and is overcome: it is
overcome horizontally by the speaker's joining himself to the fellowship
of all Israel, and vertically by his joining himself to the past and the
future.

> But thou art holy, thou that art enthroned
> upon the praises of Israel.
> Our fathers trusted in thee:
> They trusted and thou didst deliver them.
> They cried to thee, and were delivered:
> They trusted in thee, and were not confounded.
>
> (3–5)

Not the transcendental moment of lonely communion is the desired end
but the trials and consolations of history as the nation experiences it. The
psalmist begs for his individual life—"deliver my life from the sword, my
only one from the power of the dog"—but when he has been answered
and delivered, he promises to leave his solitude behind and make his
ordeal an occasion of rejoicing for the community: "I will declare thy
name to my brethren; / in the midst of the congregation I will praise
thee" (22). The ending of the psalm establishes once again the vertical
connection between the individual sufferer and believer—now liberated
from his solitary state—and the generations yet to come: "A seed shall
serve him; / it shall be told of the Lord to the coming generation" (30).
The story of his deliverance will be recounted to "a people yet to be
born" (31).

III

As noted earlier, it has been the tendency of critical scholarship in the
past century—especially in the work of Hermann Gunkel and his pupil

Sigmund Mowinckel—to stress the cultic aspect of the Psalms. This is consistent with what I have termed the horizontal widening of the "I" of the Psalms. Individuality is breached as the speaker's lament or thanksgiving takes on a collective character expressing itself in ritual practices. While Gunkel himself excluded the strongly personal psalms such as 3, 13, and 22 from the setting of the cult, seeing them as more genuinely "spiritual" and "individual,"[20] later form-critics have found cultic situations even for these. We are not here concerned with the archeology of the text, that is, with reconstructing the cultic setting if any, the original "scene" or *Sitz im Leben* of this or that psalm—even if so doubtful an enterprise were really possible—but with establishing the kind of discourse that is involved. We have noted that the collective worship in the Temple matters to the psalmist, but is it true, as the form-critical school maintains, that we have here a mode of discourse in which the individual voice is all but eliminated? Are the Psalms unambiguously the expression of a group, what in modern literary theory is sometimes termed a *sociolect*?[21] Now, it is clear that such a reading does not do justice to the inward meditative character of the Psalms, which we noted earlier, the *śîḥâ* or *higgāyôn* in which the lonely worshiper takes counsel in his soul, sorrows in his heart daily (13:2). For the fact is that, if psalms tend to move from the "I" to the "We" as we have maintained, *they also move back again,* thus preserving the full interior quality of the "I." Indeed, the trials and struggles of the community often take on the character of a lonely, individual ordeal in which the suffering soul cries out to God and is answered. What one would want to say is that, paradoxically, the ongoing covenant drama involving God and people is constantly interiorized to become the drama of a lonely soul, crying in anguish, trusting and despairing. The people in short take on the marks of lyrical subjectivity, giving us idiolect and sociolect all together.

We may take Psalm 103 as our example of such a dialectical combination of the personal and the impersonal. It starts with the praise of one worshiper who has been saved from personal danger. It is a formulaic beginning but deeply stressed nonetheless: "Bless the Lord, O my soul: / and all that is within me bless his holy name" (103:1). Here *qĕrābay* (all that is within me) are more literally "my internal organs," the very physical components of one's personality, the very bodily substance of the "I." In verse 6 the poem moves into the plural form as the salvation granted to the individual is widened to become a paradigm for the justice done on behalf of "all that are oppressed." The "I" of the opening is explicitly replaced by the plural form "we." "He has not dealt with us according to our sins; / nor repaid us according to our iniquities" (v. 10). But in verse 13 we get a dialectical movement in the other direction: this merciful

dealing with the community now takes on all the pathos and intimacy of
the most personal of relationships:

> As a father pities his children,
> so the Lord pities those who fear him.
> For he knows our frame;
> he remembers that we are dust.
>
> (13–14)

The term *raḥēm* (pities) is of the same stem as *reḥem*, "womb." One effect
of this is to give to the love of God a maternal rather than an exlusively
paternal character,[22] but it also takes us back to the imagery of the
opening verse. Just as the individual worshiper expresses the praise of
God through his internal organs, so the love of God for a people is
expressed in terms of physicality of an essentially private and intimate
kind. God and the people have a womb relationship. It is not too far-
fetched to see this aspect further enforced by the language of verse 14—
"for he knows our frame; he remembers that we are dust." *Yāda'*, the
term for "knows," often has the association of carnal knowledge (a parallel example would be Hos. 2:20). God's sense of the human condition is
as deep and intimate as a man's knowledge of his wife. In short, the
qĕrābay (my inward parts) are as relevant to the we/Thou relationship as
they are to the I/Thou. And we may add that the interior organs that
"praise his holy name" are not the entrails of an animal being sacrificed
in accordance with the cult, but the constitutive parts of the *nepeš*, the
throbbing vital inwardness of the personality as subjectively revealed in
meditation. The physicality of our own person—the very ground of our
self-awareness—serves here to bridge the gap between individual and
community—it is somehow common to both.

   The last verses of the psalm continue to grapple with the antinomy of
the broader and narrower forms of dialogue. The contrast is stretched to
its uttermost. God has established his throne in the heavens. The hosts of
heaven perform his *dābār*, carry out his will. Relationality has its cosmic
dimension as the words of blessing rise up "from all his works, in all
places of his dominion." But we come back in the end to the still center,
where the praise is a function of the organic soul of the individual worshiper—"Bless the Lord, O my soul." The first words of the psalm are
here repeated at the end to form an *inclusio*.[23] We are back, it seems, with
lyrical subjectivity. The truth is that this is neither an idiolect nor a
sociolect. When properly understood such a psalm stultifies the very
distinction itself. We will have to find different terms for defining its
mode of discourse.

   We may start with the *inclusio* or framing device itself in Psalm 103,
i.e., the phrase *bārĕkî napšî 'et-YHWH*, "Bless the Lord, O my soul," which

occurs twice in the opening verses of the psalm and once again in the last verse. By this device the note of lyrical subjectivity is struck at the end as at the beginning. All the hosts of heaven praise the Lord, but in the end, as we noted, we return to the still small voice of the soul itself. But what is the nature of that voice? We may now note that the same phrase occurs as a framing device also in Psalm 104 (1, 35) and that it occurs with a variation (*halĕlî*, "praise," instead of *bārĕkî*, "bless") in the opening verse of Psalm 146. In other words, what we have here is a formula. The phrase seems to signify an individual spasm of feeling, the expression of a personality; nevertheless, it points to itself as a traditional phrase, an item of received poetic language. It is remarkable how many of the most intimate expressions of feeling in the Psalms are in fact formulaic. Psalm 142 gives us as piercing a cry of pain as any in the Psalter:

> I cry to the Lord with my voice;
> with my voice I make my supplication to the Lord.
> I pour out my complaint before him;
> I declare my trouble before him . . .

and yet Robert C. Culley has shown in a valuable study that no less than 65 percent of the phrases in this psalm are formulaic—they can be matched in other psalms.[24] If we had a larger corpus of psalm-poetry from the same period, the percentage would probably be higher. Psalm 71 with its equally passionate expressions of lament and praise—"Cast me not off in the time of old age; / forsake me not when my strength fails me . . ."—is 36 percent formulaic. The reader then as now responds to well-known and well-tried patterns of language. From this point of view, it is decidedly not individualized composition. Culley's conclusion from his careful survey of these formulaic patterns is that we have to do with "oral poetry" and "oral composition."[25] This present study is not much concerned with how these texts were originally composed or delivered; we will simply note in passing that while the claim for "oral composition" is arguable, it can also be maintained that a formulaic style is equally in place in written literature.[26] There is nothing to stop a writing poet from making use of traditional and conventional phrases. We know from medieval liturgical poetry in Hebrew and other languages—surely the work of writing poets—how liberally such poetry draws on well-known and well-expected phraseology. It afforded reader and writer alike the joy of recognition, the pleasure of meeting an old acquaintance.

A more important conclusion to be drawn from such a formulaic phrase as "bless the Lord, O my soul" and many others like it is that no presence is here evoked by the personal "I": what is evoked is the power of the phrase itself as it resonates with other occurrences, the power of its own enunciation as that is shared in by singers of times past and times present. The term I would wish to propose for defining the nature of this kind of poetry is "covenantal discourse." The words become the sign of a covenant of praise, binding together a community on the horizontal plane and, on the vertical plane, binding generation to generation. We should remind ourselves that in the covenant mode the individual, no matter how solitary he is, is bound up in the solidarity of the group and the group, no matter how solidary, is addressed in the second-person singular (cf. Exodus 20), each and every member being as it were charged with personal responsibility. The text of the Psalms often affirms this by way of testimony—"I will declare thy name to my brethren; / in the midst of the congregation I will praise thee" (22:22)—but the text also enacts this interplay of solitude and solidarity through its own mode of discourse. The text as poem becomes the locus of an encounter between God and poet and between poet and people. Something like this is implied in the account of David's election in 2 Samuel. David is "raised up on high," "anointed" to be "the sweet singer of Israel" (2 Sam. 23:1); in the same context (23:5) David speaks of God's everlasting covenant with him. It is not too far-fetched to suggest that the covenant has reference to the poetry itself that David is, as it were, chosen, anointed to deliver. It becomes in a deep sense elective poetry,[27] in which God chooses the voice that will sound the song, in which God is said to be "enthroned on the praises of Israel" (22:3), giving ear while Israel performs its task of praise, his own presence and power vouched for by that song. This is a dynamic, even one might say, a dramatic concept of discourse. The action of offering and acceptance takes place not in the cult but in the poetry. But the text is also the locus of an encounter between speaker and reader. The reader too is called into the fellowship of that covenant, participating in the covenantal mode of discourse. We have the cry of an "I" that calls out to, and is answered by, the "I" of the reader. "Bless the Lord, O my soul"—a phrase read and reread by thousands every day—becomes their words, the expression of their individuality on each and every occasion of reading or singing. It is in a sense written anew for every new context and occasion, remaining at all times sociolect and idiolect, an individual cry and a collective affirmation, a spontaneous overflow of feeling and a formula speaking to us of what we have always known.

Formulae draw attention to themselves. The signifiers are here all-important, affirming their power as words, reminding us of the other occasions and contexts in which the same words were potent. If, as we have been taught, poetic language involves "the maximum foregrounding of the utterance," according to which "the act of speech itself is placed in the foreground,"[28] then this is truer of the Psalms probably than of any other poetry. Every phrase in the Psalms is a kind of quotation; there is an intense play of signifiers as words and phrases and images demand that we take cognizance of them. Many of the Psalms belong to the so-called wisdom-literature but the wisdom sought and gained is very much bound up with language, with cunning speech and verbal echoing.

To put it very simply, we could say that we have here a kind of poetry reflexively conscious of the importance of poetry. An extraordinary number of terms in the Psalms are related to the activity of singing, praising, performing songs to musical instruments, etc. Almost every psalm has some reference to itself as poem, as though poetic composition were in itself the most important matter in the world, as indeed in a way it is, both for the psalmist himself and for the later Hebraic tradition. There is nothing of greater moment than textuality and poetic texts are the supreme example of textuality. One midrashic saying has it that

> Were it not for the poetry and song that they [all flesh and blood] recite before me daily, I would not have created the world; and whence do we know that the Holy One, blessed is he, only created the world on account of poetry and song? From the verse which says (Psalm 96:6), "Honor and majesty are before him, strength and beauty are in his sanctuary." That is to say, honor and majesty are before him in heavens, but strength and beauty arise from his sanctuary on earth. . . . And whence do we know that the Holy One, blessed is he, created the heavens for the matter of poetry? From the verse which says (Psalm 19:1), "The heavens declare the glory of God. . . ." And whence do we know that Adam opened his mouth in a song of praise? From the verse which says "A psalm, a poem for the Sabbath day. It is good to give thanks to the Lord, and to sing praise to thy name, O most high!" (Psalm 92:1).[29]

This ninth-century midrash identifies a large number of terms in the Psalms as having reference to poetic activity. The "strength" (*'ōz*) and "beauty" (*tip'eret*) that belong to the worship in the sanctuary are seen as functions essentially of verbal production; the heavens, which "declare" (*měsappěrîm*) the glory of God in Psalm 19, really do so by means of a psalm of praise; Adam (traditionally regarded as the author of Psalm 92) was not only the first man but also the first poet, and he opens his mouth in praise by referring reflexively to the virtues of poetry: "A Psalm, a Poem for the Sabbath-day. / It is good to give thanks to the Lord, and to sing praise to thy name, O most High." The terms *mizmôr, šîr, lěhôdôt,* and *lězammēr* in this passage (psalm, poem, give thanks, sing praise) all have reference to the poetic activity itself.

But here we approach a further dimension of the covenantal mode of discourse. Textuality is, in the midrashic passage quoted above, balanced by creation. For the sake of poetry, we are told, the world is created: the song of men ascends to heaven in poetry and, when they are created, the heavens "declare" the divine glory in a poem of praise, in fact in Psalm 19! Now if we take the notion of poetic production as seriously as this passage intends us to, we are to take the notion of world-production no less seriously. What is being offered us here is not the romantic, Coleridgean notion of poetic "creativity," of the power of the poetic imagination to "create" its own interior universe of consciousness. We do not draw a magic circle around the inspired artist to isolate him from the world. In the covenant mode of discourse, world and word stand over against each other, bound together in mutual testimony. As noted earlier, in connection with the summoning of heaven and earth to witness in the song of Moses (Deuteronomy 32), world and word bear witness to each other.[30] If poetry is intensely important, it is because implicit in it is the word of power that brought the world into existence. That word still reverberates. If "day to day utters speech" (19:2), it is because the same *'ōmer* (speech) was at work in the bringing into existence of the same *yôm* (day) at the first act of creation when God said *(wayō'mer)*, "let there be light," and he called the light "day" *(yôm)*. Constituted by a word of power, nature as word enters into the poetry, bestowing on it something of its own power.

IV

A closer examination of Psalm 19 will make clearer the nature of what is here termed covenantal discourse.

Psalm 19
For the Chief Musician. A Psalm of David

1. The heavens declare the glory of God;
   And the firmament proclaims his handiwork.
2. Day to day utters speech,
   and night to night expresses knowledge.
3. There is not a speech, nor are there words,
   of which the sound cannot be heard;
4. for their echo is gone out through all the earth,
   and their words to the end of the world.
   Therein he has set a tent for the sun,
5. which is like a bridegroom coming out of his chamber,
   and rejoices like a strong man to run a race.
6. Its rising is from the end of the heavens,
   and its circuit to the ends of it:
   and there is nothing hidden from its heat.
7. The Torah of the Lord is perfect, restoring the soul:
   the testimony of the Lord is sure, making wise the simple.

8. The statutes of the Lord are upright, rejoicing the heart:
   the commandment of the Lord is bright, enlightening the eyes.
9. The fear of the Lord is clean, enduring for ever:
   the judgments of the Lord are true, righteous altogether.
10. More to be desired than gold, than much fine gold:
    sweeter also than honey, and the honeycomb.
11. Moreover by them is thy servant enlightened:
    in keeping them there is great reward.
12. Who can discern errors?
    cleanse me from hidden faults.
13. Keep back thy servant also from presumptuous sins;
    let them not have dominion over me:
    then shall I be blameless,
    and I shall be clear of much transgression.
14. Let the words of my mouth, and the meditation of my heart,
    be acceptable before thee, O Lord, my rock, and my redeemer.

It will be seen that the psalm falls into three well-marked sections: 1–6, 7–10, and 11–14. Each section has its distinctive rhythm and its distinctive thematic focus and yet the three parts are bound together by verbal echo and cross-reference. The first six verses present us with an image of the natural order, with the sun, the most powerful feature of that order, marking out the rhythmic alternations of day and night. The lines are slow and regular; in the Hebrew there are approximately four words to each half line. Order and intelligence are the mark of these verses as well as of the phenomena contemplated by them. The day "utters speech" (*'ōmer*), night "expresses knowledge" (*yĕḥawweh-dāʿat*), the sort of knowledge or intelligence that goes into the making of the poem. Verse 3 is generally translated: "There is no speech, nor are there words; / their voice is not heard." This, however, directly contradicts what precedes and what follows. It is more reasonable to assume with several commentators [31] that the double negative makes a positive. We then read 3 and 4 as follows:

> There is not a speech, nor are there words,
> of which the sound cannot be heard;
> for their echo is gone out through all the earth,
> and their words to the end of the world.[32]

In short the heavens indeed "declare" the glory, they utter articulate speech; we in a manner hear "their *words*" (*millêhem*) (4b). It is, we may say, a verbalized cosmos. The impression made by the sky and the sun encamped in its midst is one of grandeur, height, and distance—this is especially the effect of verse 6—

> Its rising is from the end of heavens,
> and its circuit to the ends of it:
> and there is nothing hidden from its heat

—but it is a cosmos that nevertheless addresses us and is addressed in language. That is the discovery that the psalmist makes and it is that which affords him his excitement. It is not a Wordsworthian awe at the grandeur of nature but the metaphysical shudder of insight that occurs when the world becomes audibly responsive to its creator, becomes a kind of text.

In the second section of the poem (vv. 7–10), the poet turns in fact to a text, namely the Torah, which is gravely hymned in six neatly balancing, stylized phrases, followed by a couplet. In their ritualistic movement and parisonic balance, the verses somewhat ostentatiously assert their poetical character.

> The Torah of the Lord is perfect, restoring the soul:
> the testimony of the Lord is sure, making wise the simple.
> The statutes of the Lord are upright, rejoicing the heart:
> the commandment of the Lord is bright, enlightening the eyes.
> The fear of the Lord is clean, enduring for ever:
> the judgments of the Lord are true, righteous altogether.
>   More to be desired than gold, than much fine gold:
>   sweeter also than honey, and the honeycomb.

As several commentators have pointed out, this praise of the Torah uses terms that properly describe the sun.[33] The commandment is "bright" like the sun (*bārâ*, cf. Song of Sol. 6:10); the fear of the Lord "endures for ever" with the permanence of the heavenly bodies or the light of creation (cf. Ps. 33:9 for the same stem *'md*); and gold and honey in the last verse of the section are archetypal analogies for the sun. We thus have a dialectical pattern whereby the heavens (and specifically the sun) have the attributes of speech, of textuality, while the Torah, in its turn, shining brightly so to speak in the moral heavens, has the attributes of taste, light, color, and physicality. The excitement is in perceiving and enjoying this dialectical interplay. There is also a dialectic of proximity and distance. The heavens declare the honor of *'EL*, the high God whom man has some difficulty in approaching (cf. Job 9:2–3); the Torah, however, in each of the verses 7–9 is the work of YHWH, the God of a nearer and more intimate revelation (cf. Gen. 12:1f.). Some critics, taking this hint, have been led to suppose that here we have two separate poems, the first, based on Babylonian mythological material, is a praise of Shamash the sun-god, the second is a later Israelite hymn in praise of the Torah. Against this disjunctive view[34] must be set the fact of the contexture of the whole poem. The various parts of the poem are linked by affinity and contrast; they illuminate one another.

"Illumination" in fact or "enlightenment" is the central term in the opening verse of the final section of the psalm: "Moreover by them is thy servant enlightened: / in keeping them there is great reward" (v. 11).

Nizhār in this verse is more often rendered "warned." The stem *zhr* can mean warned or enlightened. Here it is evidently a homonym—it means both. The sun enlightens, the Torah warns; or rather both perform both actions; the term is ambiguous. But it is not the light of the sun or the precepts of the Torah taken separately that the verb *nizhār* acknowledges but rather the privilege, the *zōhar* or "splendor" of bringing the two together. The use of the term represents a species of metaphysical wit. More than that, in this phrase, "by them is thy servant enlightened/warned/gloriously privileged," the poetic activity is itself celebrated. It is poetic meditation that makes possible the connection of the two spheres, that of ʾEL and that of YHWH, of world-creation and of revelation and of both with praise and song.

Wordplay is the mark of this section. In verse 12 the phrase "cleanse me from hidden faults *[nistārôt]*" links this section once again with what has gone before. The same participial *nistār* had occurred in verse 6 in the phrase "there is nothing *hidden* from his heat"—i.e., from the heat of the sun. As though to say that, as against the public sphere of creation, where nothing is hidden, we have here a more private, intimate sphere, but here too YHWH is at work illuminating the hidden places of the soul. The next verse introduces two further examples of metaphysical wordplay:

> Keep back thy servant also from presumptuous sins;
> let them not have dominion over me:
> then shall I be blameless,
> and I shall be clear of much transgression.
>
> (13)

The opening verb "keep back" (*ḥăśōk*) suggests by paronomasia the very like-sounding *ḥōšek*, meaning "darkness." This may have been suggested by *nistār* (hidden) in the previous verse. It takes us back to the imagery of light (and by implication, darkness) in the first two parts of the poem. While the public realms of creation and Torah are, so to speak, drenched in light, the more private realm to which the final verses have reference implies an absence of glare, a more covert encounter. As another psalm has it—"He that dwells in the secret place of the most High, / shall abide in the shadow of the Almighty" (91:1). In the second half of the verse quoted above, the phrase "then shall I be blameless *[ʾêtām]*" (introducing the same root *[tmm]* as in *tammātî*, "my perfect one," Song of Sol. 6:9), takes us back to the praise of the Torah in verse 7—"The Torah of the Lord is perfect *[těmîmâ]*, restoring the soul." Contemplating the "perfection" of the sun's movement and the parallel "perfection" of the Torah, the poet himself aspires to something of the same quality of purity or blamelessness.

Covenantal discourse in this poem takes the form of bringing together the testimony of the heavens with that of the moral law, the Torah. It should not come as a surprise to learn that the world of nature is bound by covenant no less than the people of Israel. Jeremiah speaks of "my covenant of the day and the night" (33:25). E. C. Rust notes that "behind God's Covenant with his chosen people lies his covenant with nature itself."[35] J. Pedersen makes a similar point.[36] The establishment of an orderly cycle of nature after the Flood is of course confirmed by setting the rainbow in the cloud "for a token of a covenant between me and the earth" (Gen. 9:13). In the Psalms such notions take the form of juxtaposing through imaginative cross-reference the "word" inscribed in the heavens with the "word" inscribed in the Torah. In Psalm 33 the juxtaposition is achieved by an intense play on the term *dābār,* or "word," as the psalmist wittily juxtaposes the *dābār* whereby God rules the moral universe with the *dābār* by which the heavens were made (33:4, 6). A similar wordplay occurs in Psalm 147: there God sends out his "word" to thaw the winter ice and in the next verse he declares his "word" to Jacob and his judgments to Israel (147:18, 19). Such perceptions, achieved through the plasticity of language, are, says the psalmist, "comely *[nā'wâ]* for the upright" (33:1). Psalm 147 adds the term *ṭôb* in parallel to *nāʿîm* and *nā'wâ.* Praise is "good," "beautiful," "pleasant" (147:1) because it celebrates the meeting of God, man, and nature through word and image. But of course it does not merely celebrate: it interiorizes, it enacts the meeting. The poem is the scene of an encounter. More than a scene, it is, through its impacted language, the indispensable instrumentality for making the encounter possible. That is what is meant by covenantal discourse.

But to return to the final section of Psalm 19. We may note here a further process of approximation. If we moved in the earlier parts of the poem from the remoteness of cosmology, i.e., the sphere of *'EL,* to the nearer realm of YHWH—the sphere of what a later generation would call "the universal moral law"—we move in this final section of the poem (11–14) to a more whispered region of inwardness. Here the urgent rhythm of prayer comes to replace the formal cadences of the opening doxology on the heavens and the Torah:

> Who can discern errors?
> cleanse me from hidden faults.
> Keep back thy servant also from presumptuous sins;
> let them not have dominion over me. . . .
>
> (12, 13)

Not only a new rhythm but also a new grammatical situation is here introduced. While the two opening sections of the poem had been conducted in the third person—the third person for God, for the heavens, and for the Torah, the last four verses introduce that special dimension of the covenant which can only be expressed by the meeting of the I and the Thou. "Cleanse me from hidden faults" is the cry of the soul that knows itself and knows that it has no one in heaven but thee. This is of course part of the dialectic of proximity and distance, the last section of the poem bringing us nearer to that 'EL and to that YHWH who had been alluded to in the third-person form of majesty up to now. But there is also an opposing dialectic, that of presence and absence. The "heavens" and the "Torah" are more concretely present in the poem than is the "I" of the latter section. That first person is constituted here by the discourse itself. It exists not as a presence but only as a grammatical sign; but this is what gives it its force for it is a sign that can be shared in, and enunciated by readers in all times and places. Here in the absence of persons is the very dramatic node or core of the covenant, that to which the grave opening passages of the poem refer. It is here made manifest in the more naked language of the last verses, which complete but also cancel out the passages of praise that have gone before—as if to say that when the witness of the heavens or that of the Torah has been heard, all that we have left are "the words of my mouth" and the "meditation of my heart" as the form in which that witness finally issues. For them the speaker craves acceptance. We may conclude that lyric subjectivity here replaces the language of report in the earlier sections. And yet it should be noted that the phrases are themselves formulaic, almost, one may say, institutional. The conjunction 'imrê pî (the words of my mouth) occurs some fifteen times in the Bible; YHWH is addressed as "my rock" in some half a dozen psalms. In short we have not a particularized speaker or occasion, not a person, but a pattern of words in which the covenantal forms are habitually realized.

One important aspect of this closing verse has been little noted by the commentators.[37] In the sentence quoted above, "Let the words of my mouth, and the meditation of my heart, / be acceptable before thee . . . ," the phrase "let . . . be acceptable" (*yihyû lěrāṣôn*) is a formulaic phrase used in the priestly law for the offering of sacrifice (cf. Lev. 1:3, 22:20, 22:21). In fact the form *lěrāṣôn* occurs some seven times in the Scriptures and, except in this one instance, always in connection with the Temple ritual. The implication of this is not that the psalm had a cultic "setting," that, as the form-critics might conclude, it served as an appendage to the cult. It is rather the other way around: language normally associated with an institution, a ritual of the Temple, is here boldly, even daringly transposed to "the words of my mouth, and the meditation of my heart." For them the "acceptance" is craved; in them the ritual will be performed. The covenantal exchange of offering and acceptance associated with the worship in the sanctuary is here interiorized as a function of language. There the action is. And as in the Temple ritual, the "I" becomes the "I" of a group and a nation. It humbly offers its tribute of praise and petition and is granted an answer likewise in the words of the poem. The poem enacts the two sides of the covenantal dialogue. It is a whispered act of devotion and meeting. That is what is meant by speaking of covenantal discourse. It is not that the words *express* some reality of dialogic encounter that precedes the enunciation of the words or takes place outside of them. The encounter of which we are speaking is itself an enunciative situation: it takes place in the language of the psalm, not in some ceremony or in some mystical transport beyond language. From this point of view the Psalms of David are not just one way of talking about the dialogue between God and Israel, between the "I" and the "Thou"; they verily constitute and bring about such dialogue. They are the focus and, in an important sense, the origin of that dynamic relationship from which covenant history itself flows. The poetry indeed makes things happen.

V

We are not concerned here with proposing a historical model according to which the Temple cult was the more "primitive" way of giving meaning to the covenant relationship while verbal offerings or psalms were the later, more "advanced" mode. They seem to be much rather parallel and reciprocal modes. Psalms 120–34, the so-called Songs of Degrees, may have been part of a songbook used to accompany the procession of the Levites to the Temple mount.[38] That would support the notion of a cultic *Sitz im Leben*. But it can work the other way. In Ps. 19:14, as we saw, the notion of sacrifice is interiorized, transferred to the "offering" of words. We are not to look for an external *Sitz im Leben*; the poetry does it all. This is entirely in accordance with the saying of Hosea: "Take with you words, and turn to the Lord: . . . so we will offer the word of our lips instead of calves" (Hos. 14:2). Even if the Septuagint reading is here adopted ("We will offer the *fruit* of our lips"—without "calves"), we still have in the term "offer" *(šallēm)* the clear notion of sacrifice, as in Jon. 2:9, Ps. 56:12, 66:13, where the same verb *šallēm* is used. In the Temple the fruits of the earth, animate or inanimate, were "offered" or "rendered" to the Creator as a gesture of thanks or supplication or contrition; in the Psalms, verbal signs are offered. "Take with you words," Hosea had said; as against the dramatic, concrete, visual mode of the Temple worship—a semiotics of act and gesture—we have here the lyrical, meditative mode—a semiotics of verbal signs. The one form is not "superior" to the other any more than lyric is superior to drama. All that can be said is that the verbal "offerings" have in practice, and in the absence of the Temple cult, proved effective as a means of giving shape to the covenant relationship. For centuries in the absence of the Temple cult, men have taken with them words and offered up forms of language to their creator instead of bullocks or first-fruits. And it has seemed to *work*, in the sense that the book of Psalms has come to function as a true mode of meeting for generations of men seeking a way of "rendering" thanks, of "performing" obligations and vows. But what does "taking with you words" really mean? We have spoken of the Psalms as performing the gestures of offering and acceptance, but what if anything is offered and accepted? Is there any "content" to the words to match the first-fruits, or wine, or oil, or animals that would be brought in the more dramatic, visual mode of offering during the Temple ceremonies? The answer is that in the Psalms the same signifiers are present. The vegetable and animal kingdom, the various aspects of nature are there in the form of images. And signs and images can be for men a more potent offering than the "things" themselves. Again we must be clear about this. When we speak of nature imagery, we do not speak of an independent or autonomous realm of nature. The world of nature is a partner in the triad: man, God, nature, and it is in a manner constituted by the dynamic structure of that relationship. The world bears witness for or against man; man in his turn attends and bears witness to the "words" emanating from the heavens and the earth. God, the author of both, summons them to their mutual task.

Psalm 92 will serve as an example of this special kind of nature imagery.

Psalm 92
A Psalm, a Poem for the Sabbath-day.

1. It is good to give thanks to the Lord,
   and to sing praise to thy name, O most High;
2. to relate thy steadfast love in the morning,
   and thy faithfulness by night,
3. upon an instrument of ten strings, and upon the harp;
   to the meditative note of the lyre.
4. For thou, Lord, hast made me glad through thy work:
   I will sing for joy in the works of thy hands.
5. O Lord, how great are thy works!
   and thy thoughts are very deep.
6. A dull man does not know;
   nor does a fool understand this.
7. When the wicked spring like grass,
   and all the workers of iniquity flourish,
   it is only that they shall be destroyed forever;

8. but thou, Lord, art most high for evermore.
9. For, lo, thy enemies, O Lord, for lo, thy enemies shall perish;
   all the workers of iniquity shall be scattered.
10. But my horn shalt thou exalt like the antelope:
    I shall be anointed with fresh oil.
11. My eye has looked upon my enemies,* that rise up against me;
    my ears have heard the evildoers.
12. The righteous man flourishes like the palm;
    he grows great like the cedar in Lebanon.
13. Those that are planted in the house of the Lord
    shall flourish in the courts of our God.
14. They will still bring forth fruit in old age;
    they will be stout and fresh.
15. To declare that the Lord is upright;
    he is my rock, and there is no unrighteousness in him.

*Reading *šûrāy* as a variant of *šōrĕrāy* (cf. Ps. 54:5).

As remarked earlier, this psalm begins with an unusually elaborate superscription in which psalmody itself is praised—praised for its beauty and for the enlightenment it affords. The opening word *ṭôb* in the phrase "it is *good* to give to thanks to the Lord" is, here as elsewhere, a synonym for "beautiful."[39] In the rather similar opening verse of Psalm 147, *ṭôb* stands in direct parallel to *nā'îm* and *nā'wâ*, regular terms for the beautiful. In the next verse of our psalm this metapoetic opening resolves itself into the less formulaic phrase: "To relate *[lĕhaggîd]* thy steadfast love in the morning, / and thy faithfulness by night." *Lĕhaggîd* is not the usual term for singing and praising but carries more the sense of "expounding" (as in 1 Sam. 8:9) or "solving a riddle" (Jud. 14:12), or "interpreting a dream" (Gen. 41:24), or "making a connection" (Exod. 13:8). In the latter example the father is bidden to explain the connection between the eating of the unleavened bread and the Exodus from Egypt. What the psalm is saying here is that to "expound" God's faithful love by means of a poem—this poem in fact—is a good and comely exercise for the inquiring mind. But what is the matter that has to be expounded, the riddle, so to speak, that has to be solved? This begins to come to light in verse 4: "For thou, Lord, hast made me glad through thy work *[bĕpā'ŏlekā]*: / I will sing for joy in the works of thy hands *[bĕma'ăśê yādêkā]*." These terms for "work" and "the works of thy hands" point forward clearly to the imagery of vegetation shortly to be introduced into the poem. That is the matter to be inquired into. But we clearly do not have here the simple contemplation of natural phenomena, as in Wordsworth's joy at the sight of the daffodils. And this is immediately made clear in the following two verses:

> O Lord, how great are thy works!
> and thy thoughts are very deep.
> A dull man does not know;
> nor does a fool understand this.

This psalm has been rightly related to the wisdom-literature.[40] It is the wise man's understanding of nature that is here the issue—i.e., what intellectual and moral profit he will derive from the consideration of the grass, the blossoms, the cedar, and the palm tree, and how he will relate them to the life and duty of man. The best gloss on these verses is in a poem by Henry Vaughan. He is meditating on a waterfall:

> What sublime truths, and wholesome themes,
> Lodge in thy mystical, deep streams!
> Such as dull man can never finde
> Unlesse that Spirit lead his minde,
> Which first upon thy face did move,
> And hatch'd all with his quickning love.

Again it is the truth of nature's witness that counts, a truth that yields itself not to the "dull man" but to the witty man who knows how to solve riddles, to apprehend the particular uses of language, to appreciate the significance of analogies, to make connections. The psalmist immediately poses his "riddle."

> When the wicked spring like grass,
> and all the workers of iniquity flourish,
> it is only that they shall be destroyed forever.

The terms for "spring" and "flourish" *(biprōaḥ, wayyāṣîṣû)*, although applied here to "the wicked," are by no means negative terms; the same verbs occur in Isa. 27:6 as signs for the marvelous growth and splendor of Israel in the latter days, when Jacob shall "blossom and bud" *(yāṣîṣ ûpāraḥ)*. The vitality of the flowers bears witness to a vital creation, one too to which man belongs or desires to belong. And yet to speak of a blossoming flower is to conjure up immediately the balancing notion of the fading flower. If in Isa. 27:6, blossoming and flowering had been the privilege of a renascent Israel, in the following chapter the wicked men of Ephraim have become the "fading flower *[ṣîṣ nōbēl]* of its glorious beauty" (Isa. 28:1, 4). Nature in short is for the biblical poet a paradoxical witness: it grants us growth, but in the very same breath it condemns us to transience, ephemerality.

The first strategy of the author of Psalm 92 is to attach this paradox firmly to the wicked, the sorcerers, the *pōˤălē ʾāwen*. It is they who flourish like the flower, "only to be destroyed forever." But the very language of the psalmist has betrayed him. We are all of us, righteous and wicked alike, involved in the transience of nature no less than in its vitality. This is implicit in the very use of the terms *prḥ* and *ṣîṣ*. We blossom and we fade; the term *nābēl* (fading) is the shadow of the word *ṣîṣ* (flower). In another chapter of Isaiah we hear that "all flesh is grass *[ḥāṣîr]*, and all its glory is like the flower of the field," but "the grass withers, the flower fades" *(nābēl ṣîṣ)*, when the breath of God breathes upon it (Isa. 40:6, 7). To utter the words that the psalmist utters—"the wicked spring like grass, / and all the workers of iniquity flourish, / but only to be destroyed forever"—is in short to condemn not only the wicked but all men to destruction. Not only is natural beauty vain, it is also deceitful when used as poetic metaphor.

To escape this trap, the psalmist now turns to the third partner in the covenant relation, to the God who stands above the world of natural vegetation. He is after all the Thou of the intimate dialogue—perhaps as such he can marvelously lift up the worshiper who turns to him and somehow raise him above these images of nature. In fact the notion of height and raising are at the center of the following verses:

> But thou, Lord art most high for evermore.
> For, lo, thy enemies, O Lord, for lo, thy enemies shall perish;
> all the workers of iniquity shall be scattered.
> But my horn shalt thou exalt like the antelope:
> I shall be anointed with fresh oil.

God is "most high"—independent of the lowly flowers that fade—and as such he can exalt and raise the man who turns to him. The same stem links the height of God *(mārôm)* in verse 8 with the exalting of the speaker *(wattārem)* in verse 10. The play of the inflections of the same verbal root links together man and God in mutual witness as both stand against the treacherous implications of the flower and grass imagery of verse 7. But the poet cannot escape from the realm of the natural; no matter how hard he tries, the very nature of his language again betrays him. The exalting referred to immediately and inevitably conjures up the horns of the antelope or the wild ox. The linking of the stem *rûm* (to exalt) with *qeren* (horn) is indeed formulaic, part of the corporate language of poetry (as in Ps. 89:17, 24). There is no abstract realm of elevation or exaltation, only the height and dignity of the antelope or the ibex as he might be glimpsed proudly stationed on the slopes of the hills rising from the Jordan valley. If it is true that the psalmist has no one in heaven but God, he has nothing to point to on earth but the witness of the natural world, animate and inanimate.

Nature thus remains, an irreplaceable witness. The *rě'êm* or antelope is therefore what he here "offers," and the mention of the horn by association suggests the oil of the final phrase[41]—likewise "offered" within the "temple" of the discourse like the oil that accompanied all the offerings in the larger Temple. From the height that he has now achieved with the help of the image of the horns of the wild creature of the hills and with the help of the anointing oil by which he feels his existence to be consecrated, he can now face the enemies who rise against him (v. 11). But the confrontation with the enemies is not quite so simple as the usual English translations suggest. RSV reads: "My eye has seen the downfall of my enemies, / mine ears have heard the doom of mine evil assailants." But there is nothing in the Hebrew text to correspond with "the downfall of" or "the doom of." Nor is there any justification for Eerdman's rendering of the first half of the verse as "My eye hath looked down upon them that rose up against me"—there is nothing in the Hebrew to correspond with "down." The speaker could just as well be looking up at the foes who look down on him—indeed the phrase "that rise against me" *(baqqāmîm ʿālay)* for enemies in 11a suggests that they, the enemies, also have the benefit of height. Briggs is faithful to the Hebrew in his more straightforward translation: "And mine eye shall look on my lurking foes; / Evil doers mine ear shall hear."[42] There is no guarantee in the verse that the raising of the speaker by means of the image of the horns of the *rěʾêm* has disposed of the threat of the enemies. The outcome of the confrontation remains undetermined. His eye will look at them, his ears will hear them. Thus while God's enemies are sure to be scattered and to perish forever (v. 9), the enemies of the speaker are not so unambiguously defeated, for height and pride are qualities that they too can achieve. A third attempt at summoning the witness of nature is thus called for. Perhaps there is a way of overcoming the treacherous quality of such images, binding the world of created things more firmly into the interiority of the covenant discourse. It is this which is achieved in the final section of the poem.

Echoing in the verb *yiprāḥ*, the blossoming flowers of verse 7, the psalmist now directs us to the palm tree in blossom, and echoing in the term *yiśgeh* the notion of height from verse 10, the psalmist directs us to the lofty cedar of Lebanon. These now become the ultimate images for the *ṣadîq*, the righteous man: "The righteous man flourishes like the palm: / he grows great like the cedar in Lebanon." It will be seen that the righteous man remains rooted in the world of nature no less than the wicked man, but the image of the tree here as in Ps. 1:3 allows him to overcome the transitoriness of the merely natural. In Psalm 1 the righteous man had likewise been compared to a flourishing tree: "And he shall be like a tree planted by streams of water, / that brings forth its fruit in its season" (1:3). He was there placed in direct contrast with the wicked, who were likened to chaff: "Not so the wicked: / for they are like the chaff which the wind drives away" (1:4). It will be seen that there the contrast is more simple and didactic than in the patterning of Psalm 92. In Psalm 92 the images of both the fading flower and the stout tree are interwoven with greater complexity, as befits a poetic exercise of which it is said that the dull man cannot know and the fool cannot understand. How complex the image of the tree is we will see if we consider the mention of the Temple in verse 13 of our psalm: "Those that are planted in the house of the Lord / shall flourish in the courts of our God." Since trees were not planted in the Temple court, this verse has been variously interpreted. Some have treated it as an eschatological vision of some future temple that in the latter days will resemble the garden of Eden;[43] others have treated the image of the trees transplanted into the Temple court as "purely figurative,"[44] the "real" subject of the sentence being the righteous man, not the tree. There is a parallel instance in Ps. 52:8 where the righteous man had compared himself to "a green olive tree in the house of God." This reference too has often been seen as mere trope or figure, as though only the righteous man and not the tree is to be located "in the house of God." But it seems that a sensitive reading obliges us to take seriously there as in Psalm 92 the mutual testimony of the tree and the righteous man, both having a relation to the sanctuary. In 92:13 we have the emphatic *šĕtûlîm* (planted) and *yaprîḥû* (they shall flourish) applied very distinctly to the trees themselves. It is they, as much as the *ṣadîq*, who are said to flourish in the courts of our God and produce fruit in their old age. This is not trope or "figure" but the summoning of nature to bear witness. Indeed the witness of the trees "transplanted in the house of the Lord" continues for three verses, beginning as simile but proceeding to the greater immediacy of metaphor. Clearly the trees are saying something of crucial importance in the poem, representing perhaps the deepest of the "deep thoughts" (v. 5) of which we are told the poem consists.

It may be suggested that the trees "transplanted" here into the house of God are no other than the cedar timbers of which the house and court were constructed (1 Kings 5:6). Olivewood and figures of palm trees were also used in the construction (ibid., 6:31, 32). The trees or timbers are thus literally "transplanted" into the house of God. It is there in the Temple that they are gathered, so to speak, into the artifice of eternity; they remain stout and fresh and bring forth "fruits" in their old age. We are talking indeed of the organic life of nature, but nature has been raised and sanctified, inserted (literally) into the structure in which God and man meet. The witness of the natural world is part of that meeting, built into the fabric of the building as it is built inseparably into the fabric of the poem. By evoking this as the final triumphant image in this poem, the cunning poet has found a term of resolution; no longer defeated and betrayed by those images and signs of growth and vitality by which man is linked to the organic life of nature, he can now establish the covenantal discourse firmly on the three foundations of man: God: nature. The best gloss on this passage is again in one of the poems of the great seventeenth-century metaphysical poets. I refer to George Herbert's "Virtue."

> Sweet rose, whose hue angrie and brave
> Bids the rash gazer wipe his eye:
> Thy root is ever in its grave,
>   And thou must die. . . .
>
> Only a sweet and vertuous soul,
> Like season'd timber, never gives;
> But though the whole world turn to coal,
>   Then chiefly lives.

Herbert is likewise in this poem seeking to define the status of the righteous man ("a sweet and vertuous soul"). The righteous man is as much a part of the natural world as the sweet rose whose root is ever in its grave but, through the image of the seasoned timber that "never gives," nature itself is raised into the sphere of Grace. Herbert's poem is part of a collection entitled "The Temple," the "seasoned timber" here as in our psalm being part of the structure of that temple. In Herbert's discourse too the temple and its forms of worship are constituted by the language and images of the poetry.

Psalm 92 ends with the same extraordinarily central and purposeful verb *lĕhaggîd* that we noted at the beginning of the poem in verse 2. Now that he has completed his exploration of these nature images and reached through that exploration a kind of resolution, the poet sums up what has been achieved in the words "To declare [or expound] that the Lord is upright: / he is my rock and there is no unrighteousness in him" (15). There is a difficulty about the subject of the hanging infinitive *lĕhaggîd* (to declare). Who declares? Most translators run the verse on from the previous verse, making the righteous man (or the trees?) the authors of the exposition or cunning speech signified by *lĕhaggîd*. But it is difficult to justify this interpretation on linguistic grounds. The verb *yihyû* (they will be) of the previous verse could not normally govern such an infinitive, i.e., "they will be (stout and fresh) to declare." Sensing this difficulty Abraham Ibn Ezra suggested an implicit subject such as "all mankind." The verse is thus saying that, as a result of what we have heard, all mankind will be led to declare. . . . But the truth seems to be that *lĕhaggîd* is a kind of absolute expression; it does not have a subject except insofar as the whole psalm is its subject. In this it is precisely parallel to the *lĕhaggîd* of verse 2, which has reference to the whole poetic exercise that it announces. We now hear that the discourse has been

satisfactorily completed and with it, the "uprightness" of God who is the
creator of man and nature has been affirmed for he has raised the
righteous man above the transience of the merely natural into the permanence of dialogue. The final *lĕhaggîd* thus strikes a note of triumph.
As though to say exposition has been achieved and it has succeeded; the
righteous man has "borne fruit" in his old age.

The two occurrences of *lĕhaggîd,* one at the beginning, the other at the
end, thus form an *inclusio:* the poem ends where it begins as in the
repeated "Bless the Lord, O my soul" in Psalms 103 and 104. But here it
signifies the completion of a more strenuous exercise in meditation. The
psalm actually consists of more than one *inclusio.* If we attend to its inner
structure we shall see that it is arranged in something like four concentric
circles forming what is sometimes called a chiasmus (see fig. 1). We have
a series of four terms or topics in the order of A, B, C, D—they are
declaring (lĕhaggîd, 2), references to the *Temple worship* (2, 3), *blossoming
(biprōaḥ,* 7), and *height (mārôm,* 8). Then in the second half of the poem
we have the same key terms or topics in the reverse order of D, C, B, A,
viz., *height (wattārem,* 10), *blossoming (yiprāḥ, yaprîḥû,* 12, 13), *the Temple (bêt
YHWH,* 13), and *declaring (lĕhaggîd,* 15). The poem is thus tightly organized: at its center is the notion of height dialectically shared in by the
righteous and the wicked. Then we have the references to blossoming (7,
12), with the tree making good the impermanence of the grass. But in
the circle beyond that we have the pieties of the Temple worship, the
dialogic space that has become the private inner space of the *ṣadîq* from
which the wicked are excluded. This is conveyed in verses 2 and 3 by the
mention of the morning and evening devotions, the sounds of the harp
and the lyre, and in verse 13 by the reference to the "trees" or timbers
"planted" in the house of the Lord. All these terms and images are finally
enclosed by the intensely active verb *lĕhaggîd,* which signifies the action
of the poem itself, its contrivance, its dynamic form, and, above all, its
purpose.

Ultimately this verb *lĕhaggîd* implies that the purpose of such a poem is
not just "to be," as Archibald MacLeish would have it, but "to declare," to
strive, to make a statement. The use of the verb in the infinitive is
comparable in fact to the infinitival *laʿăśôt* from Gen. 2:3 referred to in an
earlier chapter.[45] The story of the creation of the world concludes with
this hanging infinitive—"which God had created *to make.*" As we noted
then, the purposeful use of the verb "to make" without a clear object
implies a lack of closure. Creation continues. Similarly in Psalm 92 the
infinitive *lĕhaggîd* denies closure. In spite of the close-knit chiastic structure of the poem, the verb *lĕhaggîd,* "to go on expounding," points beyond the limits of the poem, even, in a manner, explodes those limits.
Not balance and symmetry remain but a continuing witness.

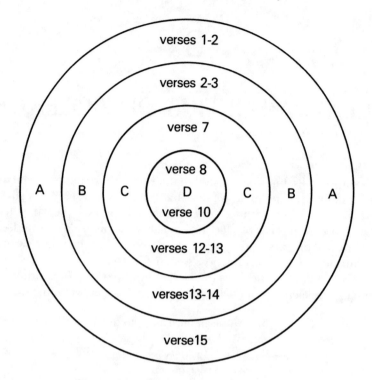

Fig. 1. The Chiastic Structure of Psalm 92

A = References to the poetic composition itself. Key term *lĕhaggîd*.
B = References to Temple worship.
C = "Blossoming" of the wicked/righteous. Key term *prḥ*.
D = "Height." Key term *rûm*.

·8·

HOSEA: A POETICS OF VIOLENCE

The example of Psalm 92 suggested that we had two structural principles in collision. On the one hand we saw that the chiasmus served to enclose the poem, giving it a rounded and balanced shape; on the other hand there was a certain lack of closure indicated for us by the untethered *lĕhaggîd*, "to go on expounding," as though to say that the poem's work is never finished. This contradiction within the structure can be seen in many other psalms. Sometimes the element of openness or continuation is stronger, the element of enclosure, weaker. Psalm 6 will illustrate this:

> To the Chief Musician on strings, to the *šĕmînît*.
> A Psalm of David.

1. O Lord, *rebuke* me not in *thy anger*,
   nor *chasten me* in *thy hot displeasure.*
2. Be gracious unto me, O Lord; for I am weak.
   O Lord, heal me; for my bones *are shaken [nibhălû];*
3. *My soul [napšî]* too is *deeply shaken [nibhălâ mĕʾōd].*
   And thou, O Lord, how long?
4. *Turn back [šûbâ],* O Lord, deliver *my soul [napšî]:*
   save me on account of thy steadfast love.
5. For in death there is no remembrance of thee:
   in Sheol who shall give thee thanks?
6. I am weary with my groaning:
   all the night I soak *my bed,*
   with *my tears my couch* I moisten.
7. *My eye* is wasted because of grief;
   it grows dim because of all my *enemies.*
8. Depart from me all you *workers of iniquity;*
   for the Lord has heard *the voice of my weeping.*
9. The Lord has heard my *supplication;*
   the Lord accepts my *prayer.*
10. All my enemies shall be *put to shame [yēbōšû]*
    and *deeply shaken [yibbāhălû mĕʾōd];*
    let them *turn back [yāšûbû]* and be *put to shame
    [yēbōšû],* in a moment.

Robert Alter has properly drawn attention to the incremental principle in Hebrew versification. There is a "dynamic movement" from one

136

half-verse to the next; parallelism is not merely the rhyming or echoing of the same idea but involves intensification, a mounting passion, as the idea or perception is carried forward incrementally.[1] But this principle does not only apply to the movement from verse to verse; as we saw in relation to the Song of Solomon, it may be said to govern large poetic structures. There the "plot" advances purposefully even as it stays with a number of central dream motifs.

Psalm 6, as set out above, exhibits the incremental principle both in the inner organization of its verses and also in the chainlike progression from one verse to the next. The links of the chain are indicated by the italics in the above version. The first verse provides a simple example: anger (*'ap*) is intensified into "hot displeasure" (*ḥamātĕkā*) in the second half of the parallelism. The "chastening" of verse 1 is linked to the more particular physical afflictions mentioned in 2. From the shaking of the bones in verse 2 we advance to the profounder anguish of the *nepeš* or life itself of verse 3, the same stem *bhl* linking the two. The *nepeš* is picked up again (like the link of a chain) in verse 4 as the speaker cries to God to save his life. The tricolon of verse 6 marks the advance from groaning to tempestuous weeping, while the notion of weeping leads by association and intensification to the actual wasting of the eye itself in the onset of premature old age in verse 7. In verse 8, YHWH is said to hear "the voice of my weeping." The weeping that had hitherto been a simple physical reflex, an inevitable response to pain, now has a voice. No longer a mere inundation, it becomes a prayer, a supplication, a language—indeed a reflexive term for the poem itself, for that is evidently what is referred to as "the voice of weeping." The final verse links up with 2 and 3 to form an *inclusio;* the verb *nibhal*—to be shaken or terrified—has now been transferred to the enemies, the evildoers who had been the agents of the speaker's trouble. It is their turn now to be affrighted and shaken (*yibbāhălû*). In fact the verb for "turn" (*šûb*) is here picked up from verse 4 to form a second *inclusio*. God was then asked to "turn back" and save the speaker's life from the dangers and terrors that threatened it. It is as a result of that entreaty that the enemies in their "turn" are now seen to "turn back." The reverses that the speaker has suffered have yielded to a reverse suffered by opponents and, in that way, the direction of the poem has itself been reversed. The verb *šûb* takes on a powerful, meta-poetic force; it also attracts to itself by paronomasia the very like-sounding stem *bôš* (the same consonants reversed), signifying the shaming or humiliating of the same enemies. The enemies not only suffer a reverse, they are put to shame. The second half of 10, which picks up the verb *yēbōšû* from the first half, thus intensifies and carries the idea forward by the deadly wordplay *yāšûbû . . . yēbōšû*, the incremental principle giving to this final verse a dynamic, expectant quality. This expectancy is raised to an even higher pitch by the extraordinary closing word, *rāgaʿ*, "in a moment," or better, "of a sudden." The poem ends on a note of astonishment, the very negation of closure. We are left wondering how this sudden, momentary reversal will take place. No explanations are offered. We must wait and see.

Closure and the denial of closure thus meet together in this final verse. A poem seemingly closed leaves us with a word hanging in the void. We must complete the idea ourselves, or perhaps we must ourselves await the historical fulfillment of which that word is an intimation. The poem exhibits an aesthetic shape but it also exhibits the denial of that shape; there is coherence, but also incoherence.

II

It sometimes seems that a true understanding of biblical poetics must do justice to this element of incoherence as a feature of what we have termed "covenantal discourse." We discern again and again in such discourse the presence of structural principles that do not fuse to form an "Aristotelian" order. To get a better understanding of this aspect we may now turn to a more extended and complex example, viz., the book of Hosea. This is a remarkably "covenantal" text. In fact, central to the whole prophecy is the image of a marriage bond that holds in spite of betrayal (3:1), of a covenant transgressed (8:1) and reforged (2:20–22), one that binds Israel to God and both to the world of natural things. At the same time the text of this prophecy with its radical mixture of prose and verse shows a remarkable degree of incoherence.[2] The editors of this book in the Anchor Bible remark that "the text of Hosea competes with Job for the distinction of containing more unintelligible passages than any other book of the Hebrew Bible."[3] Seemingly disconnected sentences, cryptic expressions, words that stand out jaggedly from their context have placed enormous difficulties in the path of form-critics looking for homogeneous literary units. Some commentators have resorted to wholesale emendation, including the radical reordering of verses and blocks of verses.[4] One of the more perceptive editors, H. W. Wolff, seeks to overcome the difficulty by suggesting that there are overall structures that he terms "kerygmatic units"; these contain within them briefer, less homogeneous "rhetorical" (i.e., literary) units.[5] There is thus an enveloping order even though its outlines cannot be clearly seen. But he never really establishes the nature of these larger "kerygmatic" structures. Freedman and Andersen frankly acknowledge "the turbulence of Hosea's thought," the absence in it of anything resembling poetic regularity. But they add that this may be "the result of an artistry far more sophisticated than anything previously suspected."[6] This points us in the right direction.

If we forget the need to establish the literary unity of the text and concentrate instead on its effect on readers throughout the generations, we surely have in Hosea poetry of great and concentrated power. He is classed among the "minor" prophets only because of the brevity of his *oeuvre*—fourteen chapters in all—but he is in every sense a major writer. Alonso-Schökel terms him very aptly "a great poet and prophet of love."[7] But Schökel chooses a relatively smooth passage (11:1–9) as his example. What we need are some categories for comprehending the power of Hosea's more typically fractured style.

We may take chapter 5 as an example. It has a truly "kerygmatic" opening, with the familiar *šimĕʿû . . . haʾăzînû* (hear . . . give ear), as of the opening of a lawsuit, which we found in the Song of Moses (Deuteronomy 32) and again in Isaiah 1.[8] As so often in this prophet, God is speaking in the first person:

> 1. Hear this, O priests;
>   and hearken, O house of Israel;
>   and give ear, O house of the king;
>   for yours is the judgment,
>   because you have been a snare on Mizpah,
>   and a net spread upon Tabor.
> 2. And the apostates are deep in slaughter,
>   and I am a chastisement to them all.

We have a glimpse of idolatrous cults on the two heights mentioned in the second half of verse 1 and the priests are charged with responsibility for this. But no clear indication of what is going on emerges. In verse 2 the spluttered alliteration of *wĕšahăṭâ šēṭîm heʿĕmîkû* is doubtfully rendered as "the apostates are deep in slaughter." There is possibly an allusion here to gangs of murderers on the highway, but the phrase is cryptic to the point of incomprehensibility. Later in the book it will be to some extent elucidated when the same syllables re-echo in 9:9 as *heʿĕmîkû šiḥētū*—"they are deeply corrupted"—speaking of Israel's crimes both in the past and in the present. Throughout Hosea words re-echo, the second occurrence often providing an antithesis, or else, as in the present instance, a momentary flash of meaning to clarify what would otherwise be totally obscure. The "lawsuit" continues with God seeming to level his bitter charges against the "house of Israel" and Israel seeming to answer them.

> 3. I know Ephraim,
>   and Israel is not hid from me:

for now Ephraim, thou hast been promiscuous,
Israel is defiled.

4. Their doings will not allow them to return to their God:
   for the spirit of harlotry is within them,
   and they have not known the Lord.

5. And the pride of Israel shall testify against him:
   Thus Israel and Ephraim shall stumble in their iniquity,
   Judah also shall stumble with them.

6. They shall go with their flocks and with their herds
   to seek the Lord,
   but they shall not find him;
   he has withdrawn himself from them.

7. They have dealt treacherously against the Lord:
   for they have begotten strange children:
   now shall a month devour them with their belongings.

It will be noted that the first-person utterance of verses 1–3 gives way in 4 to the third person. The judge or plaintiff now seems to distance himself from the accused, who have not only played the harlot but "have not known the Lord." "Knowing the Lord" is a primary category in Hosea.[9] Ephraim's not knowing the Lord is reflected in the arrogance of his reply ("the pride of Israel shall testify against him"), though the content of that reply is only hinted at as a "stumbling in iniquity" (5). In verse 6 there is a sharp reversal. Swerving aside suddenly from the tale of Israel's iniquities, the prophet recalls for us the great desert trek with the people departing from Egypt "with their flocks and with their herds" (cf. Exod. 10:9); we get a fleeting image of the loving bride going out to seek her divine bridegroom as in Jer. 2:2. An evil and retrograde generation momentarily becomes something like the Shulammite in the Song of Solomon as they go out "to seek the Lord; but they shall not find him; he has withdrawn himself from them." It is a poetry of love and estrangement, but neither can be entertained without the other. That is the special agony of Hosea. An angry God—and he is never angrier than in Hosea's prophecies—is nevertheless haunted by his own unsubjugated affections. It is this oscillation of love and hate, nearness and distance, already intimated for us in the story of Hosea and his estranged wife in chapters 1 and 3, that shatters continuities. Images of love carry with them their dark antithesis. Images of anger are menaced and arrested by memories of devotion. The summarizing judgment comes in verse 7. The very children of the estranged bride are of doubtful paternity (cf. 2:4) and so the sentence of death is pronounced: a month will suffice to devour the people and their gods. The language is again elliptic, obscure; its violence comes across more clearly because of the tremendous resistance that the words have to overcome.

These verses of chapter 5 are by no means the most difficult in the book. The last three verses of chapter 4 or the first three verses of chapter 8 or the latter half of chapter 12 are even more entangled and compressed. In Psalms too, we found the tensions and drama of the covenant relation but nothing as cryptic (Jerome's word is *commaticus*) and as discontinuous as this tormented language of Hosea. Perhaps the reason for this lies in the special angle, or what is nowadays termed the "implied speaker" of this prophecy. If Psalms gives us man addressing God, then Hosea more than any other book of the Bible (even more than Jeremiah or Isaiah) gives us God's side of the relationship. It is dominated by the first-person mode of address as God himself cries out, cajoles, reprimands, mourns, and debates with himself. If the Psalms give us the inner zone of human meditation, Hosea gives us fundamentally "the prophet's reflection of, or participation in, the divine pathos,"[10] as that pathos is directed toward man. It is as though we were viewing the dark side of the moon or rather as though we were viewing the earth from the direction of the moon. The strangeness of the view accounts for the strangeness of the discourse.

When viewed from the godward side, the tensions that characterize the covenantal relation are profounder and more agonizing than those which characterize the human side of that relationship. The passage just cited will give us an idea why. We may consider again the remembered moment of devotion in verse 6, a devotion remembered only to be at once rejected and spurned.

> They shall go with their flocks and with their herds
> to seek the Lord;
> but they shall not find him;
> he has withdrawn himself from them.

It will be seen that the verse announces an alternative to relationality, viz., withdrawal, absence. "He has withdrawn himself from them." This is no longer even the dark side of the moon; here we have a God who is liable to orbit into stellar regions where the earth itself is forever lost to view. It is such absence that is threatened in the phrase "they shall not find him; he has withdrawn himself from them." The language of Hosea opens up for us the abyss of divine absence. Further down, the notion of threatened withdrawal and absence is repeated with even greater violence:

> For I will be to Ephraim as a lion,
> and as a young lion to the house of Judah:
> I, even I, will tear and go away;
> I will take away, and there shall be none to deliver.
> I *will go and return to my place*,

till they acknowledge their offence, and seek my face:
in their affliction they will seek me.

(5:14–15)

God's "returning to his place" *('āšûbâ 'el-mĕqômî)* is the "turning" to end
all turnings. The verb *šûb* in its various inflections occurs more than
twenty times in this prophet.[11] In particular Hosea is the prophet of
"turning" in the sense of repentance (see 14:2, 4, etc.). But here we have
a turning *away* that seems to negate the very possibility of repentance, of
a restoration of bonds. Ominously, God will return to his "place," a place
where there is neither covenant nor the language of covenant. No longer
a shepherd, no longer a loving husband, not even an offended husband,
he has become a ravening lion who tears off the flesh of his victim and
retires with it to his "place." The abyss of absence is that which here
threatens the prophet's audience. It is an absence in which the House of
Israel will be lost, its identity gone. But no less it is an abyss that, so to
speak, threatens God himself. It is this dread prospect that accounts for
the tormented quality of the language and for the deep pathos of this
prophet. He has sensed the agony of God himself as he seeks to hold on
to the human bond that is all that stands between himself and the void of
absence:

> How shall I give thee up, O Ephraim?
> How shall I surrender thee, O Israel?
> how shall I make thee like Admah?
> how shall I set thee like Zeboim?
> My heart is overturned within me,
> all my compassion is kindled.
>
> (11:8)

This is the accent of "divine bafflement, of God's struggling with himself."[12] It issues in the familiar imagery of the overthrow of the Cities of
the Plain (Admah and Zeboim are the twins of Sodom and Gomorrah;
see Deut. 29:23) and also the familiar stem *hpk*, signifying the "overthrow" of those cities. But in one of those extraordinary inversions of
language so characteristic of Hosea, the term is used for God himself. He
is, so to speak, threatened by that same punishment—"my heart is over-
turned *[nehpak]* within me." To destroy Israel in the manner of Admah
and Zeboim is for God to condemn himself to a kind of "overthrow," to
negation. For God's need of Israel is no less than Israel's need of God. If
it is true that the "I" of Psalms is constituted by the covenant relation and
that nature itself is likewise not so much a presence as a functioning part
of a covenant drama, then it is even truer to say that God himself, the
third partner in the covenant, is only "present" in the sense that he is

given existence for us by that relation. It is when Israel hears, that God may be spoken of as One (Deut. 6:4). Without that hearing and that bond, God himself is inaccessible. Moreover, the bond of which we speak is a bond of language. In discourse God is present to man. God speaks to us through words and in words. God's "person" is for the rabbis inseparable from Torah. Beyond words there is simply the interstellar space, the "place" so ominously hinted at in 5:15a. There we will seek God in vain and there too he will seek us in vain.

We now begin to see why words are so important to this prophet, not words in organized "wholes" but words thrown out, rescued from the abyss, tormented into a meaning that will make possible some reciprocity between God and Israel. They are inadequate, but they are all we have. Through them we can still somehow reach out to him ("Take with you words and turn to the Lord," 14:2); through them God can still make a desperate bid to reach us. This is what happens in the desert, the *midbar*, referred to in chapter 2. It is a place of terror but also of assignation:

> Therefore, behold, I will allure her,
> And bring her into the desert *[hammidbār]*,
> and speak *[dibbartî]* to her heart.
>
>   (2:14)

Desert and speech are here joined by the wordplay of *midbār . . . dibbartî.* The two, say the rabbis, are the same.[13] The desert is a place of absence but there are words in it, voices that echo as we wander erroneous in its emptiness and desolation, like the voice that Isaiah speaks of: "A voice cries out in the desert: / Prepare the way of the Lord" (Isa. 40:3). Hosea returns in chapter 13 to the dialectic of presence and absence in the desert, recalling once again the Exodus from Egypt and the great trek across the wilderness of Sinai: "I knew thee in the desert, / in the land of great drought" (13:5). In the desert we have a verbal encounter divorced almost from physical circumstances. In "a land of great drought" God "knew" us and we "knew" him. Of course, it is much easier to find a settled land and there to worship according to established, less naked forms, with a shrine, a ritual, a sustaining myth of seasonal care and fertility. But there in the settled land the word itself may be forgotten, the word of pure naked summons and response. That word and the forgetting of the word are very much the theme of the prophet Hosea:

> When they were fed, they became sated
> When they were pastured, they became full;
> they were filled, and their heart was exalted;
> therefore they have forgotten me.
>
>   (13:6)

In the desert void the word is sounded; in the fullness of Canaan it is forgotten. The prophet Hosea seeks to mediate that word, to recall us to it in its intensity, its ambivalence, its fugitive luminosity. We are at a great distance here from the Greek logos, for the words of which we speak often lack a rational form or *telos;* they are to be found in isolation from one another with great gaps in between, their meanings undetermined, contradictory, discontinuous—wandering signifiers that return upon us with a dreadful pertinacity.

III

The naming of names is the very matter of Hosea's prophecy. It is the act with which the book begins. After he has married Gomer, daughter of Diblaim, Hosea is commanded to give highly enigmatic names to their three children. The search for the meanings hidden in those names will continue through the fourteen chapters. Their first child, a son, will be called Jezreel—"God will sow." It is first taken as a name of menace— "for yet a little while, and I will visit the blood of Jezreel upon the house of Jehu" (1:4). The whole bloody history of the Northern Kingdom and its rulers going back to the time of Ahab and Jezebel would now reach a culmination in the turmoil that followed the reign of Jeroboam the son of Joash, grandson of Jehu (2 Kings 15). By an ominous wordplay of *yiśrāʾēl/yizrĕʿeʾl* the fate of Israel as a whole will be involved in the blood visited upon the house of Jehu, "for I will break the bow of Israel in the valley of Jezreel" (1:5). The name with its dread echo will reach out to embrace the scattering of the Northern Kingdom, when Israel would be overthrown and exiled to Asshur (2 Kings 17:6). Then God would sow indeed; he would sow the name in the valley of Jezreel and from it would spring up armed men. The second child, a daughter, would be called *Lōʾ-Ruḥāmâ,* "Unpitied"—"for I will no longer have mercy on the house of Israel, to forgive them at all" (1:6). The third child, a son, will receive the name *Lōʾ-ʿAmmî,* "Not-My-People"—"for you are not my people, and *I will not be your* God" (1:9). Actually, a fourth name is embedded in this last verse. The God who had identified himself in his first encounter with Moses by the name *ʾEhyeh* (I-will-be) (Exod. 3:14) now announces his new, more dreadful name of *Lōʾ-ʾEhyeh* (I-will-not-be). The dark abyss of absence is here glimpsed in this negation of the name whereby God had been known and his promise given. *Yizrĕʿeʾl, Lōʾ-Ruḥāmâ, Lōʾ-ʿAmmî,* and *Lōʾ-ʾEhyeh* now come together as the signs of a non-meeting, an encounter between a No-People and a No-God. The dreadful reversal of all norms is here glimpsed, the day of Jezreel indeed, a day of sowing and scattering the storm and of reaping the tempest (8:7).

But all these names contain their own antitheses. In fact they are themselves antitheses, names that exist only by virtue of that which is denied. We are haunted by their contraries just as God in his anger is haunted by his own unsuppressed and unsuppressible love. *'Ehyeh* echoes again in the lyrical closing chapter, *'ehyeh kaṭṭal lěyiśrā'ēl:*

> *I-will-be* like the dew to Israel:
> he shall flower like the lily,
> and cast forth his roots like the Lebanon.
>
> (14:5)

'Ehyeh will reassert himself just as *Yizrě'e'l* will become the sign of a new growth of bounty and blessing. "Sow to yourselves *[zirě'û]* righteousness, reap by love," the prophet would declare (10:12).[14] Already in the second chapter, *Lō'-'Ammî* and *Lō'-Ruḥāmâ* have slipped into their opposites: "Say to your brothers, *'Ammî;* / and to your sisters, *Ruḥāmâ*" (2:1). Words are essentially reversible, they can be turned around. That is the great turning around of which the final chapter speaks, the "turning" of God's anger (14:4) and the "turning" of the people to God (ibid.). And as this happens, so Unpitied becomes Pitied—"for in thee the fatherless finds mercy *[yěruḥam]*" (14:3). Indeed, paradoxically, we discover God's unconditioned love only through the negating of it. It is then that it sweeps across us to haunt and importune us. In the sign *Lō'-'Ammî* we discover the trace of its opposite. Negation is itself negated. Through the language of denial, God's overmastering love is manifested. It cannot be overcome, nor can the name *'Ammî* be eradicated. The attempt to eradicate it simply establishes it and confirms it:

> And my people *('Ammî)* are bent on turning away from me; . . .
> But how shall I give thee up, O Ephraim?
> how shall I surrender thee, O Israel?
>
> (11:7, 8)

'Ammî, we may say, proves to be more powerful than its opposite.

The densest wordplay in this prophet involves the name Ephraim.[15] Salvation seems to come to Ephraim as a result of the ambiguities lodged in that amazing name. The punning of the vocables spurts out in all directions. Chapter 7 opens with the linking of *rop'î* (I would heal) with the name *'Eprayim.* Ephraim suggests healing but there will be no healing; far from seeking health, Ephraim is "full of adulterers *[měnā'ăpîm]* like an oven heated by the baker *['ōpeh]*" (7:4). The imagery of the baker's oven draws to itself by association images of devouring, of the heat of wine, and of "a cake not turned," the baking of an evil mixture in which Ephraim's identity is lost among the nations (7:8). In the next chapter Ephraim is linked by popular etymology to the term *pere'*, a wild ass—"a wild ass wandering alone" hiring lovers in Assyria (8:9). The metaphors are violently mixed but they are held together by the thread of consonantal wordplay, paronomasia. In 9:16, Ephraim will "bear no fruit" *(pĕrî)*, for "their root is dried up." But the word for fruit, in spite of the negative syntax, has here attached itself to Ephraim just as the word for healing *(rop'î)* had earlier on. In chapter 14 both of these etymologies will "return" as positive signs for the salvation of Ephraim. Then God will say, "I will heal *['erpā']* their backsliding" (v. 4), and he will turn to Ephraim and declare, "from me is thy fruit *[peryĕkā]* found" (v. 8). Ephraim, whose fertile countryside makes the name a synonym for lush vegetation, will now "blossom *[yiprah]* like the lily." "Those who *dwell* in his shadow shall *return* [with a play on *yāšūbû . . . yōšĕbê]*; they shall revive like corn, and blossom like the vine" (14:7). The newfound fertility of Samaria in the bounteous time to come has been attained by means of the play of phonemes in intense conjunction. Fertility is thus the final word for Ephraim but it has been prepared for by its opposite. If Ephraim is said in 9:16 to bear no fruit, that is a way of talking about fruitfulness. The poem will "heal the backsliding" of the word just as it will "heal the backsliding" of Israel (14:4). If in 13:15 Ephraim is said to flourish *(yaprî')* like the marsh plants that quickly shrivel when the hot desert wind blows from the east, then that language too can be redeemed and Ephraim can flourish indeed, like a rich garden, in the blessed time to come (14:7). Not only can the people be turned about, transformed, but language can be redeemed, can "turn," can reveal its unseen potentialities. Indeed, the very language of reproof and chastisement can become the key of promise. Hosea might have said with Feste in *Twelfth Night*, "A sentence is but a chevril glove to a good wit. How quickly the wrong side may be turned outward." But unlike Feste, Hosea plays in earnest; if he turns images and words inside out, it is because he has a purpose; the signs he seeks are marks of salvation. Wordplay is in this case a matter of life and death, for the prophetic function itself operates through and by the engagement with language.[16] "Inspiration" comes to the prophet as he manipulates words, and if we can in our turn disentangle the complexities of his language, we may come near to recovering some part of that same "inspiration."

IV

Ephraim primarily denotes fertility. This had been the etymology handed down from the patriarchal age: Joseph called his second son *'Eprayim* because "God has made me fruitful *[hipranî]* in the land of my affliction" (Gen. 41:52). If in Hosea Ephraim is in fact condemned to sterility, threatened with the emptiness and dryness of the desert waste, such images do not annul the notion of fertility. Fertility remains embedded in the name even though it may be negated or caricatured. The "wild ass *[pere']* wandering alone" to which Ephraim is linked in 8:9 is an image of unbridled sexuality. Elsewhere (in Jeremiah) the same creature is described as one that "snuffs up the wind in her desire; in her lust who can turn her away?" (Jer. 2:24). Conception is a blessing but not as Ephraim may conceive. In such turns of sound and sense it will be seen that fertility, though caricatured, is not left behind. The same applies to the strange obstetric imagery of 13:12–13. Ephraim's iniquity is "bound up"; though his mother is ready to give birth, "he could not present himself at the mouth of the womb." An infant arrested in the womb, a cake burnt on one side, a dried-up spring—all these strange images have reference to fertility even as they seek to deny it. Israel turns to the *Bĕʿālîm* "that give me my bread and my water, my wool and my flax, my oil and my drink" (2:5). For that Israel is condemned. But YHWH's ultimate promise to his people includes a reference to the same blessings. YHWH is not a vegetation deity—his Word was spoken in the desert—nevertheless, Israel has to know that "it was I who gave her the corn, and the wine, and the oil, and multiplied silver and gold for her" (2:8). The God who calls Ephraim to his high destiny is one for whom all natural gifts are transitory: he condemns Israel for failing to transcend the natural, for being "like a morning cloud and like the dew that passes early away" (6:4, 13:3). But paradoxically, when he turns back to Israel, he announces that he will *himself* be "like the dew to Israel" (14:5)—the transitoriness of the dew forgotten and only its freshness and blessedness remaining! His rain clouds will then bring fruit and abundance. There is here a dialectic of denial and accommodation. In the Book of Esther, we saw that the wealth and opulence of the Persian court are beheld in the critical perspective established by the actions (or inactions) of Mordecai and Esther. But the book will end with the Jews decreeing a feast as lavish as those of the Persians themselves (Esther 9:18f.). Similarly, after seeming to condemn the vanities of the earthly kingship of Ahasuerus, the chronicler will in the end record Mordecai's elevation to the rank of Grand Vizier (10:3). Here, likewise, in Hosea, YHWH stands at a maximum distance from the *Bĕʿālîm*, the gods of the earth; their powers are scorned; nevertheless, YHWH also preempts their function and privileges for himself.

This is the paradox with which Hosea grapples, quite consciously it would seem. He fiercely condemns the Baal-worshipers for their idolatrous rites, performed "on the hills and under oaks and poplars and terebinths, because the shadow thereof is good" (4:13), but when Israel finds its way back to the God of the desert, she will be granted the shade and scent of the great forest trees of Lebanon (14:7). More than that, God himself will, astonishingly, be seen to compare himself to a tree—the only time in scripture that he does so! "I am like a leafy cypress tree; / from me is thy fruit found" (14:8). It is no wonder that, after exercising his "wit" in so paradoxical and riddling a discourse, the poet/prophet should sum up the work in a metapoetic fashion reminiscent of Ps. 92:5–6 and say, "Whoever is wise, let him understand these things: / whoever is prudent, let him know them" (14:9). How are we to understand these paradoxes? If it is a problem for the biblical theologian, it is no less a problem for the student of literature.

But the most extraordinary of these contradictions has yet to be considered. It is that relating to the "sacred marriage." As is well known, at the heart of the Baal cult is the union of Baal with his sister-consort Anat: it is this *hieros gamos* that guarantees rain and fertility and it is this union that also helps to assure the cyclical order of the seasons. No prophet, hardly even Elijah, who personally slew the prophets of Baal after a spectacular contest on Mount Carmel (1 Kings 18), expressed fiercer opposition to this aspect of Baal worship than Hosea. Hosea's particular emphasis is on the sexual excesses that accompanied it (2:10, 4:13–15, 5:3). And yet the fundamental starting point for his own prophecy concerns Hosea's marriage with Gomer, which is intended to symbolize God's "marriage" with his consort, Israel![17] The name of their first child, "God sows," would also suggest to Hosea's auditors the "sowing" function of Baal, who plants his seed in the earth to assure fertility. As H. W. Wolff aptly remarks, Hosea develops a dialogue with the mythology of his day "in a remarkable process of adaptation of and polemic against this mythology." The shape of Hosea's imagery, he says, "is suggested by that which is condemned."[18] Israel's "whoring" after strange gods is beheld under the figure of Gomer's adultery and this in turn is to be seen as dramatizing the betrayal by Israel of her divine husband, i.e., the violation of a sacred marriage, which itself seems to have owed something to the Canaanite myth of Baal and Anat! The more strongly the union of husband (God) with consort (Israel) is insisted upon, the more heinous does the Canaanite myth and ritual appear. The Canaanite myth is thus used to attack the Baalist religion. It is affirmed and dissolved at the same time; it is, so to speak, deconstructed.

E. Jacob, who first pointed out this logical impasse, also suggested a way of comprehending it. After all, the story of Gomer and Hosea and by direct inference that of God and Israel, though a kind of "sacred marriage," is of a special kind. It is marked by rupture (or divorce) followed by remarriage. Union and reunion are due not to a cyclical movement but to a freely undertaken act of renunciation and then of repentance and return by the parties. We do not have seasonal repetition as in the fertility myths, but a new event, a creation. "This transfers the site of the marriage from nature to history and transforms a seasonal phenomenon into a unique event . . . the myth is overcome by being transcended."[19] The Canaanite mythologoumenon is here, but it has been destroyed from the inside.[20] Baal and Anat, we may say, cannot act freely; they are imprisoned in nature. By contrast, Israel is through her "divine marriage" made free from nature. Hence the marriage is contracted in the wilderness, where the blessings of the natural world are absent. But paradoxically those blessings will return as a result of obedience to a calling God who stands outside the automatic rhythm of nature. He calls and Israel answers or does not answer (2:15); he calls and the earth answers (2:22). Both man and nature retain their autonomy in the face of a God who is not a *ba'al* but an *'îš* (2:16), i.e., a husband in the sense of a partner to whom one is freely contracted and bound.

There is a poetic correlative to this aporia or ironical tangle that we have been considering. A myth based upon unique events, contractual relations, history, and creation will yield a poetics significantly different from the myths of an uncreated nature cycle. The latter will be marked by roundedness and closure, the former, by discontinuity and violence. Ultimately, the myths of nature, typically those of Anat or Ashterot, as these were known to the Hebrew prophets, are myths of the Great Mother. In their ambience we know no separation or absence; we are enclosed. This has advantages but it also has limitations. Geoffrey Hartman has perceptively remarked that "too much is anchored in the mother as beginning and end, womb and ultimate repose, principle and limitary horizon. Closure, inspired by her, could become idealized incest, claustrophobic vision."[21] Poetry cannot do without closure any more than men can do without nature, but the greatest poetry also escapes closure, opens itself to the abyss. And Hosea's work of prophecy belongs to the greatest poetry.

V

The first four verses of chapter 6 show us Hosea confronting the limits of nature mythology and the poetics of roundedness and closure that it yields. As noted earlier, God has threatened the people that if they do not seek him, he will leave them and go to "his place" (5:15). In the face of this radical threat of divine absence, Hosea now supposes a scene, a dialogue, in which the people do seek him; they make a gesture of seeming to "return" but God's response is one of frustration and distrust:

1. Come and let us return to the Lord:
   for he has torn, and he will heal us;
   he has smitten and he will bind us up.
2. After two days he will revive us;
   on the third day he will raise us up,
   and we shall live in his presence.
3. Let us therefore know, let us press on to know the Lord:
   his going forth is sure as the morning;
   and he shall come to us as the rain,
   as the latter rain that waters the earth.
4. O Ephraim, What shall I do with thee?
   O Judah, what shall I do with thee?
   for your love is like a morning cloud,
   and like the dew that early passes away!

Seen in relation to the text of Hosea as a whole, this passage is remarkable for its smoothness. The speech given to the people is, if anything, too smooth; the lines are of uniform length, neatly balanced, and they conclude with a fine flourish—"he shall come to us as the rain, / as the latter rain that waters the earth." It is all a good deal too pat, like Bildad's first speech to Job:

> If thou wilt seek God,
> and make thy supplication to the Almighty;
> if thou be pure and upright;
> surely now he will rouse himself for thee,
> and reward thee with a just habitation
> Though thy beginning was small,
> yet thy end will be very great.
>   (Job 8:5–7)

Both speeches suggest that we need only go through the motions of "seeking God" and the reward is "in the bag." The history of God's dealings with man has the rounded, inevitable quality of myth: thy beginning is small, but thy end will be great; when he is duly propitiated, God's blessing is inevitable; the early rain and the later rain are then sure to come. What is missing from such formulations is the untidiness, the undetermined quality of historical time, the openness of the covenant, the fearful freedom granted to both parties. The people have understood the problem of returning in terms of a seasonal cycle, as of a dying and rising god: "he has torn us, and he will heal us . . . after two days he will revive us; and on the third day he will raise us up." The language would work, as James Ackerman has pointed out, for a vegetation deity like Baal or Tammuz. The verses in fact are ironical, a piece of satire: "The repentance liturgy of the people is heavily ironic. YHWH is exasperated by it because Israel perceives her god as a vegetation deity whose return is as sure as the spring rains—not dependent on Israel's return to and respect for covenant law. Biblical literature is capable of highly sophisticated irony...."[22] When the passage is read in this way, God's reaction to Israel's repentance is seen to underscore the unsatisfactory nature of that repentance:

> O Ephraim, what shall I do with thee?
> O Judah, what shall I do with thee?
> For thy love is like a morning cloud,
> and like the dew that early passes away.

The divine bafflement expressed in the words "O Ephraim, what shall I do with thee?" is not only at Israel's failure to "know God" but at their failure to find a language appropriate to such knowledge. These rounded forms you are using, he seems to say, will not do. YHWH is not a rain god or a dew god, and yet on the other hand if you find the right response to his call, rain and dew will not be lacking either. They are, after all, necessary for survival in the world. Finding the right mode of discourse, indeed, one that will establish a due reciprocity between man, God, and nature and will yet guarantee their freedom and autonomy, becomes a survival issue.

VI

In the last two chapters of Hosea's prophecy we have the most violent negation of the myth of a pastoral bounty guaranteed by the return of the seasons, and at the same time we have the most emphatic preemption by YHWH of his role as source of natural blessing. There is no attempt at synthesis, but we are given words, words that we can "take with us." Chapter 13 exhibits once again the fundamental antithesis with which this prophet is constantly engaged:

> 6. When they were pastured, they became full;
> they were filled, and their heart was exalted;
> therefore they have forgotten me.
> 7. Therefore I will be *[wā'ĕhî]* like a lion to them;
> like a leopard I will lie in wait *['āšûr]* for them by the wayside.
> 8. I will meet them like a bear bereaved of her whelps,
> and I will rend their closed up heart,
> and there will I devour them like a lion:
> the wild beast shall tear them.

In verse 6 the Lord is a shepherd and the sheep shall not want; they have abundant pasture. But then the shepherd suddenly turns round to attack the flock; he has become a ravenous beast, a lion, a leopard.[23] Hidden in the words is the full irony of this reversal. *Wā'ĕhî* (I will be) resonates with *'ehyeh*, the divine name of promise.[24] But *'Ehyeh* has now become a beast of prey. This is not even the abstract negativity of *Lō'-'Ehyeh* as in 1:8, but something more dangerous, more terrifying. The actual source of danger is hinted at in verse 7 in the powerful paronomasia of *'āšûr* (I will lie in wait) and *'aššûr* (Assyria). The Assyrian threat has been lurking behind all these oracles, literally "lying in wait" for Ephraim (5:13, 7:11, 10:6). That threat now reveals itself as an enraged animal, a leopard, a lion, a bear deprived of its whelps, ravaging the people of Israel with privy paw. But behind the face of the leopard is *'Ehyeh* himself. It is he, the shepherd, who has become the devourer. The violence of the imagery is matched by the violence of the transitions. There is no "therefore" at the beginning of verse 7 in the Hebrew, just the connecting *wāw* (and). The poem itself is torn, fragmentary.

This is even more marked in the continuation of the above passage:

> 9. Thy corruption! Israel!
>   For against me, against thy help!
> 10. Where is/I am [*'ehî*/] thy king now?
>   that he may save thee in all thy cities?
>   and thy judges of whom thou didst say,
>   Give me a king and princes?

Andersen and Freedman very properly note on this passage that "its form-critical character . . . whether a speech or a fragment, cannot be established."[25] It cannot, in brief, be forced into a literary mold. *Šiḥetkā yiśrā'ēl* (Thy corruption! Israel!) of verse 9 recalls Deut. 32:5, *šiḥēt lô lō' bānāyw mûmām*, "not his the corruption, but the blemish of his sons." Here as there we have ambiguity; as we noted in an earlier chapter, the stem *šḥt* can signify the ruin inflicted on the people (as in the matter of the Flood or the overthrow of Sodom) or it can refer to the corruption of the people themselves that brings about that ruin. Most editors emend the texts so as to make the word fit smoothly into one meaning or the other. But it is probably more correct to see the language as to some extent out of control; meaning is not assured, like something existing prior to the composition. The prophet is seeking through words, through their plasticity and also through their refractoriness and the surprises they constantly spring, to gain a hold on a God-man relationship that has gone wildly wrong. God enters the sentences as he does in "normal" covenantal discourse and yet he stands outside, letting us destroy ourselves. To read the text unambiguously as "I will destroy you, O Israel" is to flatten out the jagged edges of the word *šiḥetkā*, which could just as easily mean, "You destroy yourself, O Israel." How can one mediate between these two meanings? Clearly it cannot be done. It is best to ignore meanings and to remain with the words and phonemes.

Likewise, *'ehî* (I am) in verse 10 is frequently emended to *'ayyê*, meaning "where," i.e., "Where is thy king?" etc.[26] Certainly the context seems to require the question "where," and such smoothing out can be justified. But we surely have in verse 10 the unsubdued and unsubduable echo of "I will be *[wā'ĕhî]* to them like a lion" from verse 7, and in verse 7 no emendation is possible. So that if *'ehî* in verse 10 is "where" it is also the *'ehî* of God himself in his fury and his mastery. *'Ehyeh* is in the poem, a formidable antagonist. The verses are saying, "Where is your king now, the one you caused to reign in defiance of me?/I will be your King./I will not be your King for you have brought destruction on yourselves./I will be your king in a way you little expect or desire." All these meanings somehow seem to be in the verses, lurking behind the potent ambiguity, indeed the incomprehensibility, of *'ehî*. God is balancing before us the possibilities of being and not being God. "To be or not to be," he seems to say, or rather, "To be *and* not to be." In verse 14 the same *'ehî* is repeated twice more. And here it is impossible not to hear the dreadful parody of the original word of promise from Exod. 3:14.[27] In a violent transition from being a redeemer, *'Ehyeh* has now become plagues and destruction!

> I would ransom them from the power of Sheol;
> I would redeem them from death.
> Alas/Where are/I will be/thy plagues, O death!
> Alas/Where is/I will be/thy destruction, O Sheol!
> Relenting shall be hidden from my eyes.
>
> (13:14)

In the dark and mysterious inwardness of God, the name *'ehî* gets twisted in many directions. It becomes a sigh, a groan ("Alas!"), a question ("Where?"), an affirmation ("I will be"), and the parody of an affirmation ("I will be death"). Blake asked in his poem "The Tyger": "Did he who made the lamb make thee?" The God of Hosea not only made both, he is both; he is shepherd and ravening beast; he redeems from death and he is our destruction in the same breath. The same signifiers bring all these meanings together. In the tempest of contradictory meanings, the only rock we can hold onto is the words themselves. *'Ehî* alone has continuity in the turbulence of its dizzily changing significations and the discontinuities of its context.

The final attempt to compel such names as *'Ehyeh, 'Aššûr, 'Eprayim,* and *Ruhāmâ* to yield a message of hope and salvation is made in the concluding chapter of this prophecy. The wordplay continues, indeed reaches a pitch of intensity that calls for the active cooperation of the reader, who

is summoned in the last verse to exercise his wit in unraveling the twisted
threads.

1. O Israel, turn to the Lord thy God;
   for thou hast stumbled in thy iniquity.
2. Take with you words, and turn to the Lord:
   Say to him, Forgive all iniquity, and take good:
   so we will offer the word of our lips instead of calves.*
3. Asshur shall not save us;
   we will not ride upon horses:
   nor shall we say any more, Our gods to the work of our hands.
   That in thee the fatherless finds mercy.
4. I will heal their backsliding,
   I will love them freely:
   for my anger is turned away from him.
5. I will be like the dew to Israel:
   he shall flower like the lily,
   and cast forth his roots like a tree of Lebanon.
6. His branches shall spread,
   and his beauty shall be like the olive tree,
   and his scent like Lebanon.
7. They shall turn that dwell in his shadow;
   they shall revive the corn,
   and blossom like the vine:
   his fragrance like the wine of Lebanon.
8. Ephraim! What more have I to do with idols?
   I answer him and look out for him:
   I am like a leafy cypress tree;
   from me is thy fruit found.
9. Whoever is wise, let him understand these things:
   whoever is prudent let him know them;
   for the ways of the Lord are right,
   and the just do walk in them:
   but the transgressors shall stumble in them.

*Or "we will offer the fruit of our lips."

Compared with chapter 13, this chapter seems at first sight to be a
smooth and oratorically rounded utterance.[28] But as soon as we try to
establish its nature and direction, it reveals itself as full of shifts and
discontinuities. Who, for instance, speaks in the first three verses? It
seems at first sight to be a dialogue between God and Israel, but if we
attend closely we see that it is only a wished-for dialogue constructed by
the prophet, in which God, referred to in the third person, invites a
movement of return, and Israel responds by abandoning idolatry and
false and empty rituals in favor of a more earnest mode of worship. At
the same time Israel is seen to give up the fateful connection with Asshur
and with Egypt ("Asshur shall not save us; / we will not ride upon

horses"). In other words, Hosea is proposing a scenario. It is an attractive, indeed intoxicating scenario, so much so that the language becomes cryptic as the phrases tumble out almost inarticulately one after the other:

> Asshur shall not save us;
> we will not ride upon horses:
> nor shall we say any more, Our gods to the work of our hands.
> That in thee the fatherless finds mercy.

In the first phrase, Asshur has been negatived, reversed *(ʾaššûr lōʾ . . .)*. The last phrase involves the healing of the dreaded name *Lōʾ-Ruḥāmâ*, for orphaned Israel now finds the way to God's mercy *(yĕruḥam)*. But how is all this to be brought about? How is Israel to say these wished-for things? Can Ephraim cease to be the "wild ass" embedded in his name and become instead the blessed "fruit of the lips" *(pārîm śĕpātênû)* of verse 2? It is a reverse as extraordinary as that desired for Gomer, who, in a scarcely-to-be-dreamt-of return to innocence, might one day become a loving and faithful wife. What comes out of 1–3 in short is not healing but the tension of a desire for such healing.

In verse 4 there is an unannounced shift as God invades the discourse, speaking in the first person. It is clear that in spite of the deceptive smoothness of the transition, this is not a reply to Israel's imagined utterance in 2–3. Verse 4a speaks not of a regenerate Israel but of a "backsliding" Israel, a people still culpable, sunk in idolatry. "Their backsliding" *(mĕšûbātām)* of 4a belongs to the same stem as the "turning" to the Lord *(šûbâ)* of 1a but it is the reversal of that reverse! We have here the same punning antithesis as in the brilliant phrase of Jeremiah, *šûbâ mĕšûbâ yiśrāʾēl*, "Return, turncoat Israel" (Jer. 3:12). Here in this passage of Hosea the antithetical wordplay underscores the discontinuity of the discourse. Israel bidden to *return* at the beginning of the oracle proves to be a *turncoat* when God pronounces his healing word in 4a. How can she then be healed? The answer to that is in the magnificent brevity of "I will love them freely." The two Hebrew words *ʾohăbēm nĕdābâ* represent a gesture of unconditioned grace. "I will love them gratis"—even, that is to say, without a gesture of turning on their part. God himself will do the turning ("my anger is turned away *[šāb]* from them"). The seasonal fertility now in which "Ephraim" will become "fruitful" and "blossoming" *(ʾeprayim . . . yiprah . . . perĕkā)* will not be the result of rituals of propitiation, nor the effect of the predetermined behavior of a god who is part of the natural process, but an unconditioned act of love. God will love Ephraim gratis. He will "answer" even unspoken acts of contrition.

In verse 8 there is a further uncertainty as to the speaker. Many trans-

lators render, "Ephraim will say, What have I to do any more with idols?"
but there is nothing in the Hebrew to correspond with "will say." The
speaker is more probably God himself, who in a sudden and unanticipated "turn" banishes idolatry. In the next phrase he neutralizes the
threat of Asshur, for the name Asshur is embedded in the words "I
answer him and *look out for him [wa'ăšûrennû]*."[29] It is as though God were
saying, "I answer him by taking care of the threat of Asshur!" The
marvelous turnabout has been achieved by violent reversals of language,
by paronomasia, by a dazzling concord of phonemes pointing now in a
new direction. He who is wise will understand these things. He will catch
the "scent of the Lebanon" in 6c. Also the scent of another text, namely
the Song of Solomon: "Honey and milk are under thy tongue; / and the
scent of thy garments is like the scent of Lebanon" (Song of Sol.
4:11). The love of God has marvelously found its voice, turning this
prophecy into a kind of Song of Songs, flooding it with tears, with dew
and rain. But unlike the ritual propitiation of chapter 6, where the
people turned to a deity who would revive them after three days and
reward them with the early and later rain, we have here an utterly free
gift. God will bestow his love unconstrained—*'ohăbēm nĕdābâ*. This does
not make for the rounded language of myth, where man and God neatly
collaborate in a well-designed *system* marked by closure. Language does
not reflect here the cycle of the seasons. We have rather words "thrown
out," fractured and urgent. But they work. "Take with you words and
return to the Lord," the prophet had urged. The words he speaks of are
the words of this very prophecy. Out of them the marvel will be produced. It is not for nothing that this chapter has become a great and
central liturgy of repentance, recited year by year on the great sabbath of
repentance preceding the Day of Atonement. The words are not mi-
metic, they do not record a process of "turning"; rather, they enact it,
they bring it about.

We remarked that verses 1–3 of this chapter represent a scenario in
which God bids Israel to turn and Israel speaks the desired words of
contrition. It was not a dialogue so much as a wished-for dialogue, the
words of an author in search of a character to act the role of penitent
who "turns" and is forgiven. When the words are truly heard and uttered
by readers down the generations, that scenario is fulfilled. This is also the
force of the startling and enigmatic phrase "I answer him and look out
for him" *('ănî 'ānîtî wa'ăšûrennû)*. The last word could be rendered: "and
I lie in wait for him." God awaits Israel's free response and he responds
with like freedom—"I will love them freely." Nature, the third partner in
the covenant, also responds when bidden, not obeying a seasonal
rhythm, but freely yielding her blessings.[30] That too, is intimated in this

striking verse: "I answer him and look out for him . . . from me is thy fruit found." That answering "answers" the answering of chapter 2:

> And it shall come to pass on that day,
> That I will answer, says the Lord;
> I will answer the heavens,
> and they shall answer the earth;
> and the earth shall answer the corn, and the wine, and the oil;
> and they shall answer Jezreel.
> And I will sow her to me in the earth;
> And I will have mercy on *Lō'-Ruḥāmâ,*
> and I will say to *Lō'-'Ammî,* Thou art my people;
> and he shall say, Thou art my God.
>
> (2:21–23)

As each covenantal partner answers the other in mutual responsiveness and freedom, the dread words of absence and negation are healed and are restored to their benign significations. If by a word the heavens and earth were created, by words the covenant is fulfilled. That is the greater miracle: the blessings of wine and fragrance and oil and dew that follow are the lesser miracle.

·9·

QOHELET: A HEBREW IRONIST

If the darker passages of Hosea show us God threatening to withdraw himself from man, then Ecclesiastes shows us what happens when man withdraws himself into the inwardness of his own consciousness and distances himself from God. Nowhere in Ecclesiastes is the I/Thou relationship evoked. God is referred to in the third person, and only as 'El or 'Elōhîm, never as YHWH, the God of intimacy and dialogue. Ecclesiastes is indeed the nearest the Hebrew Bible gets to pure monologue. It gives us the wise man cultivating his garden, striving for a kind of stoic self-sufficiency in which man has his own independent space. Of the Psalms we said that, though they are subjective, personal, they are never auto-biographical. The "I" is there the function of a relationship in which the reader can share; it is not the sign of an autonomous ego. By contrast, Ecclesiastes gives us a radically individualized statement. The speaker identifies himself for us in autobiographical fashion early on: "I, Qohe-let, was king over Israel in Jerusalem. And I gave my heart to seek and search out by wisdom concerning all things that are done under the heavens" (1:12). A little later on he lists some of his personal achieve-ments: "I sought in my mind how to stimulate my body with wine. . . . I made great works for myself; I built myself houses, I planted myself vineyards, I made myself gardens and orchards . . . I made myself pools of water to water a forest of trees . . . I also amassed for myself silver and gold . . . many mistresses . . ." (2:3–8). The concentration of first-person pronominal forms is without parallel elsewhere in Scripture. Qohelet could have said with Montaigne, "It is my portrait I draw . . . I am myself the subject of my book." What he mainly has to tell us of course in this extended discourse of the self is not the account of material achieve-ments—we hear little of these after the sentences quoted above from chapter 2—but the account of his mental voyaging, his self-discoveries in the region of "Wisdom" or ḥokmâ. He gave his heart, he tells us, to seek and search out by wisdom concerning all things that are done in the world (1:13). He is an observer of man and—like Bacon—of what men do, rather than what they ought to do. From this point of view his book is the nearest thing to humanism that the Bible has to offer, even a radical humanism. *Ḥokmâ* has many connotations in the Hebrew Bible. In many places it is equated with the fear of God (e.g., Ps. 111:10; Prov. 9:10; Job 28:28); elsewhere *ḥokmâ* is personified as God's partner in the work of creation (Prov. 3:19; 8:27). In Job 28, it is a divine mystery "hidden from the eyes of all living"; only those gifted beyond the reach of ordinary mortals can gain access to it. But here in Ecclesiastes, *ḥokmâ* is in the main a thoroughly human acquisition and includes a good measure of "wisdom for a man's self." Far from being a mystic path, *ḥokmâ* is more like the path of self-knowledge, a wisdom of experience in the course of which we learn something of our strengths and limitations. Far from enabling us to "know God," it leads us to recognize that we *cannot* know him, for "no man can find out the work that God has done from the beginning to the end" (3:11)! Such a wisdom leads to a detached appraisal of human possibilities and impossibilities. It is a disenchanted view that Qohelet offers us. He has advice for sure, in particular advice on how not to overstep the bounds that God has set for us. Watch your step, he says, when you go to the house of God, be careful how you speak, "for God is in heaven and thou upon earth: therefore let thy words be few" (5:1–2). In effect he says with Alexander Pope, "Know then thyself, presume not God to scan; / The proper study of Mankind is Man."[1] A breath of sober realism blows through these pages in which an aging king sums up his life and the things he has learned in it.

The great humanistic texts of the Western tradition that have celebrated such voyages of self-discovery have on the whole been felt as liberating, even joyful documents. Montaigne's *Essays* have been mentioned. They look back to Seneca's *Epistles* and forward to Rousseau's *Confessions* and Goethe's *Wilhelm Meister*. Here is the working-out of what has been termed "the Renaissance discovery of Man"—a discovery felt to be as momentous as the discovery of America or of the secret of planetary motions. To realize such experience to the full, to develop one's personality without commitment to system, dogma, or any aim beyond the magic circle of the self—all this has been seen, at least until our own century, as largely a positive quest, the final distillation of that wisdom derived from the oracle of Apollo himself in the dictum "Know thyself." The sages at Delphi had added the words "Nothing in excess." Qohelet seems to have caught the echo of both these *dicta* but how totally different they sound coming from the lips of this Jewish sage! If these are the aims of *ḥokmâ*—and he seems to agree that they are—then they lead not to joy and fulfillment, not to that gemlike flame of intenser life that Pater promised the studious artisan, but ultimately to *hebel*, i.e., vanity, nothingness, futility. It is the word that, reiterated some thirty times in the course of the book, sums up its lesson. It is *ḥokmâ*'s judgment on *ḥokmâ* itself: "Vanity of vanities, says Qohelet, all is vanity. . . . See I have acquired more and greater wisdom than anyone before me in Jerusalem; and my heart has seen much of wisdom and knowledge. . . . And I perceived that this also was a striving after wind" (1:2, 16, 17). Later on (2:15) he notes in a tone of world-weariness that there seems to be little to choose between the fates of the wise man, the *ḥākām*, and the fool. Why then, he asks, did I turn to *ḥokmâ*? That too he says is *hebel*. And he continues: "For of the wise man as of the fool there is no enduring remembrance; seeing that which now is, shall, in the days to come be entirely forgotten" (2:16). The wisdom that turns in upon itself and finds its aim as well as its origin in man himself is a wisdom without remembrance; in days to come it will be forgotten. That is why it is *hebel*, a mist, an emptiness. Qohelet turns again and again to this emptiness of a world without history, a world in which a man cannot tell what shall be after him under the sun (6:12), in which the dead are forgotten and have no continuance (9:5), in which there is no memory even of the exploit of a wise man who through his wisdom had saved a city from destruction (9:15). Human effort that exhausts itself in the realm of man is blighted. It yields a moment of significance, of celebration; there is a report in the daily paper and then all things return to the darkness from which they had emerged.

In this book Qohelet seems to be contemplating the very same phenomenon to which Pater had addressed himself in his conclusion to *The Renaissance*. He was speaking there of the impressions gathered by the individual mind:

> Every one of those impressions is the impression of the individual in his isolation, each mind keeping as a solitary prisoner its own dream of a world. Analysis goes a step farther still, and assures us that those impressions of the individual mind to which, for each one of us, experience dwindles down, are in perpetual flight; that each of them is limited by time, and that as time is infinitely divisible, each of them is infinitely divisible also; all that is actual in it being a single moment, gone while we try to apprehend it, of which it may ever be more truly said that it has ceased to be than that it is.[2]

But for Pater, to give oneself up to the flux of changing sensations is to live to the full; it is essentially life-enriching, carrying with it no aftertaste of futility. Above all, living in the actuality of the single moment is ultimately an aesthetic ideal, indeed *the* aesthetic ideal, as Pater himself clearly proclaims in the sequel to the above-cited passage: "Of such wisdom, the poetic passion, the desire of beauty, the love of art for its own sake, has most."[3] In devoting himself to *ḥokmâ* viewed in very much this fashion but in seeing it at the same time as *hebel*, utter futility, Qohelet defines for us the precise nature of the paradox with which this study is concerned. The aesthetic ideal is beheld, pursued, achieved, and also rejected. To follow *ḥokmâ* in the sense of the aestheticization of existence, the enjoyment of the moment, to catch the grace of each fleeting day is also Qohelet's stated aim. In one place he links together the good and the beautiful where *ṭôb* (good) takes on the aesthetic value that we noted earlier.[4] Here *ṭôb* and *yāpeh* (beautiful) are discovered in the zest of daily experience and work to which we give ourselves up without thought for anything beyond: "It is good and comely *[ṭôb 'ăšer-yāpeh]* for one to eat and to drink, and to enjoy the good of all his labour in which he toils under the sun all the days of his life, which God gives him: for it is his portion" (5:18). But over this ideal of the beauty of the achieved moment, the shadow of futility falls, for he sums it up with the remark, "For he should remember that the days of his life are not many, in which God provides him with the joy of his heart" (20). This is only one way of rendering that rather arcane Hebrew sentence. RSV plausibly reads it as a piece of advice on how to *forget* the brevity of life: "For he will not much remember the days of his life because God keeps him occupied with the joy in his heart." According to this rendering, the absorption in the joy of the moment and with it the aesthetic quest are a way of hiding oneself from our time-bound existence. But of course the implication is that such a hiding cannot long succeed. The mind cannot keep as a solitary prisoner its dream of a world, as Pater thought. Instead of joy and fulfillment we shall find panic and emptiness, in a word, *hebel*.

But the emptiness that now threatens is one more total and absolute than that signified even by *hebel;* it is death, the ultimate negation. It levels man and beast (3:19), the *ḥākām* and the fool (2:14), indeed, it levels the stillborn infant with the man who lives a thousand years (6:4–6). Death for Qohelet is not conceived in images of horror as it is for Job; he is not obsessed with the pit and with the worm that feeds sweetly on the dead in Sheol. On the contrary, the onset of death in chapter 12 of Ecclesiastes has a certain melancholy beauty. But Qohelet is haunted by death as absence, by the nothingness that awaits all human endeavor, that cancels out children, riches, beauty, and wisdom itself. The human voice, the memory of our being, is simply lost in the void. This is where his meditation has brought him, the final truth about man viewed simply as man.

> It is better to go to the house of mourning,
> than to go to the house of feasting:
> for that is the end of all men,
> and the living will lay it to his heart.
>
> (7:2)

Whatever thy hand finds to do, do it with thy strength, for there is no work, nor thought, nor knowledge, nor wisdom in Sheol, whither thou goest. (9:10)

Death as absence or negation, which is what he strives to communicate in these verses and the many others like them from the latter part of his book, corresponds to God's threatened absence as intimated in those grimmer verses from Hosea quoted in the previous chapter. What holds God to us is relationality, the bond of his covenant with man; when that is lost or threatened, we have the dreadful prospect of God disappearing from us into a void or an abyss, what I have termed the interstellar space. There we will never reach him and he will never reach us. When, as in Ecclesiastes, we see man turned in upon himself, when life is conceived from a human perspective without relation to that which is beyond man, then man and all he has lived for disappear into another void of total absence, that of the darkness of the grave, where no word will ever reach us. Such is human destiny, viewed without the aspect of covenant. Nothing is said directly of covenant in Ecclesiastes. That bond of relation which gives meaning to a world, purpose to human life, and shape to history, is implied by a kind of pointed silence, by an absence that seems to cry out and draw attention to itself. It defines itself, paradoxically, through the bleakness and emptiness of an existence in which it is never affirmed.

II

In this matter of relationality and the absence of relationality, special interest attaches to the sharp differences, the *swerves* that Ecclesiastes exhibits when it is set beside other books of the Bible to which it seems to be intertextually related. We mentioned Qohelet's envying the stillborn infant who "comes in vanity and departs in darkness" but who is better off than the man who had lived long and begotten many children but had died ignominiously (6:3–4). The same thought had come to Job: if only he had been an untimely birth, he would have been spared a lifetime of anguish and trouble (Job 3:16f.). He returns to the notion in chapter 10: "Why then hast thou brought me forth out of the womb? / Oh, that I had perished, and no eye had seen me!" (Job 10:18). But even as he pronounces his dreadful wish for nonbeing, Job has a sense of an intimate, indeed, unbreakable bond with a God in whose hands he always is in anguish or in joy, in life or in death: "Thy hands have made me and fashioned me together round about; / yet thou dost destroy me" (10:8). Job almost wishes he were not always in the hands of God, that he were not an objective of such immediate personal attention to a Creator who had poured him out like milk and curdled him like cheese. By contrast Qohelet has a sense of human existence turned in upon itself; the stillborn and the long-lived alike have their beginning in vanity, their end in darkness. Their significance terminates in their own being; they both arrive at one place and are alike forgotten. Qohelet seems to glance again at Job later in the same chapter. "It is well known that man is but man," he says, "nor may he contend with one who is mightier than he" (6:10). O. S. Rankin remarks that this may be a reflection on the dialogue in Job.[5] Job was that man who, claiming a direct bond of relation with God, dared to summon God to a lawsuit (Job 13:22). By contrast, Qohelet's essential skepticism is based upon the sense of an unbridgeable gap between God and man. No man can contend with God or summon him to a lawsuit. Man is but man, or as he says in another place, "God is in heaven and thou upon earth: therefore let thy words be few." It is Qohelet's answer to Job—a brave answer, but it leaves man facing the darkness alone. He cannot confront his maker "face to face."

In a later verse Qohelet seems to echo a famous saying of Micah. Micah had said,

> He has told thee, O man, what is good *[higgîd lĕkā 'ādām mah-ṭôb]*;
> and what does the Lord require of thee,
> but to do justly and to love true loyalty *[ḥesed]*,
> and to walk humbly with thy God?
>
> (Mic. 6:8)

Here is YHWH making his essential demand on the creature he has formed. What he desires of man is *ḥesed*, "troth" or "true loyalty," the very expression of the covenant bond that here links God and man, a humble "walking," an intimacy of unbroken dialogue. Qohelet seems to parody this verse with its resounding opening proclamation—"he has told thee, O man, what is good"—in Eccles. 6:12. "For who knows *what is good for a man [mah-ṭôb lā'ādām]* in this life, for the count of the days of his vain life which he spends like a shadow? *for who shall tell a man [yaggîd lā'ādām]* what shall be after him under the sun?" (6:12). In place of Micah's confident and joyful affirmation of what is good for man, because God has told him so, we have Qohelet's skeptical questions, "who knows what is good for a man? . . . who shall tell a man?" Seen from the side of man himself, from his isolated human perspective, we discover not *ḥesed*, i.e., that mutuality of a covenant love that makes suffering endurable, bestowing a meaning on our transient and painful existence, but rather a few days of vanity and emptiness, no more. In short, the *ḥākām*, or philosopher, surveys God, studies his doings, but he does not, like the man evoked in Micah's prophecy, walk hand in hand with YHWH. The difference in their postures is all important.

Again, in 8:17, Qohelet tells us that he has seen "all the work of God" *(kol-maʿăśeh hāʾĕlōhîm)*, but that it is ultimately incomprehensible. Again the phrase *maʿăśeh 'ĕlōhîm* or *maʿăśeh YHWH* has a rich and varied intertextual resonance. In Psalms it is a formulaic phrase for God's creative activity. Those who go down to the sea in ships see YHWH's works and wonders *(maʿăśê YHWH wĕniplĕʾôtāyw)* in the deep (Ps. 107:24); in Ps. 118:17, the speaker will live and not die so as to be able to recount God's works *(maʿăśê YH)*; in Deuteronomy and elsewhere the same verbal combination signifies God's triumphs in history (Josh. 24:31, Deut. 11:7); it can also be used as a synonym for the covenant itself, for the fullness of God's revelation to Moses and Israel (Exod. 34:10). In all these places, "the work of God" is something we see, know, and behold and, in seeing it, we are inwardly transformed. The Exodus passage is the most solemnly and grandly assertive of them all: "and all the people among whom thou art shall see the work of the Lord that I will do with thee, that it is tremendous."[6] In 8:17 Ecclesiastes seems in his skeptical fashion to be responding to such assertions. He has, he says, taken a philosophical survey of "all the work of God" and it has come to be for him not a transforming vision, an encounter with all reality, but an attempt to attain what is ultimately unattainable, "because though a man labour to seek it out, yet he shall not find it." Neither here nor anywhere else in his book does he deny this *maʿăśeh ʾĕlōhîm*, this "work of God." He is as sure as any biblical author of God's being and power, of the fact indeed of his government of the universe. Where he seems to go his own way is precisely on the matter of our being able to *know*, to *behold*, to be in communication with the omnipotence of the deity. As von Rad maintains, God for Qohelet is "beyond men's perception and comprehension. . . . Man never achieves a dialogue with his surroundings, still less with God." Here is Qohelet's point of departure from the other biblical teachers of wisdom.[7] Can we know the work of God? Through his language, through his echoing of other biblical texts, he raises precisely this kind of question and either leaves the question open or concludes that we cannot know and that the frustrated search itself merely confirms the emptiness and vanity of our human condition.

But of course there *is* a search. Qohelet is not a Stoic who has identified God with the *mundus* and is content to dissolve once again into its elements. He does not have the Stoic apathy or indifference. He is agitated by thoughts that wander through eternity. The absence of the dialogue relation is a felt absence; it is the negation of a something, of a presence that haunts the text and seeks to be defined. In chapter 3 there is an enigmatic verse that says: "He has made everything beautiful in its time: also he has set the mystery of the world in their heart, so that no man can find out the work that God has made from the beginning to the end" (3:11). "He has made everything beautiful in its time *[yāpeh bĕʿittô]*." If only we could be satisfied (Pater-like) with that moment of grace in which everything is beautiful! But we are made in such a way that the part does not satisfy us, that aesthetic delight in the beauty of the moment. It is the whole that we seek, "the work that God has made from the beginning to the end." Again a reference to the formulaic *ma'ăśeh 'ĕlōhîm*—"the work that God has made." But here it is clear that the search goes on for the meaning of that work; it is a restless and unsatisfied search. God has "set the mystery of the world" in the human heart. This translation is based on the Targum, which relates the word *'ōlām* (world) to the stem *'lm*, meaning to hide or conceal. This serves to link our verse with Exod. 3:15, where God, introducing himself for the first time to Moses by the ineffable name YHWH, says, "this is my name forever *[lĕ'ōlām]*." According to the rabbis, the defective spelling of *lĕ'ōlām* (here as in Eccles. 3:11) requires us to read the announcement as "This is my Name to be concealed."[8] The Targum and many Jewish commentators read the verse from Ecclesiastes in like fashion,[9] suggesting that Qohelet is pointing to a "hidden" element in the world, a hiddenness at the secret heart of reality that haunts the philosopher, so that, try as he will, "no man can find out the work that God has made from the beginning to the end." The mystery of revelation is never invoked in Ecclesiastes but in this verse it is tantalizingly close, "concealed" indeed in the "world" that he has set in our hearts. But the mystery we are speaking of is not only concealed in the "world," it is also concealed in the text. YHWH, the God who is never named in Ecclesiastes, is concealed in the absences of this extraordinary verse if we link it intertextually with Exod. 3:15. "This [i.e., YHWH] is my Name to be concealed." In Ecclesiastes the name is indeed concealed, or rather it is half concealed and half revealed in the mysterious verse we are discussing.

Such a dialectic of presence and absence resembles that in the Book of Esther. There the God of Israel never named in the text is "concealed" by, but also discovered in, the ninety times repeated mention of "the king." As the authority of the earthly king, so often invoked, is gradually emptied of content, so behind that word *hammelek* we come to see the shadow of a divine King who is only defined through his absence from the overt text.[10] God is of course not absent from Ecclesiastes in the same way; his power and the respect we should have for him are very much discussed. It is the name YHWH, the name of names by which he reveals himself to Israel, that is absent from the overt text. And YHWH, we should remember, is the God of dialogue, of hope and memory. It is to him that we call and he answers us in our distress (Ps. 120:1). In Qohelet he is absent, or rather, mysteriously hidden.

Qohelet faces this very absence, this emptiness. Indeed, he bids us face it and accept it also. But even as he does so the term *hebel* betrays him. We die and are forgotten. But can that be all? Man, says Qohelet, is leveled with the beasts—"as the one dies, so the other dies; yea, they have all one breath; so that a man has no preeminence over a beast: for all is vanity" (3:19). But beasts do not write books about the vanity of their existence! Even as he makes his most negative affirmations, the shadow of their antithesis falls upon him. It is as though not *hebel* is the issue but the emptiness of *hebel* itself; the negations demand also to be negated, to be shown up as vanity, as themselves empty and hopeless.

III

As a final example of *hebel* and its implications, we may consider Qohelet's brief but very sharply drawn vision of the cosmic order. Like Hosea, who through the imagery of chapter 6 confronts the seasonal order of nature as conceived by the fertility religions of his time, only to reject it as worthless and unprofitable ("O Ephraim, what shall I do with thee?"), so Qohelet in chapter 1 confronts the cyclical order of a world without history and without the presence of a creator God to whose word heaven and earth might bear witness. It seems that when man isolates himself in this way from that which is outside man, the universe too becomes a mighty stranger; it becomes not the universe of Psalm 19, 98, or 148, which joyfully responds to the word of its Creator, but one that turns upon itself in a ceaseless monotonous round like the Greek cosmos. Qohelet may well have had the Hellenic world-picture in his mind.[11] He evokes such a world-picture, even affirms it, but the weariness with which it fills his soul signifies not only the vanity of the world and the vanity of human wishes, but the vanity and hopelessness of such a picture of the world:

> One generation passes away, and another generation comes:
> but the earth abides for ever.
> And the sun rises and the sun goes down,
> and hastens to its place where it rises again.
> The wind goes to the south,
> and veers to the north;
> round and round goes the wind,
> and on its circuits the wind returns.
> All the rivers run into the sea;
> yet the sea is not full;
> to the place where the rivers flow,
> thither they return.
> All things are full of weariness;
> man cannot utter it:
> the eye is not satisfied with seeing,
> nor the ear with hearing.
> That which has been, is that which shall be;

and that which has been done is that which shall be done:
and there is nothing new under the sun.

(1:4–9)

Never has the notion of world cycles and nature cycles been so graph-
ically formulated. The passage catches the essence not only of so much
ancient Greek thinking, but also of the world systems associated later
with the Italian philosopher Vico, with the poet W. B. Yeats, and with
the historian-philosopher Oswald Spengler. "That which has been, is
that which shall be." But equally, never before have the utter hopelessness and wearisomeness of such conceptions been so vividly rendered. It
is not just that the rivers run into the sea and the sea is not full, but that
such thoughts run back into themselves and never find a liberating out-
let. The thinking itself is trapped, enclosed. When that which has been is
that which shall be, the mind itself becomes oppressed with the monotony of its own circular movement. That seems to be what is meant by
saying that "the eye is not satisfied with seeing, nor the ear with hearing."
The eye that only sees the same repeated process, the ear that only hears
the same myths retold can never find satisfaction. In a word Qohelet
finds himself in a condition of spiritual claustrophobia. The recognition
of circularity involves for him a recognition of how intolerable such a
state is and how desperately we need to escape it.

According to the Jewish-German philosopher Franz Rosenzweig, such
claustrophobic attitudes characterize the world view of paganism, in particular that of the Greeks. The gods live by themselves in the world of
myth, inaccessible to man; man (and supremely the tragic hero) lives in
the utterly self-contained zone of his selfhood than which there is no
greater solitude; and the world is a self-generating cosmos pursuing its
own unchanging order, impervious to either man or God. The three
realms are mutually exclusive.[12] Qohelet contemplates the cyclical monotony of such a universe with the deepest pessimism. Those who have
argued for or against a Greek influence in the verses above have, it
seems, missed the point. It matters little whether he drew the image of
such a cosmos from Hellenic or pre-Hellenic sources; what matters is the
implicit recoil from such a world view. We noted earlier[13] that the sense
of eternal recurrence and the passive adaptation to it are of the essence
of the pastoral tradition going back to the Greeks, to Theocritus and
Bion. The ever-returning spring consoles us for death itself. But Qohelet
knows no such consolation: "all things are full of weariness, man cannot
utter it." This is not a borrowing from Greek, or Egyptian, or Babylonian
wisdom, but a judgment on it.

We may take a formulation by Epictetus, an author far too late to have
been a "source" for Ecclesiastes, but he exhibits well these commonplaces

of ancient wisdom and more particularly the contented attitude to them, to which Qohelet is here reacting:

> Such was and is and shall be the nature of the universe, and it is impossible that what happens should be other than it is. And this process of revolution and change is shared not only by mankind and the other living creatures upon earth, but also by things divine; yes, and even by the four elements themselves, which turn and change upwards and downwards, earth turning into water and water into air, and this again into ether; and similarly the elements change from above downwards. If a man endeavours to adjust his mind to this and to persuade himself to accept necessity with a good will, he will live out his life very reasonably and harmoniously.[14]

The imagery is very close to that of the verses quoted above from Ecclesiastes, chapter 1. That passage also featured the eternal motions of the four elements (earth, water, wind, and the fire of the sun). But how different was Qohelet's tone! Unlike Epictetus, who "accepts necessity with a good will," Qohelet is appalled by the thought that "there is nothing new under the sun." How weary, stale, flat, and unprofitable he seems to say are the uses of a world that lacks the new thing, from which the potentiality of change, of miracle is absent. It is not that Qohelet affirms change and miracle: he does not. But it is their absence that cries out to him and that provides the basis for his eternal discontent. He offers for our contemplation a universe in which there is no recording angel to preserve the memory of our deeds, no promise, nothing at the end of the day to distinguish the life of the wise man from that of the fool, where the stillborn infant and the man who lives a thousand years twice told alike have no remembrance and arrive at the same place (6:5–6). Marcus Aurelius will say the same things several centuries later—in fact he seems almost to be echoing Qohelet—but like Epictetus, he will say them with a complacency that is utterly lacking in the Hebrew author:

> These two things then thou must bear in mind; the one, that all things from eternity are of like forms and come round in a circle, and that it makes no difference whether a man shall see the same things during a hundred years, or two hundred, or an infinite time; and the second that the longest liver and he who will die soonest lose just the same. For the present is the only thing of which a man can be deprived, if it is true that this is the only thing that he has, and that a man cannot lose a thing if he has it not.[15]

A straight line connects this passage with the words of Walter Pater quoted earlier. All that is actual, he said, is the single moment. In the instant, beauty is achieved. It is all that we have. Here is the Stoic-

Epicurean response to a cosmos that has withdrawn from man into its self-contained circularity.

But all this is something of a simplification of the position of Marcus Aurelius. One can discern among the Stoics a quite contrary response also. As well as giving themselves up passively and contentedly to the daily movement of the cosmos, they also paradoxically taught their disciples that a philosopher should not be governed by the periodic movement of the universe but should detach himself from it and affirm his freedom.[16] In fact philosophical contemplation itself implies a critical distance. This point is made powerfully in the continuation of the passage just quoted:

> Of human life the time is a point, and the substance is in a flux, and the perception dull, and the composition of the whole body subject to putrefaction, and the soul a whirl, and fortune hard to divine, and fame a thing devoid of judgement. And, to say all in a word, everything that belongs to the body is a stream, and what belongs to the soul is a dream and vapour, and life is a warfare and a stranger's sojourn, and after-fame is oblivion. What then is that which is able to conduct a man? One thing and only one, philosophy. But this consists in keeping the daemon within a man free from violence and unharmed, superior to pains and pleasures, doing nothing without a purpose. . . .[17]

To keep the daemon within a man free from violence and unharmed means to stand outside, even in a manner to raise oneself above the processes of natural flux and change. While the Stoic sees the *mundus* with its cycle of change as the all-enveloping reality, he also, through his self-awareness, sets a distance between himself and the *mundus,* maintaining the independence of the "daemon within him." This reflexivity marks the stance of the philosopher. We may say that here we have a fundamental irony or aporia: even as the philosopher contemplates himself as the passive *object* of a universal *process,* his active contemplation of this process in the language of philosophy detaches him from the process, affirms his freedom and independence as a *subject.* We are in fact somewhere near the very ground and origin of all irony.

The mark of the ironic mode of existence is self-division. Paul de Man takes from Baudelaire the useful term *"dédoublement."* Anyone can laugh at another person who trips and falls in the street: the ironist sees it happening to himself and smiles. This self-duplication or *dédoublement* is "the characteristic that sets apart a reflective activity, such as that of the philosopher, from the activity of the ordinary self caught in everyday concerns . . . it designates the activity of a consciousness by which a man differentiates himself from the non-human world."[18] Irony brings together man as object, immersed in the world, and man as a subject, capable of rising superior to pains and pleasures—as Marcus Aurelius phrased it. But of course there is no reconcilement of the two aspects. Irony holds them apart, lighting up the irreconcilable division between human dignity and human insignificance, between everyman as victim and everyman as god. Irony rests on "an endless alternation of thesis and antithesis"; it has little or nothing of synthesis in it.[19] In this sense it is fundamentally and characteristically Greek and, by the same token, fundamentally and characteristically non-Hebraic. The Greeks and after them the Romans found in irony a way of holding on to a perception of the two contrasting aspects of human nature that the Hebrew poet had dramatized in the two creation stories of Genesis 1 and 2. In the one version man is made in the image of God and raised majestically above all the brute and vegetable creatures, but in the other version he is scraped together from the dust of the earth and animated by a breath— the same breath that was breathed into the nostrils of the beasts. The contradiction is resolved for the Hebrew genius by a deeply conceived doctrine of creation. A creator God makes man out of clay as a potter fashions a vessel but he also calls him into fellowship with him, thereby marvelously raising him above the process and order of nature. The Greeks sensed the same paradox but, lacking a sense of a dialogue relation that guarantees a partnership between God and man in spite of their apartness, they kept alive the contradictions through the mechanism of irony. Man, the world, and God remain separate in their isolation from one another. Man as part of the cosmos does not become one with man as autonomous self, and neither enters into a covenant with a creator God. Thus irony brings us the wit and wonder of human self-division. The ironist beholds his own comic fall as he slips in the mud and he preserves the delicious contradictions involved; he is both the god who sees and stands superior to what he sees and the mere shred of protoplasm overcome by the simple laws of gravity. There is no resolution or synthesis. Oedipus is both the wisest and most foolish of mortals: though he solves the riddle of the Sphinx, the chorus rightly terms him a fool. In this he represents the absolute form of irony. His only way out is self-mutilation and, ultimately, death.

But death itself is, for the Greeks, the ultimate irony. This can be seen most clearly in the Stoic teaching about readiness for death as set out by Marcus Aurelius himself. It is clear that, on the one hand, death is the loss of individuality, the dissolving of the "person" into the elements of the cosmos. Marcus Aurelius concludes his second book of meditations, from which the extracts cited above are drawn, with that very thought. Death, he says, is "nothing else than a dissolution of the elements of which every living being is compounded."[20] Just as the elements constantly change into one another, so human beings dissolve into the inorganic life of the *mundus*. We are part of the order of the world itself, rolled round in earth's diurnal course with rocks and stones and trees. And yet in this very same context he calls upon his followers to "wait for death with a cheerful mind," to cultivate the Stoic readiness for death, the essence of which is philosophical detachment, indifference, even defiance. The philosopher, we may say, is that man who can look death in the eye and by so doing can differentiate himself from the mere life of nature, the empirical order of things. Montaigne many centuries later was going to write a famous essay with the title "To Philosophize is to learn to die." Here is the ultimate expression of Irony itself, that prime invention of Hellenic man and his chief legacy to the modern world in literature and thought. Irony is integral to the perception of the tragic hero. He is the man whom we pity because he is helpless, passive, mortal like ourselves; but we look up to him with awe because he has also learned to preserve his selfhood, Prometheus-like against the stream of mere natural process. His death is his fundamental defiance; he dies but he does so in a gesture of independence of death itself. Romeo catches the true tragic note—"Then I defy you stars!" He is doomed, caught in the net of inevitabilities, but ironically the moment of his fall is that in which he asserts his freedom, "his maximal canonization as hero, the utterly locked and closed 'enselfment' of his selfhood."[21] The self-divisions of which we are speaking can thus yield a tragic form but they have, more often, in the Western tradition, yielded a comic form. There the ironic antitheses are left to be enjoyed and endured. Alexander Pope in his "Essay on Man" was to catch the contradictions we are discussing in a series of brilliant epigrams that might stand as a summary of the ironic mode of perception and self-perception:

> Placed on this isthmus of a middle state,
> A being darkly wise, and rudely great:
> With too much knowledge for the sceptic side,
> With too much weakness for the Stoic's pride,
> He hangs between: in doubt to act or rest;
> In doubt to deem himself a god or beast;
> In doubt his mind or body to prefer;
> Born but to die, and reasoning but to err;
> Alike in ignorance, his reason such,
> Whether he thinks too little or too much:
> Chaos of thought and passion, all confus'd;
> Still by himself abus'd or disabus'd;
> Created half to rise, and half to fall;
> Great lord of all things, yet a prey to all;
> Sole judge of truth, in endless error hurl'd:
> The glory, jest, and riddle of the world![22]

IV

Ecclesiastes, we may say, is the Bible's "Essay on Man." The word *'ādām* is repeated some fifty times, more almost than in any other book of the Bible. What is man? Qohelet seems to ask, and the answer is a series of contradictions not unlike those in Pope's poem. Thus in 7:1 he tells us that the day of death is better than the day of birth, but later on he tells us that a living dog is better than a dead lion (9:4)! From time to time, we hear that the best thing to do is to eat and drink and enjoy each day as it comes, but elsewhere the speaker thoughtfully reminds us that God has put the "mystery of the world" in our hearts so that as a consequence we are forever worrying about beginnings and endings (3:11)! In more than one place he bids us fear God and not overstep the bounds set for us (5:6, 8:5, 12:13), but elsewhere he ponders wryly on the unwisdom of being "righteous overmuch" (7:16). From this point of view, Qohelet is the Hebrew ironist,[23] not only gazing ironically on the world without, but gazing quizzically within in that typically reflexive posture of ironic self-awareness and self-division. Often as we have seen the vanity of *ḥokmâ* itself becomes the issue, as the *ḥākām* ponders the idleness of his own pursuits. It is true that, unlike the fool, the wise man has eyes in his head, but then they suffer the same fate in the end (2:14). The thought turns back and reverses itself, and this is reflected in a style both winding and inconclusive: "So I said in my heart, As it happens to the fool, so also it happens to me; so why was I then more wise? Then I said in my heart, that this too is vanity" (2:15).

On the question of style, it has been suggested that there is a resemblance in Ecclesiastes to the Stoic-Cynic style of argument.[24] There is the same tendency to break the sentence into short-breathed phrases, the same interior argument, the interpolated questions. Qohelet sometimes shows an even greater affinity with a later Stoic philosopher, Seneca. As with Seneca we have here a style of monologue ("so I said in my heart") as the mind spirals around its own axis, seeking enlightenment from within. All this is not a matter of indebtedness in the usual sense (Seneca is obviously later than Ecclesiastes) but evidently one of a common, almost international style for Wisdom writing, the mark of which is a winding, aphoristic, disjunctive mode of discourse, giving us "separate units often forced together without any clear link in meaning."[25] Inner contradictions are quite in place in such a discourse. Qohelet does not develop a rounded thesis but tries out different points of view, often contradicting himself as he goes along. What we have here in short are not rounded thoughts but a mind thinking, moving spirally toward a conclusion, where the conclusion itself is a subject for further self-questioning. It is the informal style of ironical reflection as practiced by the

Greek and Latin masters of this style and their European imitators later on[26] and as invented (or reinvented) by Ecclesiastes for his own purpose.

Many critics, noting the antitheses and contradictions in the book, have been moved to suppose a multiple authorship. Thus one author—a pessimist—would be responsible for saying that it is better to go to a house of mourning than a house of feasting (7:2), while another author —an optimist—would be responsible for telling us that to be alive is always better than to be dead (9:4); one pious author would be telling us to live in the fear of God, while another, not so pious, would be telling us not to be righteous overmuch. But in the kind of interior monologue or debate practiced by the Senecan essayists such antithetical movements of the thinking mind are entirely in place within a single consciousness. Bible critics are more at home with dogmatic statements, the mode of kerygma. But this is not what Qohelet gives us; in the ironical play of consciousness the mind is constantly in motion, trying different possibilities as it circles and seeks conclusions. And what matters is the search rather than the conclusions.

This, however, is not quite the whole story. Qohelet's style of discourse has a richer mode in reserve, a more poetic mode. In the more poetic passages we sense the limits of irony itself. Stoical self-sufficiency breaks down and a more passionate asseveration takes its place, marked (as we noted occasionally in Esther) by the rhythm of the parallelism. Thus in 3:16 Qohelet inveighs in a most unironical fashion at social injustice. It might almost be the prophet Amos speaking:

Moreover I saw under the sun,
that in the place of judgment, even there was wickedness;
and in the place of righteousness, even there was wickedness;
I said in my heart, God shall judge the righteous and the wicked . . .
                    (3:16–17)

In such verses we reach the limits of irony as the mind vibrates to a different need and a different purpose. For a moment the ego-centered direction is abandoned and another takes its place—a disinterested indignation at the world's wrongs, a quite nonphilosophical passion for judgment and righteousness.

From this point of view, Qohelet is and is not an ironist. This is the only book of the Bible that has something of the playfulness, the sense of being amused at one's own expense that are the mark of the ironic consciousness. But he does not take this all the way in the manner of the true ironist. Friedrich Schlegel noted the infinite doubling back on itself of the ironical mind; since nothing is taken seriously and no stable existential ground is anywhere affirmed, irony is ultimately all engrossing; it

ironizes the whole world! "Which gods," he asks, "can rescue us from all
these ironies?" Even the stars cannot be trusted—they are liable to turn
into something fantastic.[27] Everything has become play, fantasy. Irony
ends up, says Paul de Man, by "reasserting the purely fictional nature of
its own universe."[28] For that critic as for Schlegel this is a supremely
commendable achievement. It gives us the aestheticization of all existence. All the world's a stage and all the men and women merely players.
Language itself becomes the ultimate fiction, unconnected with an external reality, uncommitted to history, existing only in the instant. The
world of the ironist is constituted by such language, language as an art
form making no claims on the empirical world, having no purpose beyond itself.[29] This is the mode that Greek antiquity has bequeathed to us,
but the Hebrew genius of Qohelet voices in the end its commitment to a
nonaesthetic, nonironic view of existence.

We could put this another way. Kierkegaard's criticism of the irony of
both the ancients and the moderns is that it negates all historical actuality
and substitutes for it a totally self-created actuality, an ego-bound system.
The ego is left observing the ego. The "infinite poetic freedom," the
doubling-back on itself of the ironic mind, the ceaseless play of contradictions ("now he is a god, now a grain of sand") lead ultimately, says
Kierkegaard, to boredom, *ennui*.[30] We may say that, from this point of
view, the final stage of irony has been reached in our time in the cult of
absurdity, often yielding in Beckett and others a succession of words and
images that seem to have abdicated all meaning. What we are invited to
see is Nothingness itself. For in the end an ironical view is based on the
essential instability of all views and positions and attitudes. There is
nothing stable under the sun. But this is deceptive, for, as Wayne C.
Booth has perceptively noted, "we find Beckett himself asserting, decade
after decade, an extremely stable commitment to absurdist views."[31] In
other words, while, as Schlegel said, the whole world might be ironized
out of existence, irony itself remains! The ironist does not shed his ironic
ego. If he did he would become something other than an ironist, something, say, more like Oscar Wilde when he came to write his "Ballad of
Reading Gaol." The modern practitioners of the absurd do not take that
step. P. L. Thorslev makes the same point using the analogy of Karl
Popper's criterion of falsifiability. The ironist, like Popper's scientific
man, treats every hypothesis, doctrine, and creed as falsifiable; he deliberately undermines his own principles of a moment earlier. This is as
true of Lord Byron as it is of G. Bernard Shaw. But he does not undermine irony itself, just as Popper does not question the principle of falsifiability!

> The Popperian scientist does not undermine the authority or utility of
> his criterion of falsifiability; nor does Socrates deny his dialectic based

on the laws of contradiction. Nor does the Romantic ironist relinquish his irony: to do so would be (in Hegelian terminology) to negate his negation and arrive at a positivity. This alone he must deny himself.[32]

Now this is precisely what Qohelet does and this is the point where he abandons the ironic mode. He negates his negation, arriving at a positivity. He is, we may say, both more and less ironic than Socrates. He is more ironic because he goes on to declare that the dialectical wisdom of the ironic philosopher is itself *hebel,* thus puncturing the ironic self-confidence of a Socrates. But he is less ironic, because having undermined the ironic stance itself, he is left with a positivity, he is propelled into affirmation: "For God is in heaven and thou upon earth: therefore let thy words be few" (5:2). The last phrase seems to be a dissuasion against too much philosophical discourse of the kind to which he is here treating us! It would be difficult to point to a Platonic dialogue in which the multiplication of such dialogues is itself dismissed as vanity, a weariness of the flesh, in the manner of Ecclesiastes: "And furthermore my son be admonished: of making many books there is no end; and much study is a weariness of the flesh" (12:12). Again, the view that would assign these closing verses of Ecclesiastes to another editor or author should be resisted. This skeptical rejection of skepticism is the final twist of Qohelet's super-irony. It gives us an ego that has ironized itself away and has abdicated the self-sufficient thinking of the *ḥākām.* Qohelet never quite says, like the author of Psalm 111, that the *beginning* of *ḥokmâ* is the fear of the Lord but his final statement seems to say that the *end point* of *ḥokmâ* is the fear of God! "The end of the matter, when all is said and done: Fear God and keep his commandments, for that is the whole of Man." This sentence differs from the more formulaic "the beginning of *ḥokmâ* is the fear of the Lord" in being more ironical. For we have here a final and pointed use of *hā'ādām,* "man." The whole book had been one continued attempt to find a satisfying and wholly *human* wisdom. The proper study of mankind is man, Qohelet seems to say. But ironically, this penultimate verse of the book explodes such a humanistic pretension. To fear God and keep his commandments becomes "the whole of Man" or, we may say, what is left of man when his ego has been ironized away. Read in this way, the verse is utterly integral to the book, its final summarizing statement. Now we understand what was meant by saying that the *ḥokmâ* of the *ḥākām* was itself vanity. Here is the positivity that emerges from the negation of the negative.

V

But irony, in particular that of the Greeks, does seem to know one way out and that is, Death. Death is the entirely adequate mode of ending for the trapped hero of Greek tragedy, and self-inflicted death has been found equally appropriate by some in our time who have followed the negative path of absurdity to its limit. Death marks the terminus of the ironic mode of existence providing it with an aesthetic closure, giving form to its formlessness. But viewed from another angle, as we noted earlier, the heroic readiness for death is itself profoundly ironic. "I am the Duchess of Malfi still," says the heroine of Webster's play as she confronts her death. Julius Caesar, a moment before we see him killed, his blood flowing from a dozen stab-wounds, declares, "I am constant as the northern star"; other men, he says, are flesh and blood but he is "unshaked of motion"! Death is thus the appropriate terminus and also the perfect and ultimate expression of irony. Irony remains after life is extinguished. At least thus the world is imagined.

Perhaps the best example of all is that of Othello in Shakespeare's great tragedy. Othello presents himself in Act V not as the murderer of Desdemona but as a noble executioner, a priest. He is bringing a sacrifice and is doing so with all the self-conscious poetic dignity that the occasion requires. But we know better, and that pose will be demolished by the raucous cries of Emilia, who bursts in upon him just as the murder is accomplished: "O gull, O dolt, / As ignorant as dirt . . . / The Moor has killed my mistress." But again we know better. Othello is no more a dolt and gull than he is a noble executioner. Rather he is both and neither—the glory, jest, and riddle of the world. His last heroic deed, in fact his only heroic deed in a play in which he is ironically denied any other exhibition of heroism, is to kill himself. He does so majestically and defiantly. He also does so for love. He has destroyed that which he loved and therefore has no way out but to destroy himself also. The circle is closed; there is no redemption or hope, only magnificent aesthetic closure: "I kiss'd thee ere I killed thee. No way but this, / Killing myself, to die upon a kiss." Here is the quintessence of the ironic. It is also the end of life, of love, and the end, too, of language: "O bloody period," says Lodovico as Othello's dagger puts an abrupt end to Othello's magnificent speeches. The most subtle of all the aesthetic categories that Greece has bequeathed to us finds its consummation in the grace of dying. It is the logical conclusion of the ironic mode.

However, Shakespeare's acceptance of the mode is somehow flawed. The conclusion of his play is neither so logical nor so satisfying as the ending of a Greek tragedy; it is the most noncathartic ending in Shakespeare. It leaves us not with peace of mind but with unassuaged pain; we sorrow for what Othello in his egoism has missed—love, dialogue, redemption. These are glimpsed in the play in Desdemona's simple devotion. But love and irony do not consort easily together and irony wins. We understand the necessity for the victory but we deplore it. We are appalled by the waste, by the violent obliteration of love and faithfulness. The shocking ending of *Othello* in fact implies a criticism of the very category of irony on which the play is built.[33] It is the way that tragedies end, but O, the pity of it! We yearn to transcend the aesthetic, the ironic, the rounded world of tragedy, to celebrate hope and joy, to pursue purposes beyond the closed life of the self, its honor and shame, its nobility and folly.

Ecclesiastes ultimately gives us access to such purposes. True, the book ends in death, but it is death with a difference, death as a warning, an incentive to effort. The meaning of the ending is contained not only in the great elegy itself but in the verses that frame it, verses that urge the remembering and doing and bearing witness *while there is yet time:*

> *Remember now thy Creator in the days of thy youth,*
> *before the evil days come,*
> and the years draw near, when thou shalt say,
> I have no pleasure in them;
> *Before* the sun, or the light, or the moon,
> or the stars are darkened,
> and the clouds return after the rain:
> in the day when the keepers of the house tremble,
> and the strong men bow themselves,
> and the grinders cease because they are few,
> and those that look out of the windows are dimmed,
> and the doors are shut in the street,
> when the sound of the grinding is low,
> and one starts up at the voice of the bird,
> and all the daughters of music are brought low;
> when they are also afraid of that which is high,
> and terrors are in the way,
> and the almond tree blossoms,
> and the grasshopper drags itself along,
> and the caperberry fails;
> because the man goes to his eternal home,
> and the mourners go about the streets.
> Before the silver cord is loosed,
> and the golden bowl is shattered,
> or the pitcher is broken at the fountain,
> or the wheel is broken at the cistern;
> and the dust returns to the earth as it was:
> and the breath returns to God who gave it.
> *Vanity of vanities, says Qohelet, all is vanity.*
>
> (12:1–8)

Never was there a gentler poem on the approach of death. "It is as natural to die as to be born," Bacon had said, echoing Seneca and Marcus Aurelius. Qohelet himself in the same spirit of Stoic acceptance had remarked, "To everything there is a season . . . a time to be born, and a time to die." Here that seasonableness is celebrated in grave images of growth and decay, the cycle of nature itself: the clouds returning after the rain, the blossoming and fading of the almond tree, the ripening and withering of the berries on the bushes. And to these are added the images of human culture, the treasures of art: the golden bowl, the silver cord, the wheel and the fountain. This is one of the Bible's few "set" pieces, an elaborate imaginative sequence. As in parts of the Song of Solomon, the imagery is here so to speak foregrounded; it draws attention to its own poetic character, its artifice. We are given not merely a work of art, but almost an allegory of art. It was with a fine insight that Henry James made of this golden bowl of Ecclesiastes an emblem of art's perfection and also of its vulnerability and treachery. Art measures itself against death as in the pastoral elegy, taking away all its horror, all its abruptness. There is no "bloody period." Death becomes a magic sequence of images, the beauty of a golden sunset. But Qohelet does not allow us to indulge ourselves in that beauty. He does not say to us, "That strain again; it had a dying fall." The requiem has to be savored, but it has to be resisted as well. Like wisdom itself, like wealth and station, so poetry and art are in the end declared to be a "vanity of vanities." We turn our back on death and beauty alike even at the moment of their maximum celebration. For they too are vanity, indeed a vanity of vanities.

But there is something beyond death and vanity. The syntax of the opening is utterly clear: "Remember now thy Creator in the days of thy youth, before . . . before. . . ."[34] What counts is the life that is given us, the remembering, the testimony. Undercutting and contradicting the grave poetry of dying is the purposeful rhythm of living, established in the first verse and picked up again in the epilogue. Life is given and we have to render an account of what we have done with it: "The end of the matter, when all is said and done: Fear God and keep his commandments, for that is the whole of Man. For God shall bring every deed into judgment, with every secret thing, whether it be good, or whether it be evil" (12:13–14). Like Job, Ecclesiastes ends not with death and darkness but with an ongoing history of testing and performance. Life is loaded with responsibility. Before the days come when the sun, the light, the moon, and the stars are darkened, we are to do our remembering, to remember beginnings and endings, to count our days. If we do well, if we "fear God and keep his commandments," we shall perhaps be remembered in our turn, even after we are turned to dust and the golden bowl is shattered and all its fragile beauty, its fascination, its charm, its near-perfection have been seen as vanity.

NOTES

Introduction

1. Cf. J. P. Fokkelman, *Narrative Art in Genesis* (Amsterdam: Van Gorcum, Assen, 1975), passim.

2. Cf. Northrop Frye, *Anatomy of Criticism* (Princeton, N.J.: Princeton University Press, 1957), p. 141.

3. *The Great Code: The Bible and Literature* (New York: Harcourt Brace Jovanovich, 1982), pp. 166–67.

4. Dr. Samuel Johnson, "Life of Waller," in *Lives of the Poets* (1781); C. S. Lewis, *The Literary Impact of the Authorized Version* (London: The Athlone Press, 1950), p. 25.

5. *Al-Khazari*, Part II, paragraphs 70–76 (see English translation by Hartwig Hirschfeld [New York: Pardes Publishing House Inc., 1946], pp. 110–12). For comment, see James L. Kugel, *The Idea of Biblical Poetry* (New Haven: Yale University Press, 1981), pp. 190–91.

6. Leland Ryken, *The Literature of the Bible* (Grand Rapids, Mich.: Zondervan, 1974), p. 25. But see Herbert N. Schneidau, *Sacred Discontent: The Bible and Western Tradition* (Baton Rouge: Louisiana State University Press, 1976), pp. 10, 50, 263.

7. Critics have had some difficulty in reconstructing the exact mythological pattern intimated in this verse. J. W. McKay ("Helel and the Dawn-Goddess," *VT* 20 [1970]: 451–64) identifies Helel with Venus, whose equivalent in the Ugaritic legends rebels against Yam and Baal; there is a mixture here of Greek and Canaanite myths. Otto Kaiser identifies Helel with Phaeton, the son of Helios and the charioteer of the sun in the Greek mythology (*Isaiah 13–39: A Commentary* [Philadelphia: Westminster Press, 1974], pp. 39–41). Brevard S. Childs finds the origin of the "cosmic battle between Helel and Elyon in the brilliant rise of the morning star in the heavens with its sudden dimming before the increasing rays of the sun" (*Myth and Reality in the Old Testament* [London: SCM Press, 1962], p. 71). Childs goes on to make the point that "in spite of the highly mythical nature of the material, the framework into which it is now placed [i.e., the prophet's virulent attack on the king of Babylon] has had the effect of thoroughly demythologizing it" (ibid., p. 72). G. B. Caird makes a similar observation on this passage (*The Language and Imagery of the Bible* [London: Duckworth, 1980], p. 225). An authoritative discussion of this tension between myth and history is that of F. M. Cross (*Canaanite Myth and Hebrew Epic* [Cambridge, Mass.: Harvard University Press, 1973]). "Characteristic of the religion of Israel," he remarks, "is a perennial and unrelaxed tension between the mythic and the historical"; and elsewhere: "The thrust of historical events, recognized crucially or ultimately meaningful, alone had the power to displace the mythic pattern"

(pp. vii, 87). Sometimes the *magnalia* of history tend to become themselves the focus for a new mythological pattern.

8. The above comments assume that the *māšāl*, from 14:4 to 20 or 21, represents a single continuous prophecy allowing us to bring verses in it to bear on one another. Most critics agree on this (see H. Wildberger, *Jesaja*, vol. 2, [Neukirchen: Neukirchener Verlag, 1978], p. 537). But not all agree. The suggestion has been made that a new poem begins with the word *ʾēk* ("How art thou fallen from heaven . . .") in verse 12 (cf. J. Blenkinsopp, "Stylistics of Old Testament Poetry," *Biblica* 44 [1963]: 356). But against this we should consider the emphatic anaphora binding verses 11 and 15 *(hûrad šĕʾôl . . . ʾel-šĕʾôl tûrad)*. This evidence of continuity is as striking as any form-critical notions of supposedly different literary units buried in the received text. And if the integrative approach that I am proposing rests on purely internal evidence, well then, so do all the disintegrative views as well.

9. Cf. H. Fisch, *Jerusalem and Albion* (London: Routledge and Kegan Paul, 1964), pp. 30–31.

10. Cf. A.D. Nuttall, *Overheard by God: Fiction and Prayer in Herbert, Milton, Dante and St. John* (London: Methuen, 1980), pp. 14–15. (Nuttall bases himself on an earlier discussion of the same topic by Stanley E. Fish. See *Self-Consuming Artifacts* [Berkeley: University of California Press, 1972], pp. 193–99, 216–23.)

11. John Bunyan, *The Pilgrim's Progress,* ed. E. Venables (Oxford: Oxford University Press, 1900), p. 9.

12. Cf. E. Auerbach, *Mimesis: The Representation of Reality in Western Literature,* trans. Willard Trask (New York: Doubleday, 1957), chapter 1.

13. John Milton, *Reason of Church Government* (1642), preface to the Second Book.

14. Cf. H. Fisch, "Hebraic Style and Motifs in *Paradise Lost,*" in *Language and Style in Milton,* ed. R. D. Emma and J. T. Shawcross (New York: Ungar, 1967), pp. 52–58.

15. Cf. Geoffrey H. Hartman, "On the Jewish Imagination," *Prooftexts* 5 (1985): 201–20.

16. Cf. by the present author, *Hamlet and the Word: the Covenant Pattern in Shakespeare* (New York: Ungar, 1971), passim, and especially, pp. 101–105.

17. See below, chap. 8, sections III and IV.

18. The phrase is that of Robert Boyle in his essay "Some Considerations Touching the Style of the Holy Scriptures" (1653).

1. Esther: Two Tales of One City

1. Cf. E. Auerbach, *Mimesis: The Representation of Reality in Western Literature,* trans. Willard Trask (New York: Doubleday, 1957), pp. 7, 11.

2. S. D. Goitein, *The Art of Biblical Narrative* (in Hebrew) (Jerusalem: The Jewish Agency, Department of Youth Aliyah, 1956), pp. 25, 27–28, 76–77.

3. *The Epic of the Kings: Shah-Nama, the National Epic of Persia by Ferdowsi,* trans. Reuben Levy (London: Routledge and Kegan Paul, 1967), p. 85, and cf. Goitein, op. cit., p. 79.

4. Cf. BT *Megillah,* 12b.

5. Elias Bickerman notes an analogy between Esther and several stories in *The Arabian Nights.* See *Four Strange Books of the Bible: Jonah, Daniel, Koheleth, Esther* (New York: Schocken Books, 1967), pp. 172, 181.

6. This makes the book of Esther dialogic in the special sense in which that term is regularly used by M. M. Bakhtin, the Russian literary theorist; only

Esther would seem to be more radically "dialogic" than the examples that Bakhtin adduces. Cf. *The Dialogic Imagination: Four Essays by M. M. Bakhtin,* trans. Caryl Emerson and Michael Holquist, ed. Michael Holquist (Austin: University of Texas Press, 1981), pp. 300, 304, 325–26 (on "double-voiced, internally dialogized discourse" in *Don Quixote*), and other writings.

7. There are many general and particular resemblances between the Joseph narrative and that of Esther. Some of the verbal links were pointed out by L. A. Rosenthal many years ago (*ZAW* 15 [1895]: 278–84). The topic is ably summed up by Sandra Beth Berg, *The Book of Esther: Motifs, Themes and Structure* (Missoula, Mont.: Scholars Press, 1979), pp. 124–26.

8. BT *Megillah,* 15b.

2. What Is Beautiful?

1. Exceptions to this include some line portraits by the gifted Austrian Jewish artist Ephraim Lilien and the illustrations by Hans Erni that accompany Robert Graves's version of *The Song of Songs* (London: Collins, 1973). These latter are, however, more in the nature of fleeting impressions than portraits.

2. Commenting on this passage in *The Interpreter's Bible* (New York: Abingdon Press, 1956), vol. V, p. 610.

3. Robert W. Fisher, "The Herald of Good News in Second Isaiah," in *Rhetorical Criticism: Essays in Honor of James Muilenberg* (Pittsburgh: The Pickwick Press, 1974), p. 129.

4. John L. McKenzie, ed., *Second Isaiah, The Anchor Bible* (New York: Doubleday, 1968), p. 127.

5. Cf. Thomas Greene, *The Descent from Heaven* (New Haven: Yale University Press, 1963), passim.

6. Robert W. Fisher, "The Herald of Good News," p. 124.

7. *Aeneid* IV, 238f., trans. H. Rushton Fairclough, in *Virgil,* vol. 1, Loeb Classical Library, p. 413.

8. Umberto Cassuto, *A Commentary on the Book of Genesis,* Part I, trans. I. Abrahams (Jerusalem: The Magnes Press, 1961), p. 59.

9. See especially *Genesis Rabbah* 1:10 (on the creation of the world by means of the letter *bet,* which is open in front); BT *Hagigah,* 12b. The phrase from the latter source "who renews daily the work of creation" is also embodied in the daily morning service of the synagogue.

10. Cf. W. Eichrodt, *Theology of the Old Testament,* vol. 2, trans. J. A. Baker (London: SCM Press, 1967), p. 110.

11. This view of the different (even contradictory) sources of the text of Genesis goes back to H. B. Witter and J. Astruc in the eighteenth century. It found its classical exponent in J. Wellhausen, *Prolegomena Zur Geschichte Israels* (Berlin: Reiner, 1883), chapter 8, and other writings.

12. There are some wise remarks by Meir Sternberg on the need to respect the line between source and discourse. While students of these two aspects of the biblical text can learn from one another, they are nonetheless involved in different enterprises: "Since they do not focus on the same questions, they do not contend for the same prize" (*The Poetics of Biblical Narrative* [Bloomington: Indiana University Press, 1985], p. 22). Robert Polzin goes somewhat further, claiming "operational priority" for literary criticism over historical and source criticism. See *Moses and the Deuteronomist* (New York: Seabury Press, 1980), pp. 6f.

13. Cf. BT *Berakot,* 55a, trans. A. Cohen (Cambridge: Cambridge University Press, 1921), p. 357. "Rab Judah said in the name of Rab: Bezalel knew how to

combine the letters with which heavens and earth had been created; for it is written, 'And he filled him with the spirit of God, in *wisdom* and *understanding* and in *knowledge*' (Exod. 35:31), and it is written elsewhere, 'The Lord by *wisdom* founded the earth; by *understanding* He established the heavens' (Prov. 3:19) and 'By his *knowledge* the depths were broken up' (ibid., v. 20)." The same idea is developed with reference to the completion of Solomon's Temple (1 Kings 7:51) in *Pesikta Rabbati*, pisqa 7. (See translation of W. G. Braude [New Haven: Yale University Press, 1968], vol. I, pp. 117, 126.)

14. Cf. *Darko shel Miqra* (Jerusalem: Mosad Bialik, 1964), pp. 55–56.

15. *A Commentary on the Book of Exodus*, trans. I. Abrahams (Jerusalem: The Magnes Press, 1967), pp. 476–83, and cf. *From Adam to Noah*, p. 62.

16. Especially, Moshe Weinfeld, "Sabbath, Temple Building and the Enthronement of the Lord" (in Hebrew), *Bet Miqra* 2, 69 (1977): 188–93, and M. Fishbane, *Text and Texture* (New York: Schocken Books, 1979), pp. 12–13 (and notes thereto). For some perceptive remarks on the interplay of temple imagery and creation imagery in Psalm 24, see David H. Hirsch and Nehama Ashkenasy, "Translatable Structure, Untranslatable Poem: Psalm 24," *MLS* XII (1982): 23, 32.

3. Job: Tragedy is Not Enough

1. Richard B. Sewall, *The Vision of Tragedy* (New Haven: Yale University Press, 1959), p. 9.

2. Ibid., p. 13.

3. Helen Gardner, *Religion and Literature* (London: Faber and Faber, 1971), pp. 58, 60.

4. Cf. Marvin H. Pope, ed., *Job, The Anchor Bible* (New York: Doubleday, 3d ed., 1973), Introduction, pp. xxx–xxxi.

5. Robert Lowth, *Lectures on the Sacred Poetry of the Hebrews*, trans. G. Gregory (London, 1787), chap. XXXIII.

6. Karl Jaspers, *Tragedy is Not Enough* (London: Gollancz, 1953), p. 38.

7. B. Kurzweil, "Job and the Possibility of Biblical Tragedy," in *Arguments and Doctrines*, ed. Arthur A. Cohen (New York: Harper and Row, 1970), pp. 332, 337, 341.

8. George Steiner, *The Death of Tragedy* (London: Faber, 1961), passim.

9. I. A. Richards, *Principles of Literary Criticism* (London: Kegan Paul, 1930), p. 246: "The least touch of any theology which has a compensating heaven to offer the tragic hero is fatal."

10. Cited by W. A. Irwin, "Job and Prometheus," *Journal of Religion* 30 (1950): 93.

11. Cf. Murray Krieger, *The Tragic Vision* (New York: Holt, Rinehart and Winston, 1960), pp. 10f.

12. Irwin, "Job and Prometheus," p. 93; and cf. H. M. Kallen, *The Book of Job as a Greek Tragedy* (New York: Hill and Wang, 1959), passim.

13. *Aeschylus*, vol. I, trans. Herbert Weir Smyth, Loeb Classical Library (Cambridge, Mass.: Harvard University Press, 1952), pp. 229–31.

14. D. D. Raphael, *The Paradox of Tragedy* (London: George Allen and Unwin, 1960), p. 51.

15. See M. Tsevat, "The Meaning of the Book of Job," *HUCA* 37(1966): 77–79; David Robertson, "The Book of Job: A Literary Study," *Soundings* 56 (1973): 461; and E. M. Good, "A Response," ibid., 481.

16. The significance of this is eloquently argued by Martin Buber. See "Job," in

Biblical Humanism, ed. Nahum N. Glatzer (London: Macdonald, 1968), pp. 195–96; cf. K. Kuhl cited by Tsevat, "The Meaning of the Book of Job," pp. 81–82, and S. Terrien, in *Interpreter's Bible*, vol. III (New York: Abingdon Press, 1954), p. 1173: "The bare event of the voice speaking from the whirlwind is a testimony to the love as well as the greatness of God"; cf. also André Lacocque, "Job and the Symbolism of Evil," *Biblical Research* 24–25 (1979–80): 13 (3.3).

17. As many readers will no doubt recognize, the distinction I am making here between the "two Adams" owes much to J. B. Soleveitchik's profound essay "The Lonely Man of Faith," *Tradition* 7 (Summer 1965): 5–67.

18. Otto Eissfeldt, *The Old Testament: An Introduction*, trans. Peter R. Ackroyd (Oxford: Blackwell, 1965), p. 463. For some trenchant remarks on the destructive tendency of form-critical analyses of Job based on the principle of "the elimination of What-Does-Not-Fit," see Robert Polzin, *Biblical Structuralism: Method and Subjectivity in the Study of Ancient Texts* (Philadelphia: Fortress Press, 1977), pp. 57–61.

19. In the sequel to *Prometheus Bound*, Aeschylus may well have given us something like an interview between his hero and Zeus. However, all we have are fragments of *Prometheus Unbound*, from which no real judgments can be made. In any case, the *Prometheus Bound* forms a complete play in its own right and it ends in the cataclysmic disappearance of the hero.

20. See Jan Kott, *Shakespeare Our Contemporary* (New York: Doubleday, 1964), pp. 104–105.

21. Franz Rosenzweig, *The Star of Redemption*, trans. William W. Hallo (London: Routledge and Kegan Paul, 1971), p. 81.

22. Cf. ibid., pp. 208–209.

23. Ibid., pp. 76, 78–79.

24. The clearest hint of this, as often pointed out, is in Kent's words at the death of Lear: "he hates him / That would upon the rack of this tough world / Stretch him out longer."

25. Cf. Northrop Frye, *The Great Code* (New York: Harcourt Brace Jovanovich, 1981), p. 176.

26. This in spite of the fact that there is no external evidence whatever to support the view that the work ever existed in any other form than the one we have. On the contrary, the oldest manuscript evidence, that of the so-called Qumran Targum, found in Cave XI at Qumran and reflecting a tradition going back evidently to the middle of the Second Temple period, brings strong support to the integrity of the masoretic text of Job. Of the last chapter of this paraphrase, fragmentary though it is, only the last six verses of the received text are missing. See Pope, *Job*, Introduction, pp. xlv–xlvii.

27. The most thorough presentation of this view is by William Whedbee, "The Comedy of Job," *Semeia* 7 (1977): 1–39.

28. Cf. J. G. Williams, "You Have Not Spoken Truth of Me: Mystery and Irony in Job," *ZAW* 83 (1971): 237f., 250; and cf. Robertson, "The Book of Job: A Literary Study," pp. 446–68: "God is the object of the poet's ironic joke."

29. Like many other students of the literary qualities of the Bible, I have benefited much from the writings of James Muilenburg. And yet it seems to me that his "rhetorical criticism" can lead us astray in its insistence that what we must always be looking for are artistic "wholes" and "unities." For instance, in his pathbreaking essay "Form Criticism and Beyond" (*JBL* 88 [1969]: 9), he remarks: "The literary unit is an indissoluble whole, an artistic and creative unity, a unique formulation." This rules out, it seems, those continuities and discontinuities which are often more important than the nuggets of wholeness (or imaginary wholeness) to found in the biblical text.

30. For further remarks on this subject, see by the present author, *A Remembered Future: A Study in Literary Mythology* (Bloomington, Ind.: Indiana University Press, 1984), chap. 8.

31. Herbert N. Schneidau, *Sacred Discontent: The Bible and Western Tradition* (Baton Rouge: Louisiana State University Press, 1976), p. 255.

32. This is S. Terrien's phrase. See "Yahweh's Speeches and Job's Responses," *Review and Expositor* 68 (1971): 501.

33. Dealt with at large in *A Remembered Future,* chap. 5.

34. Cf. Shalom Spiegel, *The Last Trial: On the Legends and Lore of the Command to Abraham to Offer Isaac as a Sacrifice: The Akedah,* trans. Judah Goldin (Philadelphia: Jewish Publication Society, 1967), pp. 46, etc.

35. Roger L. Cox, "Tragedy and the Gospel Narratives," in *The Bible in its Literary Milieu,* ed. John Maier and Vincent Tollers (Grand Rapids, Mich.: Eerdmans, 1979), pp. 316–17. Cox states his view as a paradox: "Christianity," he declares, "is so profoundly and uncompromisingly tragic that it ends by seeming to lose its tragic character, by coming out on the other side."

36. BT *Baba Batra,* 14b.

37. Cf. David M. Gunn, *The Fate of King Saul: An Interpretation of a Biblical Story* (Sheffield: Journal for the Study of the Old Testament, Supplement Series 14, 1980), p. 118.

4. Prophet and Audience: A Failed Contract

1. Meir Sternberg has written perceptively of the tension between the aesthetic and nonaesthetic modes, or rhetoric and ideology in biblical discourse (*The Poetics of Biblical Narrative* [Bloomington: Indiana University Press, 1985], pp. 42 and 483f.). But though he mentions the "rough handling of the audience" by the prophet Jeremiah, his examples are almost always drawn from narrative, for instance, the story of Saul's fall in 1 Samuel 15. I am concerned in this study with an equal if not greater tension to be discerned in psalm, prophecy, and wisdom. For apt remarks on audience-speaker conflicts in Isaiah, see also Y. Gitay, "Isaiah and His Audience," *Prooftexts* 3 (1983): 227–28.

2. Cf. S. R. Driver, *Introduction to the Literature of the Old Testament* (New York: Scribners, 1891), p. 497.

3. RSV here, leaning on the Greek version, renders 37b as "I will let you go in by number." With a sounder instinct the translators of NEB revert to the Hebrew and render the phrase as "I will . . . bring you within the bond of the covenant." It is not merely that the Hebrew original has greater authority but, in this case, the reading is supported by the wordplay *(habbĕrît ûbārôtî)* that is so essential a feature of the prophet's discourse.

4. Editors are generally insensitive to such wordplay. W. Eichrodt and W. Zimmerli consider our text here to be the result of confusion and dittography. With a finer literary instinct, the most recent editor, M. Greenberg, *Ezekiel I, The Anchor Bible* (New York: Doubleday, 1983), p. 373, supports the masoretic text by reference to "the high incidence of repetition and alliteration in verses 33–40."

5. Cf. Stanley E. Fish, *Is There a Text in this Class?* (Cambridge, Mass.: Harvard University Press, 1980), p. 11.

6. Cf. BT *Shabbat,* 88a and parallels.

7. Such radical relativism, for instance, characterizes the hermeneutic philosophy of Hans-Georg Gadamer. (See his *Wahrheit und Methode* [Tübingen: Mohr, 1960], pp. 159f.). There is no unchanging core of meaning, for we are inevitably caught in the historicity of our being, which is conceived not as continuity but as

flux. Gadamer was arguing against the assumptions of the earlier philological-historical school of German criticism, which believed in the possibility of recovering some absolute starting point *(Anknüpfungspunkt)* by which meaning was permanently governed. That is not what is meant here by continuity either. Moses would not have grasped Rabbi Akiba's interpretations of his book, but one would like to argue for a continuity between them nevertheless.

8. Cf. G. E. Wright, "The Lawsuit of God: A Form-Critical Study of Deuteronomy 32," in *Israel's Prophetic Heritage,* ed. B. W. Anderson and Walter Harrelson (London: SCM Press, 1962), pp. 26–67; G. E. Mendenhall, *Law and Covenant in Israel and the Ancient Near East* (Pittsburgh: Biblical Colloquium, 1955), p. 34. S. R. Driver, *The International Critical Commentary . . . On Deuteronomy* (Edinburgh: T. and T. Clark, 1895), p. 349, argues, however, that in Deuteronomy 32 "heavens and earth are invoked, not as witnesses, but as forming an audience."

9. In their comment on these verses, the rabbis had actually anticipated this notion of the calling of heaven and earth to witness as though in a court of law. See *Sifre, Ha'azinu,* Section 306, ed. Meir Ish-Shalom (Jerusalem, 1978), p. 131:

> "Give ear O heavens," R. Banaah was wont to say, when you are found guilty, only the witnesses raise their hand against him (i.e., the guilty party) as it is said, "The hand of the witnesses shall be first against him to put him to death" (Deut. 17:7), and then the others come on afterwards, as it is said, "and afterwards the hand of all the people" (ibid.). When Israel fails to carry out the will of the Omnipresent, what is said of them? "And the anger of the Lord (will) be kindled against you, and he (will) shut up the heavens, so that there be no rain" (Deut. 11:17). And the rest of the punishment will come on afterwards as it said, "and you (will) perish quickly off the good land" (ibid.). And when, conversely, Israel carries out the will of the Omnipresent, what is said of them? "And in that day, says the Lord, I will answer the heavens . . . and the earth shall answer the grain . . . and I will sow him for myself in the land" (Hos. 2:21–23).

10. J. Milton, *The Doctrine and Discipline of Divorce,* in *Works* (Columbia ed., New York, 1931), vol. III, p. 440.

5. The Song of Moses: Pastoral in Reverse

1. RSV renders *šîrâ* here by "song." "Poem" seems to me more correct. Cf. A. J. Levy, *The Song of Moses* (Baltimore: Scientific series of *Oriens—The Oriental Review,* no. 1, 1925), p. 59.

2. From William Berg's translation in *Early Virgil* (London: The Athlone Press, 1974), p. 85. Subsequent citations from Virgil are from this same edition.

3. From Bion's first idyll in *The Idylls of Theocritus, Bion and Moschus,* trans. J. Banks (London: Henry G. Bohn, 1853), p. 169.

4. L. Lerner, *The Uses of Nostalgia* (London: Chatto, 1972), p. 64; and cf. H. N. Schneidau, *Sacred Discontent,* p. 162: "Whereas the pagan world was settled in inevitable nostalgia, looking to the past for its ideal, the Hebrew conception of history opens towards a vague but fulfilling future."

5. Lerner, *Uses of Nostalgia,* p. 65.

6. Cf. W. Empson, *Some Versions of the Pastoral* (London: Chatto, 1935), pp. 20, 262.

7. Ibid., p. 23.

8. Berg, *Early Virgil,* p. 14.

9. Ibid., p. 22.

10. Rainer Maria Rilke, Ninth Elegy, in *Sonnets to Orpheus and Duino Elegies,* trans. Jessie Lemont (New York: Fine Editions Press, 1945), p. 106.

11. Cf. Bruno Snell, *The Discovery of the Mind* (Oxford: Blackwell, 1953), pp. 298f.

12. Rilke, Ninth Elegy, ed. cit., pp. 107–108.

13. Jonathan Culler's comment on Shelley's poem with its opposing apostrophes is highly pertinent. He speaks of its "dialectical alternation between attitudes of mourning and consolation, evocations of absence and presence. . . . Moving back and forth between these two postures, *the poem displaces the temporal pattern of actual loss* and, focusing on these two apostrophic commands [i.e., 'weep for Adonais' and 'mourn not for Adonais'], makes the power of its own evocativeness a central issue." *The Pursuit of Signs* (London: Routledge and Kegan Paul, 1981), p. 150.

14. Cf. N. H. Snaith, *Studies in the Psalter* (London: Epworth, 1934), pp. 53, 71; Dov Rappel, "A Commentary on Haazinu" (in Hebrew), *Bet Miqra,* no. 31 (Tammuz 5727): 22–26.

15. Cf. Rappel, "Commentary"; S. R. Driver, *The International Critical Commentary . . . on Deuteronomy* (Edinburgh: T. and T. Clark, 1895), pp. 348–49. To affirm the link between Deuteronomy 32 and Isaiah 1, where the former is seen to underlie the latter, naturally involves taking a position about the date of Deuteronomy 32. For those (such as G. von Rad and S. H. Hooke) who regard it as a later text than Isaiah, such influence is impossible. Others, however (Otto Eissfeldt, W. F. Albright, U. Cassuto), take the view that the Song of Moses is very ancient. So many dates have been suggested that one can really take one's pick. Literary criticism may even have something to contribute by way of "evidence." The feeling the reader has when the two poems are set side by side is of a powerful interrelationship, where the words of Deuteronomy 32 stand out as the primal text. This is not "external" evidence, but then von Rad and Hooke themselves have little "external" evidence with which to support their speculations.

16. See *Midrash Tanhuma,* ad loc. section 2. The coupling of *ha'ăzînû* and *šimĕ'û* is very common throughout the OT (see U. Cassuto, *A Commentary on the Book of Genesis,* Part I, pp. 239–40). What makes the present instances rather special is the doubling also of *šāmayim* and *'ereṣ* in both places.

17. Cf. A. Kaminka, "Melisot Mosheh umizmorey tehillim . . . ," *Leshonenu* (Tammuz 5688–1928): 41; and see *Mekhilta of R. Yishmael,* ed. J. Z. Lauterbach (Philadelphia: Jewish Publication Society, 1933), p. 91.

18. Cf. chap. 4 above, n. 8. And see also H. B. Huffmon, "The Covenant Lawsuit in the Prophets," *JBL* 78 (1959): 285–95; R. B. Y. Scott, "The Literary Structure of Isaiah's Oracles," in *Studies in Old Testament Prophecy,* ed. H. H. Rowley (Edinburgh: T. and T. Clark, 1950), p. 179: "This type of opening [i.e., Isa. 1:2] is derived from the manner of the adjudication of disputes and the hearing of complaints 'in the gate'. 'Hear ye . . . Give ear . . . ' introducing a complaint, calls for the attention of witnesses."

19. Cf. Geoffrey H. Hartman, "On the Jewish Imagination," *Prooftexts* 5 (1985): 203. This point is made by the rabbis in the midrash, where they relate the witness role of heaven and earth to that of the witnesses mentioned in Deut. 17:7. There it is said that when a man or a woman has heinously transgressed the covenant, "the hand of the witnesses shall be first against him to put him to death." And see chap. 4 above, n. 9.

20. Cf. Rappel, "Commentary," p. 13.

21. The authors of Luke 17 and 2 Peter 2 link the two narratives together, thus underlining the analogy.

22. Source critics might wish to explain this anomaly by saying that, unlike the story of the overthrow of Sodom, the Flood narrative has a large core (6:9–22) of

so-called P material originating from priestly circles of later date than the composition of Isaiah 1 or Deuteronomy 32. But even these critics would admit that other crucial portions of the Flood narrative belong to earlier strands of narration. The evidence in fact is so contradictory that we may safely offer our own view of the reason for the relative silence of the prophets in regard to the Flood.

23. On the mother-ocean archetype in western literature, see by the present author, *A Remembered Future: A Study in Literary Mythology* (Bloomington: Indiana University Press, 1984), pp. 131–35.

6. Song of Solomon: The Allegorical Imperative

1. Cf. Leland Ryken, *The Literature of the Bible* (Grand Rapids, Mich.: Zondervan, 1974), pp. 217–30, 234–35; and Francis Landy, *Paradoxes of Paradise: Identity and Difference in the Song of Songs* (Sheffield: The Almond Press, 1983), pp. 26–32, 174.

2. Landy, ibid., p. 27.

3. *The Idylls of Theocritus, Bion, and Moschus . . . Literally Translated into English Prose, by Rev. J. Banks, with metrical versions by J. M. Chapman* (London: Henry G. Bohn, 1853), from Chapman's metrical version, p. 261. Cf. Marvin H. Pope, ed., *Song of Songs, The Anchor Bible* (New York: Doubleday, 1977), p. 336. For an Egyptian analogue, see S. D. Goitein, *Bible Studies* (in Hebrew) (Tel-Aviv: Yavneh, 1957), p. 289.

4. "Greek Analogies to the Song of Songs," in *The Song of Songs: A Symposium,* ed. Max L. Margolis et al. (Philadelphia: The Commercial Museum, 1924), pp. 3f.

5. Robert Graves, *The Song of Songs: Text and Commentary* (London: Collins, 1973), p. 7.

6. From Chapman's metrical version of Theocritus's sixth idyll, ed. cit., p. 225.

7. First proposed by J. G. Wetzstein in 1868 and developed by Karl Budde, *Die Fünf Megillot: Das Hohelied . . .* (Freiburg: Mohr, 1898), pp. XVII–XX. For critical comment see Goitein, *Bible Studies,* pp. 287f. Goitein argues that the Egyptian parallels are of greater antiquity and also more relevant. The Egyptian material has been examined more recently in a major study by Michael V. Fox, *The Song of Songs and the Ancient Egyptian Love Songs* (Madison: University of Wisconsin Press, 1985), passim. Fox argues for "fundamental similarities and probable genetic linkage" (p. xxiv).

8. Cf. Pope, *Song of Songs,* pp. 641–42.

9. Edmund Spenser's "Epithalamion," lines 167–84, is a particularly notable example. And see also his *Amoretti,* sonnet 64, and *The Faerie Queene,* Book VI, 8:42. For discussion, see I. Baroway, "The Imagery of Spenser and the *Song of Songs*," *JEGP* 33 (1934): 23–45. Spenser had earlier attempted a poetic paraphrase of the Song of Solomon.

10. This is obviously true of the scores of such descriptive catalogues to be found in *The Arabian Nights.* They are essentially interchangeable. But there are seeming exceptions. In a *wasf* from a 20th Dynasty papyrus to be found in the Chester Beatty collection, the ancient Egyptian poet opens his poem of praise with the words "One alone is my sister, having no peer." This is strikingly like the verse we are discussing (see Michael V. Fox, *The Song of Songs,* pp. 52, 153). But in its context it suggests no more than that the girl is superlatively and incomparably beautiful. Our verse in the Song of Solomon has overtones of transcendence lacking in the Egyptian lyric.

11. Noted also by S. D. Goitein (*Bible Studies,* p. 293) as marking an important difference between the technique of repetition in the Song and the more mechanical use of repetitions and refrains in early Egyptian love poetry. The refrains in Theocritus are also essentially repetitive rather than incremental.

12. C. Rabin, "The Song of Songs and Tamil Poetry," *Studies in Religion* 3 (1973–74): 210.

13. Goitein, *Bible Studies,* pp. 271, 288, 300.

14. *Mishnah, Yadayim,* 3:5.

15. The dream character of the Song is occasionally noted in the literature; see especially S. B. Freehof, "The Song of Songs. A General Suggestion," *JQR* 39 (1949): 399–402. "A dream cannot be explained . . . by the categories of waking life. It must be interpreted according to its own strange laws" (ibid., 402). Cf. also Rabin, "The Song of Songs," pp. 213, 219.

16. Cf. M. Z. Segal, *Mebo Hammiqra,* vol. III (Jerusalem: Kiriat Sefer, 1967), 676–78; Goitein, *Bible Studies,* pp. 284–86; Michael V. Fox, *The Song of Songs,* pp. xx, 220; and Roland E. Murphy, "The Unity of the Song of Songs," *VT* 29 (1979): 436–43.

17. Developed by H. G. A. Ewald in his study of the Song of Solomon (1826) and adopted by a large number of later writers, including the influential Meir Leibush Malbim in his Hebrew commentary on the Song (1860), in which he combines this plot with an interpretation of the Song as moral allegory.

18. Anton Ehrenzweig sees traditional art as seeking to overcome the undifferentiated, Gestalt-free vagueness of the dreaming consciousness. It does so through style and structure, thus combining Gestalt-bound and Gestalt-free forms. (See *The Psycho-Analysis of Artistic Vision and Hearing* [New York: Julian Press Inc., 1953], pp. 31–33, 63–67.) The Song of Solomon would seem to provide a rather special example of this process or something like it. (I am indebted to Professor Wolfgang Iser for this reference.)

19. Leo Krinetzki, *Das Hohe Lied* (Düsseldorf: Patmos, 1964), p. 63, and cf. W. Kayser, *Das Sprachliche Kunstwerk* (Bern: Francke, 1963), p. 124.

20. E. M. Good, "Ezekiel's Ship: Some Extended Metaphors in the Old Testament," *Semitics* I (1970): 94–96. See also some pertinent remarks by Michael V. Fox on the imagery of the Song; "the images," he says, "become independent of their referents and memorable in themselves" (*The Song of Songs,* p. 329).

21. Yaacov Fichman, "The Song of Songs," in *An Anthology of Hebrew Essays,* selected by I. Cohen and B. Michali (Tel-Aviv: Massada, 1966), vol. I, p. 88.

22. *Midrash Rabbah: Shir Hashirim,* ed. S. Donsky (in Hebrew) (Tel-Aviv: Dvir, 1980), p. 150 (trans. H.F.). And cf. *The Midrash on Psalms,* trans. W. G. Braude (New Haven: Yale University Press, 1959), II, 244 (to Psalm 118:23).

23. In particular the Targum and the rabbinic commentators, but also some modern commentators including André Robert in a series of articles from 1944 onwards. (For bibliography, see Pope, *Song of Songs,* pp. 180–82, 279).

24. The linking of the *ṣĕbî* of 2 Sam. 1:19 with the gazelle of the Song is also suggested by Yehuda Kil in his edition of Samuel (*II Samuel,* ed. Yehuda Kil, *Daat Miqra* [Jerusalem: Mosad Harav Kook, 1981], p. 317).

25. See Morton W. Bloomfield, "Allegory as Interpretation," *NLH* 3 (1971–72): 302f.

26. See Barbara K. Lewalski, "Thematic Patterns in *Twelfth Night,*" *Shakespeare Studies* 1 (1965): 176–78.

27. See T. J. Meek, "The Song of Songs and the Fertility Cult," in Margolis, *The Song of Songs: A Symposium,* pp. 54–57, 62. Marvin Pope in the somewhat eccentric introduction to his edition of the Song (especially pp. 210–29) leans toward a

cultic reading of the images. He includes also some dozen plates, mainly bas-reliefs of gods and goddesses in various poses, often indecent, to each of which he attaches a verse from the Song that the picture is supposed to illustrate. All rather like reading Lady Macbeth's "out, damned spot" as clear evidence that she worked in a laundry.

28. See W. H. Schoff, "The Offering Lists in the Song of Songs and their Political Significance," in *The Songs of Songs: A Symposium*, pp. 114–20.

29. I am here echoing a remark of Jonathan Culler on G. M. Hopkins's poem "The Windhover." "The reader of poetry knows," he says, "that when such metaphorical energy is expended on a bird the creature itself is exalted and becomes metaphor" (*Structuralist Poetics* [London: Routledge and Kegan Paul, 1975], p. 90).

30. Cf., for instance, H. H. Rowley, *The Servant of the Lord and Other Essays on the Old Testament* (London: Lutterworth, 1952), pp. 189–91. Seeming evidence for this notion is a third-century source (*Abot Derabbi Natan*, 1:4) that speaks of the "Men of the Great Synagogue" "interpreting" Proverbs, Ecclesiastes, and the Song of Solomon so as to make them acceptable.

31. Gerson D. Cohen, "The Song of Songs and the Jewish Religious Mentality," in *The Samuel Friedland Lectures 1960–1966* (New York: The Jewish Theological Seminary, 1966), p. 16.

32. Cf. BT *Sanhedrin*, 101a. See also *Tosefta, Sanhedrin*, 12:10, in the name of R. Akiba.

33. *Mishnah, Yadayim*, 3:5, *Tosefta, Yadayim*, 2:14, etc. Modern discussion of this topic has not yielded a consensus. S. Z. Leiman has argued that there was a fixed canon already in the Maccabean period (*The Canonization of Hebrew Scripture, Transactions of the Connecticut Academy of Arts and Sciences*, vol. 47, February 1976, p. 135). S. Zeitlin and others have argued for a much later date (see Zeitlin, "An Historical Study of the Canonization of the Hebrew Scriptures," *Proceedings of the American Academy for Jewish Research* 3 [1931–32]: 121–58). George Foot Moore argued that the question of a canon proper, i.e., a dogmatically fixed boundary of exclusiveness, only arose among Jews as a result of the rise of Christianity and the need to exclude the Christian Scriptures. (See "The Definition of the Jewish Canon and the Repudiation of Christian Scriptures," in *C.A. Briggs Testimonial Essays in Modern Theology* [New York, 1911], pp. 101, 125.)

34. He said it was inspired by the holy spirit, but it did not "defile the hands" (BT *Megillah*, 7a). The curious regulation about sacred books defiling the hands was introduced it seems to prevent the scrolls' being damaged by mice. Cereal foods set aside for the priests *(těrûmâ)* would often be kept in the same cupboard as the sacred books and these attracted mice, which were then liable to attack the scrolls as well. Determining a low-grade defilement for sacred books meant that *těrûmâ* could not be brought near to them, and they would consequently be safe from mice! This is as near as the ancient Jewish rabbis seemed to get to a concept of "canonicity."

35. Robert Gordis, *The Song of Songs and Lamentations* (New York: Ktav, 1974), p. 99; Pope, *Song of Songs*, p. 667.

36. Dr. Max N. Pusin, quoted by Pope, *Song of Songs*, pp. 133–34.

37. Cf., by the present author, "The Dreaming Narrator in S. Y. Agnon," *Novel* 4 (Fall 1970): 49–68; *S. Y. Agnon* (New York: Ungar, 1975), pp. 40, 68–83, 93–94.

38. See André Neher, "Le Symbolisme conjugal: Expression de l'histoire dans l'A.T.," *Revue d'Histoire et de Philosophie Religieuses* I (1954): 33–49.

39. Trans. H.F.

7. Psalms: The Limits of Subjectivity

1. John Milton, *The Reason of Church Government* (1641), preface to Book 2; the notion is associated in more modern times with H. G. A. Ewald (*Das Hohe Lied Salomos*, 1826).

2. Cf. Northrop Frye, *Anatomy of Criticism* (Princeton, N.J.: Princeton University Press, 1957), p. 272.

3. Ibid., p. 250.

4. Cf. M. H. Abrams, *The Mirror and the Lamp: Romantic Theory and the Critical Tradition* (New York: Norton, 1958), pp. 58–61 and passim.

5. Cf. Geoffrey H. Hartman, *The Unmediated Vision* (New Haven: Yale University Press, 1954), p. 30.

6. Cf., among other discussions of this topic, L. L. Martz, *The Poetry of Meditation* (New Haven: Yale University Press, 1954), passim.

7. See, by the present writer, *Jerusalem and Albion: The Hebraic Factor in Seventeenth Century Literature* (London: Routledge and Kegan Paul, 1964), pp. 50–54, 56–62; and see C. A. Patrides, "A Crown of Praise: The Poetry of Herbert," preface to his edition of *The English Poems of George Herbert* (London: Dent, 1974), pp. 9–10.

8. Cf. M. H. Abrams, "Structure and Style in the Greater Romantic Lyric," in *From Sensibility to Romanticism: Essays Presented to Frederick A. Pottle* (London: Oxford University Press, 1965), pp. 527–60.

9. See below, p. 125.

10. Cf. the perceptive remarks of M. Weiss in his analysis of this psalm. *The Bible from Within: The Method of Total Interpretation* (Jerusalem: Magnes Press, 1984), pp. 299, 313.

11. Mitchell Dahood, ed., *Psalms I, The Anchor Bible* (New York: Doubleday, 1966), p. 77.

12. B. D. Eerdmans, *The Hebrew Book of Psalms* (Leiden: Brill, 1947), p. 134; Artur Weiser, *The Psalms*, trans. Herbert Hartwell (London: SCM Press, 1962), p. 163.

13. D. Robertson, *The Old Testament and the Literary Critic* (Philadelphia: Fortress Press, 1977), p. 67.

14. J. C. Ransom, "Poetry: A Note in Ontology," reprinted in *The Great Critics*, ed. J. H. Smith and E. W. Parks (New York: Norton, 1951), p. 781.

15. For a useful summary, see A. R. Johnson, "The Psalms," in H. H. Rowley, ed., *The Old Testament and Modern Study* (Oxford: Oxford University Press, 1951), pp. 162–207.

16. Weiser, *The Psalms*, introduction, pp. 23–35.

17. R. E. Prothero, *The Psalms in Human Life* (London: Nelson, 1903), p. 13. Prothero's "lyrical" appreciation of the Psalms as containing "the whole music of the heart of man" (ibid.) represents the point of view that I am seeking here to correct.

18. Sigmund Mowinckel, *The Psalms in Israel's Worship,* trans. D. R. Ap-Thomas (Oxford: Blackwell, 1962), vol. II, pp. 126, 134. Mowinckel's chapter is aptly entitled "Traditionalism and Personality in the Psalms."

19. Helmer Ringgren, *The Faith of the Psalmists* (London: SCM Press, 1963), p. 26.

20. See Hermann Gunkel, *The Psalms: A Form-Critical Introduction*, trans. T. M. Horner (Philadelphia: Fortress Press 1969), pp. 19–22, 33–36.

21. Cf. Antony Easthope, *Poetry as Discourse* (London: Methuen, 1983), p. 160.

22. Maternal imagery is more common than is customarily realized (cf. Isa. 66:13, 49:15). On this aspect, see Leila L. Bronner, "Gynomorphic Imagery in Exilic Isaiah," *Dor leDor* XII (Winter 1983/84): 71–83.

23. Cf. Dahood, *Psalms III*, p. 30 (quoting D. N. Freedman).

24. Robert C. Culley, *Oral Formulaic Language in the Biblical Psalms* (Toronto: University of Toronto Press, 1967), pp. 102–103.

25. Ibid., p. 113.

26. Cf. Ruth Finnegan, *Oral Poetry* (Cambridge: Cambridge University Press, 1977), pp. 70, 128–31.

27. Moses and Israel are, according to the Midrash, chosen singers. The *Mekilta Derabbi Ishmael* relates 2 Sam. 23:1—"but sweet are the songs of Israel"— to the covenant formula in Deut. 26:18, 17—"the Lord has avouched thee this day," and "thou hast avouched the Lord this day" (*Mekilta*, trans. J. Z. Lauterbach, vol. II [Philadelphia: Jewish Publication Society, 1963], p. 23. From Tractate *Shirata*, section 3). The blessing on the morning psalm-reading in the standard Jewish daily service concludes with the telling phrase "Blessed art thou . . . who makest choice of song and psalm" *(habbōḥer bĕšîrê zimrâ)*. This makes it exactly parallel to the blessing on the election of Israel, which comes later in the same service. (*The Authorized Daily Prayer Book of the United Hebrew Congregation . . .* , trans. S. Singer [London: Eyre and Spottiswoode, 1929], pp. 26, 40.)

28. Jan Mukarovsky, "Standard Language and Poetic Language," in Paul L. Garvin, ed., *A Prague School Reader* (Washington, D.C.: Georgetown University Press, 1964), p. 19. Robert Alter draws our attention to such foregrounding in the Psalms. See *The Art of Biblical Poetry* (New York: Basic Books, 1985), pp. 133, 135. Alter's book arrived too late for his findings to be incorporated in the earlier chapters of this study.

29. *Midrash Otiyyot Derabbi Akiba*, chap. 1, ed. S. A. Wertheimer (Jerusalem, 1914), pp. 1–2.

30. See above, chap. 5, p. 67.

31. Cf. Eerdmans, *Hebrew Book of Psalms*, p. 165; Moses Buttenwieser, *The Psalms Chronologically Treated with a New Translation* (New York: Ktav, 1969), pp. 170, 177.

32. *Qawwām* in 4a is usually rendered "their line," which gives doubtful sense. Dahood, *Psalms I*, pp. 121–22, plausibly suggests "their call," basing himself on an earlier study by Jacob Barth of the Hebrew stem and its various uses. NEB reads "their music." See also Eerdmans, *Hebrew Book of Psalms*, p. 166. I am suggesting "their echo."

33. Cf. H. Fisch, "The Analogy of Nature, A Note on the Structure of Old Testament Imagery," *The Journal of Theological Studies*, n.s. 6 (1955): 171; M. Fishbane, *Text and Texture: Close Readings of Selected Biblical Texts* (New York: Schocken Books, 1979), p. 87; Dahood, *Psalms I*, p. 121, who concludes from this interconnection that "the author of both parts of the psalm was the same poet"; cf. also Amos Haham, *Daat Miqra: Sepher Tehillim*, I (Jerusalem: Mosad Harav Kook, 1983), p. 104 (summary).

34. W. O. E. Oesterley, *The Psalms* (London: S.P.C.K., 1955), p. 167, for example, speaks of "two originally independent psalms," the first of which is adapted from a Babylonian praise of the sun-god. All agree, however, that the text as we have it was put together by a "redactor" who evidently knew what he was doing. Meir Sternberg's words on the necessary difference between the discussion of source and discourse deserve to be pondered (see above, chap. 2, n. 12). Others have made the same point. Cf. Adele Berlin, *Poetics and Interpretation of Biblical*

Narrative (Sheffield: Almond Press, 1983), p. 81, and David Jobling, *The Sense of Biblical Narrative: Three Structural Analyses in the Old Testament* (Sheffield: *JSOT*, Supplement Series 7, 1978), p. 27.

35. E. C. Rust, *Nature and Man in Biblical Thought* (London: Lutterworth, 1953), p. 64.

36. J. Pedersen, *Israel III–IV* (London: Oxford University Press, 1940), pp. 617–18.

37. But see Weiser, *The Psalms*, p. 204.

38. Cf. *Mishnah, Sukkah*, 5:4.

39. See above, chap. 2, p. 20. And see Weiser, *The Psalms*, p. 615.

40. Weiser, ibid. (notes 1 and 2).

41. In 1 Sam. 16:13 Samuel takes a horn of oil to anoint David, and cf. 1 Kings 1:39.

42. C. A. and E. C. Briggs, *The Book of Psalms. International Critical Commentary, II* (Edinburgh: T. and T. Clark, 1907), p. 283.

43. Cf. Dahood, *Psalms II*, p. 338; Haham, *Daat Miqra*, II, p. 183, n. 15.

44. Cf. Oesterley, *The Psalms*, p. 413; Buttenwieser, *The Psalms Chronologically Treated*, p. 842, n. 14.

45. See above, chap. 2, p. 21.

8. Hosea: A Poetics of Violence

1. Robert Alter, *The Art of Biblical Poetry* (New York: Basic Books, 1985), pp. 10, 11, 23, etc.

2. Cf. Francis I. Andersen and David N. Freedman, eds., *Hosea, The Anchor Bible* (New York: Doubleday, 1980), p. 69.

3. Ibid., p. 66.

4. For example, H. L. Ginsberg in his reconstruction of chapter 12. ("Hosea's Ephraim, More Fool than Knave," *JBL* 80 [1961]: 339–47.)

5. H. W. Wolff, *Hosea: A Commentary on the Book of the Prophet Hosea*, trans. Gary Stansell (Philadelphia: Fortress Press, 1974), pp. xxiii, 110, etc.

6. Andersen and Freedman, *Hosea*, pp. 70, 71.

7. Luis Alonso-Schökel, *The Inspired Word: Scripture in the Light of Language and Literature*, trans. Francis Martin (London: Burns and Oates, 1967), p. 191.

8. See above, chap. 5.

9. Cf. A. J. Heschel, *The Prophets* (Philadelphia: Jewish Publication Society, 1962), p. 60; B. Uffenheimer, "Amos and Hoshea: Two Paths in Israelite Prophecy" (in Hebrew), in *Zer Ligeburot* (Essays in Honor of Z. Shazar) (Jerusalem: Kiryat Sepher, 1973), p. 315.

10. Heschel, *The Prophets*, p. 27; Uffenheimer, "Amos and Hoshea," p. 310.

11. Cf. Uffenheimer, ibid., p. 311.

12. David J. A. Clines, "Story and Poem: The Old Testament as Literature and Scripture," *Interpretation* 34 (1980): 126. A parallel though briefer example is God's lament in Jer. 12:7f.

13. See *Midrash Exodus Rabba*, 2:4.

14. Cf. James L. Mays, *Hosea: A Commentary* (London: SCM Press, 1969), p. 27. The name "Jezreel," says Mays, "has a tantalizing opaqueness—it could mean weal or woe"; cf. also Yehuda Kil, *Daat Miqra: Hosea* (Jerusalem: Mosad Harav Kook, 1973), p. 29; Uffenheimer, "Amos and Hoshea," p. 313.

15. Cf. M. J. Buss, "The Prophetic Word of Hosea: A Morphological Study," *BZAW* 111 (1969): 39–40, 47.

16. Cf. L. Alonso-Schökel, *The Inspired Word*, p. 189: "He listens to the sound of his words as he combines them . . . as he works, he receives new insights . . .

and as he manipulates words, his meaning becomes clearer, richer, and more delicately blended."

17. Cf. H. Wheeler Robinson, *Two Hebrew Prophets: Studies in Hosea and Ezekiel* (London: Lutterworth Press, 1948), p. 18.

18. Wolff, *Hosea*, pp. xxvi, 15.

19. E. Jacob, "L'héritage canaanéen dans le livre du prophète Osée," *Revue d'histoire et de Philosophie Religieuses* 43 (1963): 252.

20. Cf. Wolff, *Hosea*, p. 44.

21. Geoffrey H. Hartman, *Saving the Text: Literature/Derrida/Philosophy* (Baltimore: Johns Hopkins University Press, 1981), p. 151.

22. James S. Ackerman, "Satire and Symbolism in the Song of Jonah," in *Traditions in Transformation: Turning Points in Biblical Faith* (Essays in Honor of F. M. Cross), ed. B. Halpern and J. D. Levenson (Winona Lake, Ind.: Eisenbrauns, 1981), p. 220.

23. Cf. Mays, *Hosea*, pp. 173–75 *(ad loc.)*.

24. Cf. Andersen and Freedman, *Hosea*, p. 635 *(ad loc.)*.

25. Ibid.

26. Thus Andersen and Freedman, Wolff, and others.

27. Cf. Kil, *Hosea*, p. 105 *(ad loc.)*.

28. Thus judged by Kil in his introduction (ibid., p. 27).

29. Cf. Kil, ibid., p. 30, and Uffenheimer, "Amos and Hoshea," p. 312.

30. Cf. Jacob, "L'héritage canaanéen," pp. 258–59.

9. Qohelet: A Hebrew Ironist

1. Alexander Pope, *Essay on Man*, Epistle ii, lines 1–3.

2. Walter Pater, conclusion to *The Renaissance* (London: Macmillan, edition of 1913), pp. 248–49.

3. Ibid., p. 252.

4. Above, p. 20.

5. O. S. Rankin, *Israel's Wisdom Literature* (Edinburgh: T. and T. Clark, 1954), p. 95.

6. G. von Rad ("Das Werk Jahwes," in *Studia Biblica et Semitica*, in honor of T. C. Vriezen [Wageningen: Veenman en Zonen NV], 1966), usefully distinguishes between *ma'ăśeh 'ĕlōhîm* as sudden and violent intervention in nature or history and *ma'ăśeh 'ĕlōhîm* as ongoing providential care, in a word, as *process*. The latter meaning is to the fore in Ecclesiastes.

7. G. von Rad, *Wisdom in Israel*, trans. James D. Martin (London: SCM Press, 1972), pp. 232–33.

8. BT *Qiddušin*, 71a and other *loci*.

9. This reading of Eccles. 3:11 is noted by M. Zer-Kavod in his edition of Ecclesiastes in *Daat Miqra: Chamesh Megillot* (Jerusalem: Mosad Harav Kook, 1973), p. 17, n. 20.

10. Cf. above, p. 13.

11. This is forcibly argued by T. Tyler, *Ecclesiastes: a Contribution to Its Interpretation* (London: Williams and Norgate, 1874), pp. 13–15; cf. also E. H. Plumptre, ed., *Ecclesiastes, The Cambridge Bible* (Cambridge: Cambridge University Press, 1898), introduction, pp. 45–46, and notes to 1:8–10. This view is contested by G. A. Barton, *Ecclesiastes*, I.C.C. edition (Edinburgh: T. and T. Clark, 1908), pp. 35–38, and by Robert Gordis, *Koheleth: The Man and His World* (New York: Schocken, 1968), pp. 51–55. M. Jastrow argued for a generalized Greek influence and background (*A Gentle Cynic* [1919; New York: Oriole Editions, 1972], pp. 147–52), and so did H. L. Ginsberg—see "Structure and Contents of Koheleth" in

Wisdom in Israel, Presented to H. H. Rowley, ed. M. Noth and D. Winton Thomas, *Vetus Testamentum,* Supplement Series, no. 3 (Leiden: Brill, 1955), pp. 148–49. Elias Bickerman regards Ecclesiastes as a third-century work strongly marked by Greek ways of thinking—see *Four Strange Books of the Bible* (New York: Schocken, 1967), pp. 144, 150, 156, 158. Much of the discussion in fact turns on the dating of our book.

12. Cf. Franz Rosenzweig, *The Star of Redemption,* trans. William W. Hallo (London: Routledge and Kegan Paul, 1971), pp. 34, 61, 68, 86–87.

13. Cf. above, p. 59.

14. "Discourses of Epictetus," Fragment 8, trans. P. E. Matheson, in *The Stoic and Epicurean Philosophers,* ed. Whitney J. Oates (New York: Modern Library, 1957), p. 460.

15. Marcus Aurelius, Meditations, book II, 14, trans. G. Long, in Oates, *Stoic and Epicurean Philosophers,* p. 500. In contrast to Epictetus and Marcus Aurelius, Seneca occasionally strikes a note of disgust when contemplating the monotony of the universal cycle of nature. But when he does so, he seems to be speaking not so much for himself as for a person too much inclined to boredom. (See *Epistles to Lucilius,* 24:26.)

16. Cf. Marcus Aurelius, Meditations, book IX, 15, 31 (ibid., pp. 556, 558).

17. Meditations, book II, 17 (ibid., pp. 500–501).

18. Paul de Man, "The Rhetoric of Temporality," in *Interpretation: Theory and Practice,* ed. Charles S. Singleton (Baltimore: Johns Hopkins University Press, 1969), pp. 194–95.

19. Cf. Peter L. Thorslev, Jr., *Romantic Contraries: Freedom versus Destiny* (New Haven: Yale University Press, 1984), p. 159 (paraphrasing Friedrich Schlegel).

20. *The Stoic and Epicurean Philosophers,* p. 501.

21. This is Rosenzweig's comment on the fate of the tragic hero. (*Der Stern der Erlösung* [Berlin: Schocken, 1930], pp. 103–104, trans. H.F.)

22. Pope, *Essay on Man,* Epistle ii, lines 3–18.

23. Cf. Jastrow, *A Gentle Cynic,* pp. 139, 182, 195.

24. A notion advanced by P. Kleinert and L. Levy at the beginning of the century, discussed and rejected by Robert Gordis, who points out that some of the chief characteristics of the Stoic-Cynic diatribe are lacking. (*Koheleth: The Man and His World,* pp. 52–53). In this study we are not much concerned with the genetic question. We are concerned with affinities rather than influences, and the affinity here is striking enough, partial though it may be.

25. M. W. Bloomfield, "The Tradition and Style of Biblical Wisdom Literature," in *Biblical Patterns in Modern Literature,* ed. David H. Hirsch and Nehama Aschkenasy (Chico, Cal.: Scholars Press, 1984), p. 24.

26. Much has been written on the Senecan style as adopted by writers in England and elsewhere in the seventeenth century, e.g., G. Williamson, *The Senecan Amble* (Chicago: University of Chicago Press, 1951); M. W. Croll, "The Baroque Style in Prose," in *Essays in Stylistic Analysis,* ed. Howard S. Babb (New York: Harcourt Brace Jovanovich, 1972). There is a briefer discussion by the present writer in *Jerusalem and Albion: The Hebraic Factor in Seventeenth Century Literature* (London: Routledge and Kegan Paul, 1964), pp. 28–29—also of the way in which the Wisdom books of the Bible often compete as a model in the seventeenth century with the writings of Seneca and Cicero (ibid., pp. 44–48). This latter point is also argued by Frank L. Huntley in "King James as Solomon, The Book of Proverbs, and Hall's *Characters,*" in *Essays in Persuasion: On Seventeenth-Century English Literature* (Chicago: The University of Chicago Press, 1981), pp. 49–56.

27. "Über die Unverständlichkeit," in Friedrich Schlegel, *Kritische Ausgabe* (Zürich: Thomas-Verlag), II, 369–70.

28. De Man, "The Rhetoric of Temporality," p. 199.

29. Cf. ibid., pp. 196–97.

30. Søren Kierkegaard, "Irony after Fichte," in *The Concept of Irony,* trans. Lee M. Capel (New York: Harper and Row, 1965), pp. 294, 298, 301, 302.

31. Wayne C. Booth, *A Rhetoric of Irony* (Chicago: The University of Chicago Press, 1974), p. 260.

32. Thorslev, *Romantic Contraries,* p. 169.

33. We are made aware in other plays of Shakespeare, notably in *King Lear* and *Hamlet,* of how the modalities of tragedy are undermined by the structure of the plays themselves. See, by the present writer, *Hamlet and the Word: The Covenant Pattern in Shakespeare* (New York: Ungar, 1971), pp. 194–204 and passim.

34. Critics have been troubled by the reference here to "thy Creator"; they feel that Qohelet is not the man to bid us remember our Creator! H. L. Ginsberg ingeniously emends the Hebrew and proposes to read the sentence as: "Remember your vigour in the days of your prime," giving an uncharacteristically tautological form to Qohelet's thinking ("Structure and Contents of Koheleth," p. 145). Critics go to strange lengths to accommodate biblical texts to their own preconceived notions of what the biblical authors ought to have said.

GENERAL INDEX

196

INDEX OF
BIBLICAL PASSAGES